ETORO SOCIAL STRUCTURE

Etoro
Social Structure
A Study in
Structural Contradiction

RAYMOND C. KELLY

Ann Arbor   The University of Michigan Press

To Mary

Foreword

Here is anthropology in its highest form. Others before have accepted the charge of bringing the most remote and exotic peoples into our own understanding of human culture by patient observation and reasoned description. But only a handful, their works standing now as permanent guideposts to the anthropological venture, have succeeded as Raymond C. Kelly in transforming the variable practice of unfamiliar custom into a more ordered conception of culture itself. The challenge presented in this respect by the Etoro of New Guinea was even something more than ordinary. Barely known to Australian patrol officers, the peoples of the southern Highlands borders were in the 1960s hardly charted by ethnography. Still it would have been comparatively easy—and occasioned no great surprise—for Kelly to fill in the anthropological map with still another of the famous "loose structures" of New Guinea: societies that have been positively characterized by the discrepancy between their ideal norms of organization and the artful dodges of action; and thus by comparison notably with African lineage systems, societies in which structure itself seemed but the certification of individual initiative. Moreover, for the student of Oceanic peoples generally, the categories of such an understanding had been firmly fixed by Malinowski's work in the Trobriands. The mark of anthropological finesse, we had learned, consists in discovery of the conflict between pragmatic interests and ideal forms —dualism of man and culture which reduced the latter to the means of a more fundamental dynamic of individual manipulation. But Kelly, by refusing to credit the discontinuity between structure and practice, norm and behavior, reverses the intrinsic logic of extinction it entails for the culture concept. He turns this very disparity into a more comprehensive statement of the cultural structure, which by its own contradictions specifies at once human actions and social representations, and among actions accounts both for those which conform to the rules and those that do not. This book is the highest form of anthropology, not only because it reveals the order in a set of complex practices, but as against the

analytic entropy of received distinctions, it enlarges the very notion of structural order.

The centerpiece of the book is a careful description and stun-
ning analysis of the Etoro social system. Whatever the position one
takes on Kelly's theoretical outlook—and the controversy this
work will provoke should not be rated the least of its merits—the
reader cannot fail to delight in the sustained deduction by which
Kelly progressively synthesizes the most specific ethnographic detail with the most general sociological argument. Essentially, the
innovation proposed in this enterprise is twofold: that the Etoro
lineage order must be viewed processually as a code of social construction and determination rather than a static form; and in the
event, the structure is seen to depend as much on a relation of
siblingship as on its apparent patrilineal descent. Ideology, especially as it rationalizes the patriliny of group form, thus conceals
what analysis reveals: that the social system is a product of the
combined play of two conflicting principles of order.

This unsuspected complexity Kelly demonstrates brilliantly.
The internal organization of the lineage itself is mediated by *matrilateral* siblingship, a brotherhood of men based on the sisterhood of
their mothers (as a result of their fathers' marriage within the same
group), or else on the commonality of mothers (as a result of the
classificatory levirate). Conversely, the failure to institute these
sibling relations presages the segmentation of the lineage, as common patrilineal ancestry by itself is no proof against the distance of
lineage brotherhood. Kelly shows the same mechanisms at work in
constituting the tribe as a dual organization of its several lineages,
those within each moiety linked by the common provenience of
their mothers and opposed to the other moiety by the marital exchange of their sisters. At another level, this system of exchange,
coupled to the strength of brother-sister ties ("cross-sex siblingship"), is realized as a dualism of residential groups, each composed of intermarrying brother lines on the same model as the tribe
as a whole. But it is impossible to do justice to the subtlety and
extent of this analysis by rehearsing it here. Attention might be
better focused on certain general issues it raises.

The work, as we see, is predicated in opposition to the classic
lineage problematic of British social anthropology. It exploits,
theoretically, certain analytic perturbations of the lineage paradigm that appear in the ethnographic works of E. E. Evans-Pritchard, Edmund Leach, and, particularly, Meyer Fortes. At the same
time, Kelly adopts a perspective that will join and clarify the issues
of current debate between "alliance" (or marital exchange) and

"descent" interpretations of the tribal social orders. "The basic precept of the kinship system," he writes, "and of Etoro social organization in general, is that relationships are defined and redefined in terms of the relations of exchange. Both the lineage's internal composition and its external relationships are finally delineated by the marriages it contracts." In this and a number of similar passages there is the same suggestion for arbitration of the controversy: that at one level, "descent" and "alliance" are complementary structural determinations, standing to each other as achieved form to organizing process respectively, the one as the constituted, the other the constituting. Yet Kelly's study carries the discussion still further, to the more basic question of the nature of "the structure" envisioned by the competing perspectives.

In opposing the traditional descent theory and its notions of functional consistency, Kelly for effectiveness argues mainly on the theoretical ground of the adversary. To the usual "principle of descent" he counterposes a "principle of siblingship," which, although rendered abstract as a relation of transitivity, continues the same discourse of phenomenal form as the "expression" of an underlying principle. On the other hand, he creatively documents a system that alliance theory will take as an expanded structure of "restricted exchange." Briefly, Kelly shows how the combination of sister exchange with a kinship rule of delayed marital return (father's sister's son's daughter's marriage) is capable of ordering a lattice network of *n* intermarrying groups within standard forms of dual organization. (Kelly's acute descriptions of marriage preference, moreover, indicate the potential transformations of this system in the direction either of a patrilateral cross-cousin balanced exchange or a matrilateral "generalized exchange.") Now for alliance theory, it is this specific form of reciprocal exchange, rather than certain principles of relationship, that comprises the structure of the situation. Hence the more basic differences in the two paradigms. The units of relationship which traditional descent theory substantializes or reifies as elementary structural principles are in the perspective of alliance the *valuations* of certain types of relation vis-à-vis others (as brother-sister vs. father-son), such as are set up in a system of exchange. The process of valuation being a Saussurian one of differential function or signification in a global system of intercourse, it is the latter, as such and in its determinate form, which becomes the object of structural concern.

But quite beyond the elucidation of structure, Kelly would give the notion a more powerful status than is accorded by most any theory. He documents how in a double sense the complex

Etoro system encompasses the empirical (to use Louis Dumont's phrase for it). First, in the sense that the structure both patterns choice or practice and consistently resumes it. For both an ideal rule (such as the prior claims of distant brothers in widow inheritance) and the systematic violations of it in "reality" (such as the common practice of true levirate) are demonstrably representations of the same structure. Practice, as Kelly puts it, amounts to a vector of contradictory principles. At the same time, in several insightful discussions of the attribution of kinship categories, he displays how the *de facto* outcome is nevertheless revaluated as a reproduction of the structure—by contrast to the prevailing anthropological empiricism which understands structure as the sediment of choice. Secondly then, Kelly's concept of structure as structuring—which is a fundamental testimony to the efficacy of culture—is extended to the encompassment of empirical events proper, to historical and contextual circumstances that are not themselves generated by the system but impose themselves from without. Here Kelly, although he disclaims extended pursuit of this dimension of the structure/"reality" problem, nevertheless gives us a number of effective resolutions. The most striking is the way the Etoro system organizes a radical population decline into social versions and limited permutations of itself. By such demonstrations of the structural orchestration of behavior and event, Kelly turns a superb ethnography into a major theoretical statement.

Not to claim that all the problems have been solved or that the solutions will escape contention. On the contrary, by concentrating primarily on the explication of practice as the vectorial product of structural contradiction, Kelly places on the anthropological agenda a new and potentially fruitful issue. For the matter has been left to some extent indeterminate, since any frequency of practice between the poles will satisfy the explanation, the simple fact of contradiction being unable to account for its precise product or vector without further specification of the forces in opposition. Here Kelly's more detailed analyses, as of the stratified model of lineage distribution favored during population decline, suggest it will be necessary to inform the concept of structural contradiction by larger considerations of system and event, including the economic and political implications given to historic circumstances by the structure in place.

One can see how far Kelly has advanced the discussion of practice beyond the state it was left by Malinowski. By dissociating cultural form from the human subject, somewhat as fiction is different from real life, Malinowski had introduced a kind of ontological schizophrenia into the discipline—which has since become the normal anthropological thought of our time. Human social life is taken to be divided against itself, made up of two different kinds of objects conceived to stand in relations of counterposition and competition. On one hand, there are the conventional forms which amount to "the culture" of the situation. They alone can have claim to this status, as they alone are described by specifically cultural properties: matrilineal or patrilineal descent, clan exogamy, mortuary rituals, payments of valuables to affines, sago production, classificatory kinship. In principle they might also be comprehended that way; that is, by a logic, at once of significance and action, developed from their symbolic or cultural attributes—as the valuation of economic goods or the categories of spiritual powers, for example, might be related to kinship classifications or marital exchanges. But the identification of cultural attributes as the "norm" or the "ideal" must condemn such an effort as metaphysical. Culture is instead subordinated to another logic—which as it does not preserve the symbolic properties cannot either give an account of them. Opposed to the cultural norm, on the other hand then, is the "actual behavior" of the people. And as specifically human, this must be described and characterized by terms drawn from another universe of discourse: the people's needs, motives, interests, and sentiments. At this point, in a sort of basic inversion of Durkheimian principles—although still in agreement with Durkheim's premise that "man is double"—Malinowski and others who follow him would displace the social dynamic onto a rationalistic and even natural level, seeking to account for it by forces situated in the individual and devoted to his utilitarian project. We have to deal with the struggle of the individual to realize his own ends in the face of constraining cultural conventions. That the ends and means are also conventional (as Kelly so well demonstrates in this monograph) could be recognized in actual fact but it is no longer relevant in theoretical principle. For meaningful analysis yields place to manipulative rationality. Theoretical attention becomes focused on the formal structure of means-ends relations grounded in an eternal teleology of human satisfactions. From this alternative vantage, culture is merely the unexplicated premise of the constituting dynamic of human purpose, and again the statistical effect of the most rational pursuit of purpose. Moreover, the individual is no longer the social being, as Marx had it, insofar as the social is specifically external to the individual being. For Malinowski, culture was only the accidental *medium* and the *milieu* of an individual existence whose basic quality was its universal (biological) pragmatism. So conceived, the interaction of "real life" and "culture" would necessarily be unequal: a relation of subject to object, active to passive, intention to effect. Behaving with a mind singular to their own best satisfactions, the people accordingly formulate and reformulate their cultural order. But the structure of culture as a meaningful order is then accordingly suspended. In theory, culture is resolved to an epiphenomenon of purposeful "decision-making processes." So does the analytic differentiation of structure and practice rob anthropology of its subject matter.

As against that impoverished outcome, herewith this book.

MARSHALL SAHLINS

Acknowledgments

The data on which this study is based were collected during a fieldwork period extending from April, 1968, to July, 1969. This field research was funded by a grant and predoctoral fellowship from the National Institute of Mental Health whose support I gratefully acknowledge.

In preparation for and during the course of my research I received valuable advice and assistance from many people. I would particularly like to thank Ralph and Susan Bulmer, William Clark, Mervyn Meggitt, John Street, C. L. Voorhoeve, and Eric Waddell for providing useful suggestions and information which facilitated my field research. I am grateful to the Research School of Pacific Studies of the Australian National University and its New Guinea Research Unit for assistance and facilities made available to me during my stay in Canberra and Port Moresby on my way to the field. I would also like to express my gratitude to the many departments and members of the administration who provided information and assistance. My wife and I are particularly indebted to Michael Eggleton, officer in charge at Komo Patrol Post, for the hospitality he extended to us and for the assistance he provided in forwarding our mail and supplies.

During the preparation of this study I have benefited from discussions and correspondence with Tom Ernst and Buck Schieffelin. Aletta Biersack, Robbins Burling, Vern Carroll, Meyer Fortes, Roy Rappaport, Marshall Sahlins, Thomas Trautmann, and Aram Yengoyan have offered many valuable comments and suggestions. I would particularly like to thank Drs. Rappaport and Sahlins for assistance and encouragement provided throughout the period from fieldwork preparation to completion of the manuscript; their comments on the latter have been especially helpful.

Insofar as a degree of intellectual biography may prove useful in placing this study, it may be noted that the concept of contradiction employed has roots in Sahlins's writings while the detailed analysis of social process through which this concept is brought to bear draws on Rappaport's cybernetic approach (here focused on social rather than ecological variables). I received my early training in kinship, social organization, and social anthropology from Aram Yengoyan and Mervyn Meggitt. There is a degree of resemblance between the present work and Meggitt's (1965) study of the Mae Enga which is a result of my use of the latter as a guide to data collection while in the field.

The fieldwork on which this study is based could not have been carried out without the assistance of my wife Mary. Due to the absence of pidgin speakers it was necessary to learn the Etoro language monolingually and Mary performed the linguistic analyses which made this possible. She also transcribed and translated several hundred pages of myths and stories which yielded information critical to the research. I am also indebted to her for assistance in compiling many of the tables herein, for typing the manuscript, and for many useful suggestions.

Finally, I would like to express my gratitude to the Etoro, and especially to Ilyawi for his friendship and his unflagging efforts to ensure that no question I asked went unanswered.

Contents

ILLUSTRATIONS

MAPS

PLATES (*following page 64*)

Introduction

This study is constituted as an ethnographic exploration of the nature of social structure, the interaction of structural principles in the social field, and the relationship between structure and actual events (or "practice"). These theoretical issues are elucidated (and interrelated) by the application of a concept of structural contradiction which is initially developed through a detailed analysis of the data of Etoro social organization and subsequently formulated as a general theory of structure—a theory which is capable of resolving the classic problem of the disjunction between norm and reality.

The ethnographic analysis consistently reveals that the empirical events and processes of Etoro social behavior are explicable only in terms of an interplay of structural principles (and of the jural rules, preferences, and social forces derived from them).[1] More precisely, the relationship between such principles is contradictory (in that their coterminous operation is productive of mutually inconsistent results). These contradictions between struc-

---

1. In my usage, the term "structural principle" is restricted to principles of relationship. A particular principle designates a specific form of connection or linkage. Insofar as structural principles are relational in essence, they possess linking and constitutive capabilities (by definition) and may be employed in a wide variety of social and cultural contexts to stipulate membership in social units, delineate unit interrelationships, define rights to (or connection with) property, specify mystical linkage between native taxa, etc. A specific formulation which invokes a particular type of relationship in a specified context may be designated as a "rule," and rules are distinguished from principles on the grounds of specificity. For example, the statement that a man is a member of the social group of his father's father is a rule. It is based on the principle of descent but restricts the application of this form of connection to a single context (group membership). Rules thus differ from principles by this characteristic feature: they incorporate a restrictive designation of the context in which a given structural principle (or type of relationship) is applicable. However, it is important to note that these context restrictions are frequently imprecise and nondiscrete and in such instances contradictions are effectively joined.

tural principles are empirically manifested in behavior such that
"practice" is the product of a double determination; the results
include violations of cultural rules (as well as conformity) and these
violations are intelligible in terms of structural contradictions in the
larger system of which such rules form a part. This constitutes a
skeletal outline of my central theoretical contention. The bulk of
what follows is an ethnography of the Etoro representing the data
from which this theory was derived and exemplifying its application within the context of a total structural system.

The contradiction which repeatedly emerges from an analytical
consideration of Etoro social structure is that between the principles of siblingship and descent. This contradiction is manifested in
the internal organization of the patrilineage, in the process of
fission through which lineage boundaries are delineated, in the role
of matrilateral siblingship as a connective bond between descent
groups in the external sphere, and in the events of widow remarriage. It is inscribed in the jurally stipulated responsibilities of
brother toward sister and played out at the residential level in
terms of cross-sex sibling co-residence versus localization of the
lineage. In many respects, Etoro social relations are ordered by the
dynamic interplay of countervailing forces which flow from these
opposed principles. Structural contradiction is itself a metaprinci-
ple of organization.

The Etoro case is a significant one for extant structural theory
because it provides both ample scope and particularly favorable
conditions for theoretical consideration of the nature of the relationship between structural principles. Distinctly different principles govern unit definition and unit interrelationship. The basic
units of Etoro society are patrilineages constituted by a rule of
recruitment based on the principle of descent. The external alignments of these units are of two types: bilateral exchange relationships (based on enduring, mutual obligations to serve as wife pro-
viders), and relations of matrilateral siblingship which link pairs of
patrilines that have parallel exchange relationships with the same
(third) lineage. Such pairs of patrilines derive their wives and
"mothers" from a common source and conceive of their relationship as one of matrilateral siblingship (exemplified by—but not
reducible to—the relation between half-siblings who have the same
mother but different fathers).

The role of matrilateral siblingship as a mode of connection in
the external domain provides the materials for a redefinition of siblingship as a principle of relationship rather than merely as a unitary
element of the internal structure of descent groups. Consideration of

formal relational properties facilitates a precise distinction and differentiation between siblingship and descent and, in addition, leads to the conclusion that elements of recruitment and alignment previously subsumed under the unitary rubric of descent are themselves based on distinctive relational qualities. The interrelationship between coordinate descent groups (within the sphere of alignment) is clearly organized by the same relational property which articulates siblings and is best understood in terms of siblingship.

The conceptual segregation of these disparate elements calls into question the received wisdom which perceives functional consistency between the constituent elements of a social system on the grounds that they are uniformly ordered by the principle of descent. The analytic construct "descent" contains two principles rather than one; hence uniformity dissolves into diversity and this raises important issues concerning the nature of the relationship between structural principles and the degree to which total structural systems conform to Radcliffe-Brown's law of functional consistency (Radcliffe-Brown, 1952:43). The Etoro case clearly indicates that such systems are ordered by a dialectical interplay of structural principles and that they manifest contradiction rather than consistency. I suggest that this interpretation has general applicability, and a reanalysis of the Nuer (Evans-Pritchard, 1940: 1951) is presented to forward that contention. This reanalysis also serves to demonstrate that the theory of structural contradiction I propose is capable of resolving the classic instance of disjunction between structure and behavior which has come to be known as the "Nuer paradox" (cf. Schneider, 1965:74; Buchler and Selby, 1968:75).

The analysis of the Etoro case and the theoretical discussion of siblingship outlined above are integrated into a general theory of structure in the concluding chapter; it is proposed that the organization of contradictions is the essence of social structure and that cultural perception of the social order expresses an ideological denial of its dialectical basis. There is a conscious contextual segregation of rule systems at the surface level while, at a deeper level, the relationship between them is contradictory. These fundamental contradictions are empirically manifested in the totality of observed behavior—which includes both conformity and deviance. The patterning of deviance is thus a product of the structure itself, not of forces external to it. In sum, I suggest that the concept of structure presented illuminates the relationship between structure and empirical events, a relationship which is obscure or problematic in current theoretical frameworks.

I have here attempted to provide only a brief overview of my central theoretical concerns and objectives since the development of these ideas is contingent upon the ethnographic data which follow. However, it may also be useful to specify some additional points of connection (and disjunction) between the issues which I address and recent developments in structural theory and in the ethnography of New Guinea societies. Both pose critical issues concerning the general nature of the relationship between structural principles and the concept of social structure per se.

Schneider has effectively criticized total-system models in which "Each little piece must be linked with every other little piece in a particular way to make a perfect constellation of a whole crystal-clear system" (Schneider, 1965:77). He argues that in place of such models (and the typologies associated with them) "We need a series of relevant elements, like descent, classification, exchange, residence, filiation, marriage, and so on; these need to be rigorously defined as analytic categories and then combined and recombined in various combinations and permutations, in different sizes, shapes, and constellations" (Schneider, 1965:78).

The program and objectives which Schneider here advocates have been broadly pursued; considerable effort has been devoted to precisely defining the analytic components of total system models and to disentangling these components from the fixed interrelationships which such models entail. (Indeed, the present study is an additional effort in this direction insofar as it deals with distinguishing siblingship and descent.) However, this dismantling of established models also poses a further and more fundamental question, namely, the general nature of the relationship between the constituent elements of structural systems (irrespective of specific permutations). One may also ask whether the widely recognized difficulties associated with total system models flow entirely from inadequate specification of components and a failure to recognize the variety of ways in which they can be combined in specific instances, as Schneider, Leach (1966:1–28), and Needham (1974:38 –71) suggest. Alternatively, is it perhaps the case that these difficulties are additionally due to a fundamental misconception concerning the *kind* of interrelationship which obtains between constituent elements? The latter perspective suggests that it is the concept of structure itself which is flawed and that "muddles" at the model level are symptomatic of more profound disabilities located in the concept of structure that informs model construction.

The present study proceeds from this alternative diagnosis of widely recognized disabilities. It is directed to the objective of exploring the potentialities of an alternative concept of structure, a concept based on a theory of structural contradiction and one which envisions an entirely different relationship between elements than that entertained by either descent or alliance theorists.

A theoretical reexamination of the general nature of the relationship between structural principles is also prompted by the accumulated evidence of an extensive body of literature on New Guinea societies; in ethnographic reports and theoretical overviews, the interaction of opposed principles (and idioms) is a significant and recurrent theme. Barnes questions the appropriateness of applying African models to New Guinea Highland societies on the grounds that the latter are characterized by cumulative patrifiliation rather than agnatic descent. He argues that " . . . in most, though not all Highland societies, the dogma of descent is absent or held only weakly; the principle of recruitment to a man's father group operates, but only concurrently with other principles" (Barnes, 1962:6). Pouwer (1964) likewise denotes a multiplicity of ordering principles as a critical feature of Star Mountains social systems. Langness maintains (contra Barnes) that African and New Guinea societies do not differ significantly in ideology or dogma per se, but in the degree to which statistical norms deviate from these. He argues that this disjunction "does not necessarily mean an absence or weakness of the dogma of patrilineal descent. What it does mean is that the dogma of patrilineal descent *operates* weakly as only one principle among several, rather than as the sole principle implied in the African materials" (Langness, 1964:171). In a review of the New Guinea literature on this subject, Kaberry also makes the point that it is " . . . because of the interplay of a number of principles that patrilineal systems of descent vary from community to community" (Kaberry, 1967:105). In an analogous context, de Lepervanche observes that (in general) "Segmentary principles are not the only determinant of the inter-relationships between social groups" (de Lepervanche, 1968:179). Wagner (1967) has constructed an analytic model of the Daribi social system in which an opposition between two main principles is seen as the key to their interrelationship. Burridge (1969) analyzes Tangu culture in terms of dialectical interactions across a series of oppositions. Strathern (1972:221–22) concludes his analysis of the Melpa by noting that there is an "interference" between the idioms of recruitment and native models for group structure which produces mixed results; he goes on to suggest that consideration of the interplay of idioms is more informative and productive than attempts to determine whether a social system can be typed or characterized as patrilineal. Although it is important to register the caveat that there are greater differences in perspective and definition of terms than these selective citations convey, the fact remains that the New Guinea literature displays widespread perception of an interplay of opposed principles (and/or cultural idioms). There is clear and consistent evidence of a general phenomenon, but one for which no general theory has been developed.

Before proceeding to the case at hand, several points should be noted regarding the nature and presentation of the data. My theoretical objectives dictate a thorough consideration of all the statistical events which constitute "practice" and my presentation reflects these data requirements. For this I beg the reader's scientific indulgence.

The small size of the Etoro tribe (numbering about four hundred) has made it possible to record tribally complete statistical data for most aspects of social organization considered herein and this obviates the problem of sampling and the potential source of error this represents. On the other hand, the total number of cases available for analysis is, in some instances, rather small. This difficulty is aggravated when a corpus of data is further subdivided in accordance with several variables under consideration, and the small size of the "sample" (in the statistical sense) diminishes the reliability of the results. I know of no remedy for this defect. It is nevertheless important to bear in mind that the "sample" represents all available data (unless otherwise indicated).

CHAPTER 1

The Ethnographic Setting

The Etoro (ɛ:t'-o-ro) are a distinct linguistic and cultural group of about four hundred people living near the southeast border of the Southern Highlands District[1] of the Australian-administered territory of Papua on the island of New Guinea. The Etoro inhabit the southern slopes of Mt. Sisa which lies along the southern edge of the central cordilla of New Guinea at approximately 6°15' south latitude and 142°45' east longitude (map 1). The north slopes of Sisa are culturally and geographically within the Highlands, while the south side of the mountain faces the Great Papuan Plateau and Mt. Bosavi, detached and isolated from the Highlands chain. The rivers within Etoro territory flow into the Rentoul and are the easternmost tributaries of the Fly-Strickland drainage system. The rivers flowing from the west side of Mt. Sisa (within the territory of the neighboring Onabasulu tribe) empty into the Gigio-Kikori drainage system. The Etoro thus occupy the intersection of major geographical boundaries between the Highlands and the lowland riverine areas on one hand, and between major river systems on the other. Their closest cultural and linguistic affinities appear to be with the peoples of the Papuan Plateau and the Fly-Strickland region to the west.

The Etoro language is classified within the Bosavi (or Papuan Plateau) language family which also includes the Beami to the west (see map 1), the Onabasulu and Kaluli, who occupy the Great Papuan Plateau, and possibly the Kasua located on the southeast side of Mt. Bosavi (Shaw, 1973). The Bosavi language family is a subgroup of the Central and South New Guinea Stock which is a subgroup of the Central and South New Guinea Phylum (Voor-

---

1. Etoro territory was within the Western District from 1951 through 1968 but has been included in the Southern Highlands District since the latter was enlarged and redefined in November, 1969.

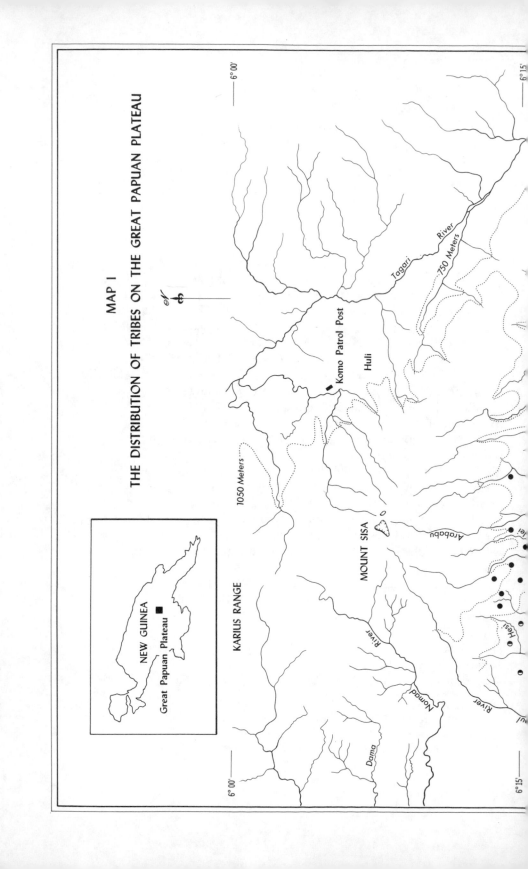

MAP I

THE DISTRIBUTION OF TRIBES ON THE GREAT PAPUAN PLATEAU

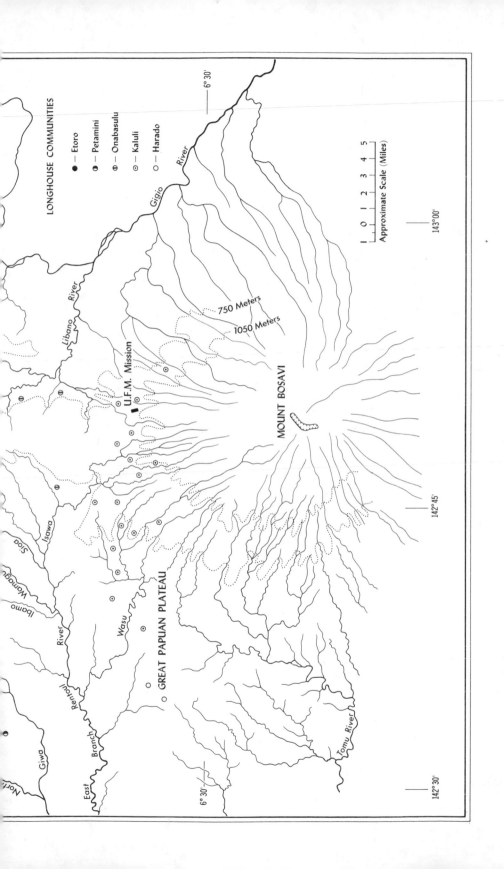

LONGHOUSE COMMUNITIES

● — Etoro
◑ — Petamini
◒ — Onabasulu
⊙ — Kaluli
○ — Harado

Approximate Scale (Miles)
1 0 1 2 3 4 5

MOUNT BOSAVI

750 Meters
1050 Meters

U.F.M. Mission

GREAT PAPUAN PLATEAU

Libano River

Gigio River

Isawa
Sioa
Womogu
Ibamo River
Wasu
East Branch
Rentoul
Giwa
North
Tomu River

6° 30'
143° 00'
142° 45'
142° 30'
6° 30'

hoeve, 1968:1–15). The Finisterre-Huon Phylum and Central and South New Guinea Phylum together form the Trans-New Guinea Phylum (McElhanon and Voorhoeve, 1970).[2]

The Central and South New Guinea Phylum is geographically the most extensive in the Papuan linguistic region. It extends along the south coast of New Guinea from Etna Bay (at the "neck" of the bird's head) to the mouth of the Kikori River, and back from the south coast to the edge of the central mountain chain throughout the area from Etna Bay to Lake Kutubu. The phylum also extends into the Highlands from the Eastern Baliem River Valley to the headwaters of the Sepik near Telefomin. In addition, the phylum includes an area covering about twenty miles of the north coast of New Guinea just west of the West Irian-Australian New Guinea border. The Central and South New Guinea Stock is geographically the largest of those within the like-named phylum. It includes an east-west strip roughly one hundred miles wide stretching from Etna Bay to Lake Kutubu. The Bosavi language family is located at the extreme eastern end of this stock area.

The Great Papuan Plateau is inhabited by five tribes which claim discrete territorial domains and which differentiate themselves from each other and their neighbors on linguistic and cultural grounds. The distribution of these tribal groups is shown on map 1. It will be useful here to briefly outline Etoro cultural affinities and social interaction with each of these groups (and with the Huli of the Highlands), as these have an important bearing on Etoro settlement patterns to be discussed below.

Culturally and linguistically, the Etoro are most closely related to the Petamini or Bedamini, who are most probably a subtribal grouping of the Beami.[3] The Etoro and Petamini languages are fairly closely related, perhaps approaching the dialect level (i.e., 70

---

2. See also Wurm, 1971.

3. Voiced and voiceless stops are allophones of the same phoneme in Etoro so that "Petamini" may also be transcribed as "Bedamini." The Etoro tend more toward voiceless pronunciation and hence refer to their neighbors as "Petamini," while the latter tend more toward voiced consonants and refer to themselves as "Bedamini." Voorhoeve employs the latter orthography. The Beami west of the Rentoul, or at least some portion thereof, also refer to themselves as Bedamini and the group designated herein is thus in all likelihood a subtribal grouping of the Beami. I will use the label "Petamini" to refer to this grouping occupying the area east of the North Branch of the Rentoul. The Beami proper call them Komifi, or "hill people," and distinguish them from the Etoro (whom they call "Edharo").

to 81 percent cognates).[4] In any event, nearly all adult Etoro men speak the Petamini language (or dialect) and there are no significant barriers to communication between the two groups. The Etoro nevertheless profess their linguistic distinctiveness, which they express by mocking imitations of the more heavily voiced consonants of Petamini speech. The Etoro also make much of the fact that members of the other tribe wear larger nose plugs. Both of these distinguishing features are themselves indicative of substantial similarities. Intermarriage is extensive, accounting for 10.4 percent (27/260) and 5.1 percent (12/235) of the unions of Etoro men and women respectively (see table 39).[5] Residence with affines and kinsmen of the Petamini tribe is not uncommon, and 3.3 percent (3/90) of (adult) Etoro men so resided during the period of fieldwork, while Petamini men constituted an identical proportion of the total adult male residents of Etoro communities (see table 25). Social interaction between adjacent communities of these two tribes is generally governed by the bonds of kinship and affinity between them. There are no discontinuities in the spacing of settlements along this border. However, more distant Petamini (and Beami) villages raided the local groups associated with the now extinct Tifanafi and Arafi lineages located in the southern part of the Etoro tribal territory (map 2) in the 1950s (indeed contributing to their extinction).

Trade between the Etoro and Petamini is currently quite limited. Before the introduction of steel tools (ca. 1955) the Etoro obtained stone axes, pineapple, disk and starheaded clubs, dog teeth ornaments (then used in brideprice), bows, and other items from the Petamini in exchange for salt and shell valuables derived from the Huli of the Highlands. About ten years before direct contact with government patrols (in 1964) steel tools became available in trade from the Highlands—to which stone tools had previously been exported—thus reversing the prior flow of goods and disrupting traditional exchange relationships. Somewhat earlier,

---

4. Shaw (1973) reports a tentative figure of 55 percent shared basic vocabulary between the Etoro and Beami while at the same time noting personal communications from several other linguists indicating the possibility of mutual intelligibility. Lexicostatistical data for the Petamini (which are currently unavailable) might resolve this discrepancy as it seems likely that Etoro-Petamini and Petamini-Beami relationships are both comparatively close (approximating the dialect level), while the Etoro and Beami—at opposite ends of the chain—are less closely related.

5. Petamini brideprice is lower than that of the Etoro, and this may account for the imbalance in the exchange of women.

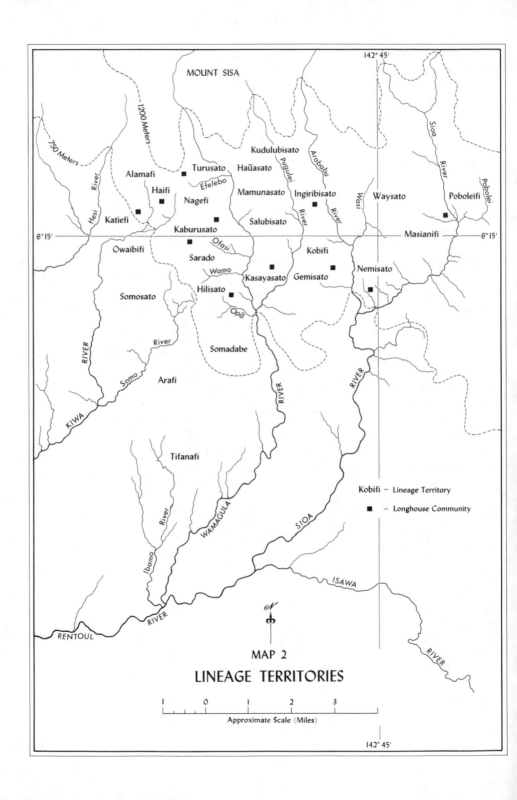

MOUNT SISA

1200 Meters

750 Meters

Hesi River

Alamafi

Turusato

Kudulubisato

Haũasato

Pugulei

Arababu

Sioa River

Poboleifi

Poboleifi

Haifi

Efelebo

Mamunasato

Ingiribisato

Wasi River

Waysato

Nagefi

Katiefi

Kaburusato

Salubisato

Owaibifi

Ofasi

Kobifi

Masianifi

6° 15'   6° 15'

Sarado

Wamo

Kasayasato

Gemisato

Nemisato

Somosato

Hilisato

Opā

RIVER

RIVER

River

Somadabe

RIVER

KIWA

Somo

Arafi

Tifanafi

Kobifi — Lineage Territory

■ — Longhouse Community

River

Ibamo

WAMAGULA

SIOA

ISAWA

RENTOUL

RIVER

N

MAP 2

LINEAGE TERRITORIES

RIVER

1   0   1   2   3

Approximate Scale (Miles)

142° 45'

142° 45'

dog teeth became rare and gradually ceased to be available from the Petamini, apparently as a result of similar disruptions in trade networks to the southwest, from whence they were derived. Mother-of-pearl shells, also obtained from the Highlands, gradually replaced dog teeth necklaces as major items of brideprice. The availability of these shells in trade quantities was probably due to their importation and disbursement by government patrol officers based in the Central and Southern Highlands. In any event, the net effect of these developments was that the Etoro came to depend on the Huli for brideprice items and axes formerly obtained from the Petamini, and trade with the latter became attenuated. Huli trading parties also traverse Etoro territory in order to trade directly with the Petamini, depriving the Etoro of their middleman role. This occurred on a limited scale in the precontact era but has greatly increased in recent times because the Huli possess quantities of the western trade goods which the Petamini desire (while the Etoro do not) and also as a consequence of the fact that the Etoro are no longer free to restrict the access of the Huli through force of arms, or the threat thereof.

Etoro territory adjoins that of the Onabasulu (Ernst, 1972) on the east, a tribe numbering about four hundred thirty. There is a more definite linguistic break along this border and the languages of these two tribes differ more in vocabulary than do Etoro and Petamini (although they are very similar in grammatical structure). However, a fair proportion of Etoro men—perhaps 20 percent—speak Onabasulu. Intermarriage and residential admixture conform to the same pattern as in Etoro-Petamini relations, but at a lower frequency. Etoro-Onabasulu marriages account for 4.6 percent (12/260) and 1.7 percent (4/235) of the recorded unions of Etoro men and women respectively (see table 39).[6] Kinship also governs social relations between border communities of these two tribes. The Etoro do not recall any raids between them, although Etoro and Onabasulu men have jointly participated in raids against the Kaluli.

There is currently little basis for trade between the Etoro and Onabasulu derived from differential resources, cultural needs, or structural position in the larger trade networks. Both tribes have

---

6. The percentages are based on a sample including women's first marriages of the past two to three generations. The figures probably understate the frequency of intermarriage in this instance due to the fact that past generation marriages are unavailable for Nemisato lineage, which contracts more marriages with Onabasulu groups than any other Etoro line.

equivalent access to Highlands goods through trade with the Huli, and both have much the same items available for exchange (although this may not have been the case before the collapse of Etoro-Petamini trade). The most important exception is a tree oil produced by the Onabasulu, but not the Etoro. This oil is an important component of the brideprice of Highlands' tribes. The Etoro obtain the oil from the Onabasulu in exchange for pearl shells and cowrie strings and export it to the Highlands where it is again exchanged against these same items (but, of course, at higher rates). In addition, all the goods involved in the Etoro-Huli trade (discussed below), with the exception of sago and pigs, are also exchanged between the Etoro and Onabasulu and may move in either direction. Those items sought by Highlanders are ultimately exported to that area by both tribes. In short, the Etoro and Onabasulu alternately play the role of middleman to each other in the Highlands-Papuan Plateau exchange.

This trade relation also has important intratribal dimensions. The exchange of unlike items does not occur within the Etoro tribe. All tribesmen are considered to be kinsmen and should be given whatever they require without expectation of a return. It follows that two men of the same village who respectively possess a cassowary bone knife and a cylindrical roll of indigenous tobacco, and each desire the other, cannot effect a direct exchange. However, they may satisfy their desires through Onabasulu intermediaries. The ban on internal trade thus necessitates external exchange relations and, more specifically, exchange with a tribe that possesses a nearly identical repertoire of goods. The prohibition may be regarded as an analogue of the incest taboo.

The Highlands on the north side of Mt. Sisa are inhabited by the Huli, ethnographically described by Glasse (1968). Extensive trade takes place between the Huli and Etoro, with the latter supplying sago, bows, arrows, feathers, hornbill beaks, net bags, string, tobacco, cassowary bone daggers, juvenile cassowaries, mature pigs, tree oil, and formerly stone tools in exchange for pearl shells, cowrie strings, piglets, and European trade goods. Salt which the Huli obtained from the Enga was formerly a major item of exchange. Huli trading parties pass through Etoro territory nearly every month, continuing on to Onabasulu or Petamini territory before returning to the Highlands. Etoro excursions into the Highlands (as far as Tari and Koroba) are undertaken only two or three times a year. The Huli have a monopoly on Etoro brideprice items as a consequence of the contact-induced disruptions of traditional trade networks. The Huli are also chief suppliers of Western trade goods to the Etoro as the latter lack cash for direct trade-store purchases. Both of these developments have augmented the volume of trade between the two tribes. Contact has also distorted relative exchange values, creating opportunities for Highlanders to reap enormous profits. For example, cassowaries which are utilized in Mendi brideprice payments could be sold in that area for seventy-five dollars or more in 1968. The same cassowaries could be obtained from the Etoro for one or two inferior pearl shells, worth only a few dollars at Mendi (due to the large quantities of such shells injected into the local economy by the Australian administration). The profit margin on these transactions was great enough so that Mendi entrepreneurs could afford the air fare to fly to Komo patrol post (in Huli territory) on government mail planes in order to carry out the trade, even though Huli intermediaries imposed a substantial markup on the cassowaries they obtained from the Etoro.

Relations between the Huli and Etoro are generally friendly and men of either group who seek to avoid intratribal revenge may take up residence with trade friends for extended periods of time. However, intermarriage between the two groups is very infrequent. (The Etoro recall that several women were married to Huli men in the past but could not place them genealogically, which suggests that the unions took place three or four generations ago.) Although there is no general state of hostility between these two tribes, conflicts periodically arise when members of Huli trading parties succumb to malaria while in Etoro territory. On these occasions, the Huli accuse their Etoro hosts of sorcery and demand death compensation on a Highlands scale, i.e., about twenty pigs. Etoro kin groups are generally unable to provide a payment of this size without seriously depleting their breeding stock and their refusal to do so has occasionally led to armed conflict. However, such conflicts are characteristically short-lived due to Huli reluctance to engage the Etoro on their own densely forested terrain, this reluctance being largely attributable to the Etoro custom of eating members of other tribes killed in battle.[7] (The Etoro are also regarded

---

7. The Etoro do not fight set-piece battles as is done in the Highlands, and the Huli were confronted with perpetual ambush when they attacked in Etoro territory. It was also necessary to fight a rearguard action over some twenty miles of trails as they returned to their own territory. A Huli tribesman related that an attacking party lost twenty men on an abortive raid against the Etoro. He also maintained that the Etoro fell upon wounded men and consumed them on the spot, their own casualties included. This is untrue, but the belief is nevertheless a deterrent.

encloses an area of about 80 square miles with an altitudinal range of 300 to 2,500 meters.[10] However, the present zone of occupation is almost entirely in the 750 to 1,050 meter range, within an area of 23 square miles. The population density of this zone is 17 per square mile.

The clustering of the population within this relatively small portion of the total tribal territory is explicable with respect to climate, warfare, and depopulation. The upper altitudinal limit of occupation (1,050 meters) is primarily determined by the influence of climatic factors on the economy. Sago palms, which provide one of the starch staples of the diet, do not grow at the cooler temperatures encountered above approximately 910 meters (3,000 feet). This is the most significant restriction on population distribution, and it is equally applicable to each of the five tribes which inhabit the Papuan Plateau, all of which depend upon sago resources.[11] Only two of the forty-five longhouse communities in this region are above the 1,050 meter line, and both of these exceptions are within a quarter mile of it (see map 1).

Gardening above this altitude is discouraged by the spatial interdigitation of the sago processing and horticultural facets of the economy (discussed in chapter 2) and also by the unfavorable gardening conditions encountered there. During the season of southeasterlies (May to August) clouds bank up against the edge of the Highlands and continually engulf the upper slopes of Mt. Sisa (above 1,050 meters) in a dense cloud cover and perpetual drizzle. This area experiences higher rainfall and reduced sunlight during other seasons as well and is consequently less favorable both for gardening and for habitation. The portion of these upper slopes which is adjacent to the zone of occupation is regularly utilized for hunting and trapping. Game is particularly plentiful along the margin of the primary and secondary forest, and this provides an inducement to locating settlements near it. (This upper portion of the tribal territory is nineteen square miles in area, of which approxi-

---

10. Numerous readings of my altimeter taken at various locations in Etoro territory revealed that contour lines on the published map (SB 54-12, edition 1, series T504) are approximately 150 meters too high, i.e., 1,200 meters is actually 1,050. Inasmuch as this instrument consistently gave correct readings at Komo and other airstrips in the Highlands, I have labeled the contour lines on maps 1 and 2 in accordance with my findings.

11. The Petamini and Beami occupy a lower altitudinal range and rely upon sago and bananas as staples while the Etoro, Kaluli, and Onabasulu depend primarily on sago and sweet potatoes.

mately six square miles are regularly exploited for hunting and trapping.)

The southern (and lower) sector of the Etoro tribal territory, from the 750 meter line to the Rentoul River, was occupied prior to the severe depopulation which has taken place in the last thirty years. The Etoro population has declined by more than 50 percent since about 1935 as a result of the combined effects of high mortality from introduced diseases (as well as traditional causes) and a low birthrate. Aerial photographs indicate that the Etoro have gradually withdrawn from the southern region during the last twenty to twenty-five years, as evidenced by a gradient of fallow succession. Informants also relate the extinction of many lineages whose territories are within this area, and the northward movement of the remnants of several others together with their co-resident affines and kinsmen. Both the lineage extinctions and general withdrawal are related to warfare.

Warfare between the Etoro and the Kaluli, Harado, and Beami characteristically took the form of raids in which small parties of warriors would attempt to surprise a few people in their gardens and sago stands, dispatch as many as possible, and return with the dismembered bodies of their victims to partake in a cannibalistic celebration. However, an imbalance in casualties between two tribes in this form of raiding led to the organization of massive retaliatory raids such as the one previously discussed. In this latter type of raid, a longhouse would be surrounded at dawn and put to the torch by a war party ideally outnumbering the inhabitants by about two to one.[12] Large "shields" sufficient to protect three or four men were used to advance on the door of the dwelling in order to secure entry, and to provide cover from which the attacking bowmen could pick off the occupants at close range as they attempted to escape the flames. In a well-organized and well-executed raid of this type there were no survivors, and defensive precautions were consequently a paramount consideration.

Protection against these large-scale raids depended upon several factors. First, a degree of security could be attained by the clustering of longhouses in relatively close proximity so that an

---

12. A war party of at least one hundred and probably one hundred fifty men took part in the devastating raid against the Kaluli discussed above. This provided about a six to one advantage over the men within the besieged longhouse. However, the offensive force also had to contend with neighboring Kaluli communities which came to drive off the attackers (although in this case arriving too late).

attacking party could be driven off by the members of neighboring communities before the conflagration forced evacuation of the house. (The smoke itself sounded the alarm and alerted even distant communities of the tribe.)[13] Second, such raids could be deterred by locating settlements at a great enough distance from enemy groups so that an attacking party would have difficulty withdrawing without losses once tribal allies were alerted. The returning warriors generally could not retreat swiftly as they would be carrying dead and wounded members of their party and, in many cases, the dismembered bodies of their victims as well. Third, the size of the community was directly related to its vulnerability. Larger longhouses had a much better chance of holding out until help arrived. Thus, in times of intensive warfare pairs of smaller Etoro communities combined into one (and the social organization of local groups definitely facilitates this). Fourth, added protection could be gained by selecting longhouse sites which offered defensive advantages, particularly cliffside locations.

All of these defensive considerations dictated the withdrawal of the Etoro from the southern part of their tribal territory once their numbers were reduced by depopulation. Small, widely separated communities could not safely be maintained within close range of enemy raiding parties. Nevertheless, many lineages attempted to hold their home ground and were consequently wiped out. For example, the Tifanafi line (see map 2) and their co-resident affines maintained a semi-isolated community in the southern region for some time but eventually succumbed to successive raids by the Beami, Harado, and Kaluli. Hence, as a result of depopulation and warfare, Etoro communities are presently relatively tightly clustered in the northernmost inhabitable portion of their tribal territory. The Kaluli have also pulled back from the frontier (judging from aerial photos) and the center of the Papuan Plateau is now an extensive, vacant tract of second growth.[14]

---

13. The large movable "shields" were to some degree a counter-ploy as they were used to enable the attackers to gain entry to the longhouse, rather than waiting for the inhabitants to be forced out by the flames.

14. The present zone of Etoro occupation very nearly corresponds with the Upper Miocene Orubadi Mudstone formation (Russel, 1953) which is bounded on both sides by Pleistocene volcanics (Mt. Sisa and also Mt. Bosavi being volcanic in origin). The southern boundary of this geological formation is evident at the convergence of the Wamagula and Pugulei rivers and about a mile below the convergence of the Sioa and

The construction and placement of the Etoro longhouse is also influenced by defensive considerations. Longhouses are traditionally located on the spur of one of the many narrow, saddlebacked ridges which fan out from the twin peaks of Mt. Sisa. The front of the house is at ground level while the rear rests on piles some twenty-five feet above the steep downward slope of the ridge (fig. 1; pls. 2 and 3).[15] Several neighboring longhouses are usually within view on adjacent ridges so that assistance can be quickly marshaled in the event of a raid.

The area in front of the house is cleared (currently scraped with shovels provided by the government) and several pits for steam-cooking are located there. The steep side-slopes of the ridge are covered by the tangled debris of fallen trees that characterize an Etoro garden. Bananas protrude above the trunks and branches and sweet potato vines cover the ground beneath. The garden generally produces poorly, since housesites are selected for defensive rather than horticultural purposes. However, the nearby source of greens, snacks, and banana leaves for cooking is convenient and the tangled debris serves a defensive function as well. The "path" through the garden winds back and forth from one slippery tree trunk to the next and those who do not know it can traverse the garden only with the greatest difficulty. Large communal gardens are located on more favorable terrain about a fifteen- or twenty-minute walk away. Sago stands are generally located near the main gardens and along the streams which flow on both sides of the ridge, converging at its base.

The outer walls of the longhouse are constructed with shingle-

---

Arababu rivers (map 2). In both locations feeder streams flow north against the extremely steep grade of Mt. Sisa. The northern boundary of this formation is located at the convergence of the Wamagula and Efelebo, and swings slightly to the south on both sides of this point. The Orubadi Mudstone Formation represents an uplift along fault lines which crosscut the slope of Mt. Sisa, producing a jumbled terrain which has been described as the most rugged in New Guinea. The soils within the occupied zone are probably somewhat different than those to the north and south, which are built up exclusively on volcanic rock and ash. However, it seems unlikely that this has significantly influenced Etoro settlement patterns since the Kaluli possess the same basic economy and occupy the same altitudinal range on the purely volcanic slopes of Mt. Bosavi.

15. The longhouses closest to the government patrol post at Komo have recently been built on level ground as these communities no longer feel threatened by raids. The communities west of Kaburusato (map 2) were not yet convinced of the Pax Australiana in 1968.

FIG. 1.   Longhouse Setting

like planks made from split logs lashed into place with rattan cane. These are backed on the inside with sago thatch, which is also used for the roof and internal partitions. The doorways can be barricaded by stacking logs one atop the other between two sets of closely spaced houseposts. The interior of the longhouse is divided into separate men's and women's sleeping quarters in the elevated rear section and a communal gathering place in the front (fig. 2). The main door opens onto a central passageway (*kamu*) which runs the length of the house, and which is, to some degree, sacred. Widows, who are contaminated by their association with male death, cannot set foot there. They enter through side doors and sit only along the outer walls of the communal section. If they wish to cross from one side of the house to the other, they must go outside and around to the other widow's door. During ceremonies, men dance the length of the *kamu*, and seances are held in the extreme rear end of it (within the men's quarters and also high above the ground).

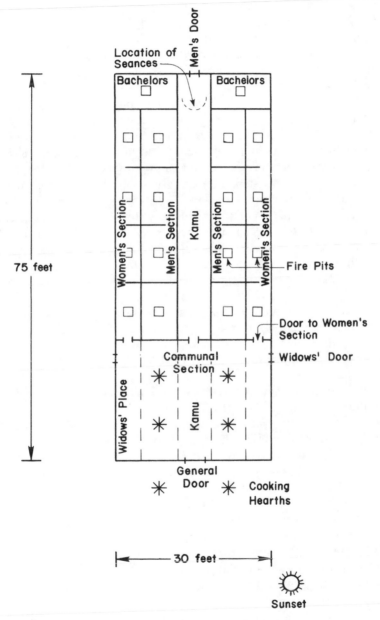

FIG. 2. Floor Plan of the Longhouse

23

In the late afternoon the main meal of the day is steam-cooked in the pits outside or, if it is raining, in similar fireplaces in the communal section. Everyone gathers here, sharing their portions of food with each other, relating the day's events, and not infrequently, retelling myths and stories. The men smoke and sometimes occupy themselves with making arrows, ax handles, or with other crafts. The older women smoke as well (although the men object to it) and invariably weave net bags. Children play and piglets scratch themselves against the houseposts. An hour or so after sunset the men retire to their sleeping platforms along both sides of the *kamu* in the rear of the house. These platforms are about five and one-half feet square and are raised eighteen inches above the floor, forming convenient benches along the central passageway. In the center of each platform is a square hole and beneath it a small fireplace which heats it from below. The bachelors sleep on the two platforms at the extreme rear which extend to the outer walls of the house. The married men sleep toward the front with the youths, who are inseminated nightly so that they might grow.

A partition extending to the ceiling separates the women's section, which lies along the outer walls, from that of the men. The women have similar, although rather smaller, accommodations. Wives sleep on platforms adjacent to those of their husbands. Boys sleep with their mothers until they are six or seven.

The symbolic architecture of the longhouse may be conceived, in general terms, as a set of concentric circles (or ellipses) which delineate progressive gradations from sacred to profane and from culture to nature. The (high) rear portion of the *kamu* where seances are held is the sacred center of the dwelling. From this point concentric circles enclose the bachelors' sleeping platforms, the men's quarters, the women's quarters,[16] the central portion of the communal anteroom along both sides of the *kamu,* the widows' sitting places along the outer walls of this communal section, the cleared ground and cooking places directly outside, the garden, the second growth forest, and (within view from the ridge) the primary forest on the upper slopes of Mt. Sisa to the north and finally the settlement of the Kaluli on the slopes of Mt. Bosavi to the south. The symmetrical floor plan also reflects the dual organization of local groups which, in terms of classificatory kinship, always con-

---

16. Thus, bachelors are more sacred than married men, all men more sacred than women, the separateness of men and women more sacred than their communal mingling, and so forth.

sist of two groups of "brothers" who have married each other's sisters. Ideally, the core of each of these groups of "brothers" will be a lineage segment and the two segments will be related as affines through a true sister exchange. (The organization of longhouse communities is discussed in chapter 6.)

Contact and Depopulation

A number of early exploratory patrols entered or crossed the Great Papuan Plateau in the 1930s. Although none of these passed through Etoro territory, the Hides and O'Malley patrol of 1935 followed the border of it and apparently contacted the Etoro at several points. Hides's route can be traced on the basis of the information he provides in his narrative account (Hides, 1973). The patrol came up the Fly, Strickland, and Rentoul rivers by canoe, and disembarked on the south side of the Rentoul about five miles downstream from the confluence of the North and East branches (map 1). Hides then proceeded along the south side of the East Branch of the Rentoul to the junction of the Sioa and Isawa rivers. The first half of this journey took the patrol through an area which is (and was) uninhabited because it is accessible to raids by four or five different tribes and is thus untenable ground. Following the river, Hides also passed through a no-man's-land between Etoro and Kaluli territories. As previously discussed, defensive considerations require that longhouse communities be located at some distance from enemy groups and apparently there has always been an unoccupied strip approximately two miles wide between Etoro and Kaluli settlements. The patrol consequently failed to contact the Kaluli, although it passed through their tribal territory.

While encamped near the confluence of the Sioa and Isawa rivers, Hides could see several longhouses to the north, probably a cluster of allied Etoro and Onabasulu border communities. He observed torches moving back and forth in the night and heard singing which resembled "the deep baying of hounds" (Hides, 1973: 49). This was in all likelihood a preraid seance in which the (*Sigisato*) spirits are invoked and promise their assistance. In any event, the following morning the patrol was confronted by a war party of fifty or more men which gathered on a ridge several hundred yards from the camp and performed a circling dance which is a traditional component of Etoro and Onabasulu warfare.[17] One

---

17. The dance is briefly performed on the clearing in front of a longhouse after the house is fired but before the occupants have become aware of it.

man (a medium) could be seen sitting on the shoulders of another, swaying, chanting, and beating a drum. This spectacle amused O'Malley who put two fingers in his mouth and gave a piercing whistle, whereupon the entire group instantly broke and ran. As chance would have it, such a whistle is the unmistakable call of a witch.

Inquiries which I made in the field failed to turn up a single Etoro who recalled Hides's expedition, all informants dating first contact with Australians to a 1964 patrol. In retrospect, I believe this was due to the fact that Hides and O'Malley were thought to be witches and have been mythologized as witch-spirits distinct from the *harigei,* or light-skinned men, of thirty years later. Schieffelin (personal communication, 1972) reports that the Kaluli say the Etoro wept upon first seeing steel tools because the chips they made were like those left by the "big witches" of the past. Moreover, the southern Etoro communities that Hides contacted were all extinct long before 1964, and it is quite possible that no one witnessed both contact patrols and hence no association between them was drawn. Also, no Etoro saw Hides at close range, or at least none who lived to tell of it.

Following this confrontation, Hides continued upstream for several hours to avoid this hostile group and then swung north, crossing the Isawa and one branch of the river which flows into the Isawa just before the latter joins the Sioa (see map 1). At the confluence of these streams, the patrol came upon the large garden clearing of a longhouse community. The elevated rear portion of the longhouse was visible on the spur of the ridge above, and bowmen on the platform which extends out from the back of the house commanded the clearing below. Hides advanced part way through the fallen timber, followed at some distance by the patrol. Two young men started to come forward to offer him a white feather headdress but were called back by the medium seen the previous day. The latter beat his drum and uttered "low voluble sounds" (1973:53), which represent the voices of the spirits speaking through a medium. As the spirits urged attack, the first arrow was released and the patrol simultaneously fired a volley over the heads of the warriors, who then fled.

Hides left a peace offering at the house and continued on, crossing the second branch of this river and proceeding up a narrow ridge line east of the Sioa (along the border of Etoro and Onabasulu territory). As Hides directed the forward carriers to unload and set up camp, a shot rang out at the rear of the line. Hides and a constable hurried back to investigate and stumbled upon two bowmen who released their arrows. Hides and the constable fired back, killing one of the men on the spot (as Hides reports, p. 55). The other evidently died shortly thereafter, as the Onabasulu say that two men, an Onabasulu and an Etoro, were killed on the Papuan Plateau (Ernst, personal communication, 1972). The patrol continued northeast through Onabasulu country and into the Highlands.

The Etoro were not contacted again until the 1960s, although several other exploratory expeditions ventured onto the Papuan Plateau in the interim. The Champion and Adamson (Bamu-Purari) patrol first contacted the Kaluli in 1936 and the Champion and Turner patrol of 1939 proceeded up the Rentoul as far as the headwaters of the North Branch of that river on the edge of Petamini territory. In 1953 a patrol from Lake Kutubu escorted a team of petroleum geologists across Kaluli territory and into the Petamini-Beami area.

A government expedition from Nomad Patrol Post passed through the northern sector of the Etoro tribal territory in early 1964, stopping in a number of communities along the way. This patrol was everywhere well received, probably due in large part to the lack of association between these newcomers and the "witch-spirits" of thirty years before.[18] In all, seven patrols visited the Etoro between 1964 and the inception of my fieldwork in April, 1968.[19] Native pastors from the UFM mission at Komo (in Huli territory) also made several short trips to the area during this same period. Missions staffed by native pastors were established at Way-sato and Ingiribisato (map 2) toward the close of my fieldwork. A single Etoro man had left the area (with Onabasulu kinsmen) to work on a plantation and returned; four other men left during the term of my fieldwork. Three Etoro men and one Onabasulu were arrested for executing an Etoro witch in 1966 and were subsequently convicted and incarcerated at Mt. Hagen, but had not returned by 1969.

The effects of these four years of direct contact prior to my fieldwork were generally not substantial. The government patrol post at Komo is about a twenty to twenty-five mile walk from the

---

18. Although such a lack of association seems improbable, it is difficult to account for this acceptance on any other grounds, since communities which are fearful generally desert their longhouses when patrols approach.

19. A medical patrol of this period is described in an article by Dr. Paul Bastian (1969).

nearest Etoro village and the presence of the administration was
experienced only once or twice a year, usually for a day or two in
each village. Although several individuals were tentatively ap-
pointed as government headmen, none had yet received the insig-
nia of office.[20] No internal conflicts had been brought to the attention of government authorities for resolution, and the indigenous
system of negative sanctions continued to operate as it had in the
past. On the other hand, outhouses were constructed, longhouses
were beginning to be built on level ground (in tacit recognition of
the government edict banning warfare), village grounds were
scraped with shovels provided by the patrol officer, platform buri-
als were largely discontinued, the marriage of prepubescent girls
was effectively prohibited, and several new crops were introduced.
There was a general awareness that a new era had begun, and that
the *harigei* represented a force with which the Etoro had to come
to terms.

Although this relatively brief period of direct contact prior to
fieldwork did not materially alter Etoro life, the preceding period of
indirect contact had very substantial effects. Trade relations were
significantly changed and the depopulation which followed the introduction of foreign diseases transformed the distribution of tribal
populations across the Papuan Plateau. Warfare ceased as withdrawal and consolidation produced disengagement along contested
frontiers. Steel tools altered labor inputs in the gardening sector of
the economy and the halving of the Etoro population doubled the
economic resources available to those who survived. It will be
necessary to describe briefly the prominent causes and magnitude
of this numerical decline as a prelude to subsequent consideration
of its effects on aspects of social organization with which I shall
principally be concerned.

The Etoro have undergone severe depopulation resulting from
the conjunction of extremely high mortality from introduced diseases and a traditionally low birthrate. The decline in numbers
probably began in the late 1930s, during the period of exploratory
patrols, and accelerated in the 1940s. Analysis of 250 blood
samples collected by Dr. D. C. Gajdusek among the neighboring
Onabasulu has revealed that antibodies for measles and a particular

---

20. Those who sought these positions were primarily mediums, who
traditionally share leadership roles with the elders of the community. The
Etoro lack leaders who are comparable to the "big men" of other parts of
New Guinea. The account of Hides's patrol accurately reflects the
significance of mediums as leaders.

strain of influenza are present in the samples taken from individuals who were over approximately twenty and twenty-one years of age, respectively, in 1969 (Gajdusek, personal communication, 1970).[21] This indicates that the tribes of the Papuan Plateau were exposed to influenza and measles in about 1948 and 1949. The effects of these sequential epidemics are clearly evident in the age structure of the Etoro population[22] (fig. 3), particularly for the twenty-one to twenty-five age group, whose members were five years of age or younger in 1948. I would estimate that these two epidemics alone produced a 15 percent reduction in population.

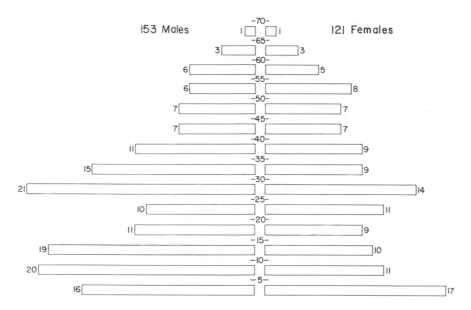

FIG. 3.   Age Structure of the Etoro Population, May 1, 1968

21. This analysis is incomplete and the results cited here are preliminary.

22. The age structure includes 71.0 percent (274/386) of the initial population of the tribal territory, the residents of eight of the eleven longhouse communities. I believe that it is representative of the entire population (see chapter 7, p. 172, for a comparison of sex ratios). The Etoro employ a specific form of address (*esama*) for persons born during the same season of the same year and are cognizant of the order of seniority of these groupings. It was thus possible to arrange individuals in birth order and group those of the same age. This material was separated into cohorts on the basis of physical appearance, taking into account sibling, parent-child, and husband-wife relationships, initiatory groups, etc.

Etoro communities experienced a 6.94 percent rate of natural decrease (from 386 to 360) during the fifteen months I was in the field. An influenza epidemic which occurred in January, 1969, accounted for 71 percent (22/31) of the mortality during this period; 5.7 percent of the Etoro population died in the epidemic, most of these during a single week.[23] In this same fifteen-month period ten children were born, five of whom survived. Even if epidemic mortality is discounted, the Etoro population would nevertheless have declined by more than 1 percent as a consequence of the low crude birthrate (21 per 1,000 per year) and high infant mortality (50 percent).

An explanation of the causes of Etoro depopulation would entail explication of complex interrelationships between many cultural and biological factors which is beyond the scope of the present work. I seek here only to describe the nature and extent of the decline as a background to discussion of its effects on residence, betrothal, etc., considered in subsequent chapters.

The magnitude of the population decline since 1935 may be estimated, on several grounds, to be in excess of 50 percent. First, informants maintain that there were twenty-one contemporaneous longhouse communities thirty to thirty-five years ago while only ten were extant in July, 1969. This suggests a 53 percent decline. If current longhouses have fewer residents than in the past (as seems likely) the decline would be correspondingly greater. Second, the southern portion of the Etoro tribal territory (below 750 meters) is currently vacant although it was occupied in 1935. Aerial photographs taken in 1961 (prior to direct contact) clearly indicate that the entire area is second growth; the outlines of gardens made ten to fifteen years earlier are distinguishable. The area of this vacant section is thirty-eight square miles of which ten square miles (at most) constituted a no-man's-land between the Etoro and their traditional enemies (or the segment of this falling within Etoro territory). The presently occupied zone of twenty-three square miles thus constitutes only 45 percent of the area utilized in the past. Projecting the 1968 population density of the occupied zone over this entire area would thus suggest a 55 percent population decline. This figure would of course be greater if the population density within the inhabited area has also decreased. Considering

---

23. Although our supplies of antibiotics were inadequate for an epidemic, I believe that they significantly reduced mortality at this time and throughout the period of fieldwork. Mortality in the 1948 influenza epidemic was undoubtedly greater.

all the data available, there can be no doubt that the Etoro have undergone an extremely severe depopulation and I consider 50 percent to be a conservative estimate. The Etoro themselves say that they are dying out. They attribute this to internal witchcraft. For each death a witch is named and a demand for compensation (or execution) follows. In an epidemic year the level of social conflict that is generated by this severely tests the social bonds which hold the society together, and this is yet another indirect ramification of contact.

CHAPTER 2

Subsistence

The Etoro economy is based on a combination of (1) sago processing, (2) shifting cultivation, (3) hunting, trapping, and collecting,
and (4) pig husbandry. Subsistence activity conforms to a seasonal
cycle which achieves a complementary articulation of these four
aspects of the economy.

The Etoro recognize two seasons: the *mugi*, or cloud season,
from about mid-April through mid-September, and the *kahẽo*, or
Marita pandanus season from late September through early April.
The *mugi* is distinguished by the availability of bush hen eggs,
wood grubs, and marsupials. During the *kahẽo*, eggs and grubs are
unavailable and marsupials are infrequently taken. *Marita pandanus* is abundant and a sauce made from the fruits is consumed
almost daily during October, November, and December and in substantial but lesser quantities during the other months of this season.

These seasons differ in diurnal patterns of rainfall and cloud
cover rather than in quantity of precipitation. The cloud season is
dominated by the southeasterlies (May to August) which bank
moisture-laden air against the southern rim of the Highlands producing low-lying clouds which envelope the southern slopes of Mt.
Sisa, particularly in the morning and evening but not infrequently
throughout the day. There is a persistent drizzle during much of the
mugi although heavy rains (of as much as five inches in twenty-four
hours) occur during both seasons. The *kahẽo* includes the periods
of prevailing westerlies (September to December) and northeaster-
lies (January to April) and is characterized by sunny days and late
afternoon or evening thundershowers. The total recorded annual
rainfall of approximately[1] 263 inches was fairly evenly distributed
throughout the year (80 inches from May to August, 95 inches from
September to December, and 87 inches from January to April).

---

1. Some of my notes were lost in a fire and I consequently lack exact
figures on total rainfall and certain aspects of subsistence which could not
be redone. The above approximation is based on my recollection of the
recorded figures for five months, and may be ten to fifteen inches too low.

This pattern is characteristic of the region along the southern edge of the Highlands (Ward and Lea, 1971:42–45). The soil is continuously wet and any slight depression provides suitable conditions for sago palms. The mean minimum temperature recorded at Kaburusato (altitude 2,500 feet) was 62°F. and the mean maximum 83°F. The lowest temperature recorded was 59°F.

The hunting and gathering facet of the economy makes an important contribution to the diet and has a significant influence on the timing of other subsistence activities. Rough estimates suggest that about two-thirds of the animal protein consumed is supplied through hunting, trapping, fishing, and collecting, while one-third is supplied by pig husbandry (table 1). Bush hen eggs are the largest single source of nondomestic protein and are available throughout the cloud season.[2] These birds build moundlike ground nests of dead leaves and twigs which are about five to six feet across and two to three feet high. The eggs are buried in the lower section of the mound and are apparently incubated by the heat given off by the decaying debris. The forest floor around the nest is "cleaned" over a sizable area in the process of construction and this, in conjunction with the size of the mounds, makes the sites clearly visible from some distance away. Locating the nests is thus relatively easy. They are found throughout Etoro territory although the most favorable collecting areas are located in the unoccupied primary forest area above 3,000 feet. The Etoro maintain that a single nest may contain as many as fifteen eggs and six to eight are frequently taken. The mounds may be opened to remove the eggs and then reclosed without causing the bush hen to desert the project. The same nest may consequently be revisited several times until the entire clutch is harvested. The final trip is sometimes made in the middle of the night in an attempt to capture the bush hen as well. The method employed is simply to creep up on the bird and grab her while she sleeps in a hollow stump or log near the nest.

Bush hen eggs are an important item in the diet in terms of overall quantity, availability in comparatively small portions over extended periods, comparatively high protein content, and high percentage of edible portion to waste. At the same time the labor expenditure in collecting is quite low, estimated yields being 4.5 ounces of egg per man-hour. In addition, snakes, frogs, wood

---

2. The number of eggs which individuals offered to sell me in various months provides a guide to seasonal availability: 9 eggs were offered in April, 26 in May, 26 in June, 39 in July, 31 in August, and 5 in September. Each egg weighs six ounces and this total of 137 equals 51.4 pounds.

TABLE 1

Estimated Proportions of Various Types of Animal Protein in the
Diet of One Etoro Community
(May, 1968, through April, 1969)

Source and Type of Animal Protein	Estimated Live Weight in Pounds	Percentage of Total
Domesticated:		
Domestic pig	550	34.4
Subtotal	550	34.4
Wild:		
Bush hen eggs	300	18.8
Wild pig	220	13.8
Cassowary	190	11.9
Marsupials	130	8.1
Fish	90	5.6
Frogs	40	2.5
Flying fox	30	1.9
Grubs	30	1.9
Other	20	1.3
Subtotal	1050	65.8
Grand Total	1600	100.2

Note: These estimates are presented as indications of the proportional contributions to the diet of domestic pork and various types of game and collectibles. (The basis for the estimates is evident in the text.) I do not believe that the total figure is sufficiently accurate to serve as a basis for quantifying individual dietary intake. Nevertheless, the age and sex distribution of the community within which this food was shared may be of interest. It included 9.17 adult males, 8.33 adult females, 1 adolescent male, 2 adolescent females, 2 children in the six- to ten-year age group, and 3 children in the one- to five-year age group, giving a total of 25.5 persons. The fractions represent individuals residing in the community for only part of the year.

grubs, mushrooms, and other edible items are frequently obtained on the same trips. Favorable locations for setting traps and snares are also noted and remembered for future reference, and previously constructed traps are checked.

Two varieties of wood grubs are collected during the cloud season (one being the larva of a beetle which is also eaten). These grubs are generally about the size of one's index finger and are found in rotting logs in sizable quantities. The tree species which they inhabit are sometimes cut and left to rot so that many grubs can be collected all at once at a particular location with the date of availability predictable in advance.[3] Several pounds can be har-

---

3. The Etoro also determine the status of the grub population by tapping the log with an ax. They say they can tell by the sound whether the grubs are ready to be harvested.

vested in as many hours by this method. Sago palms are similarly felled in order to provide an environment for a population of larva (which is harvestable in about fifty-two days). The grubs produced from sago are like miniature sacs of vegetable oil and are highly prized. (Two foot-long packages of sago in which large quantities of these grubs have been cooked are exchanged between prospective WF [wife's father] and DH [daughter's husband]). A large grasshopper which is found among the fronds of felled sago palms is also regularly consumed.

Maturing sweet potato gardens are sometimes used as "bait" to attract wild pigs which are taken by bow and arrow or by placing a spike at the point where they have previously jumped the fence. Men who employ this method of using the garden itself as a pig trap select sites near the margins of the primary forest—some distance from the longhouse community—in areas frequented by wild pigs but generally beyond the foraging range of their domestic counterparts. The garden must be watched almost daily during the latter part of the five-month harvest period and this entails a protracted stay at the small garden dwelling. The disadvantages of being away from the more comfortable longhouse and the social center it constitutes are offset by the hunting and trapping opportunities in the adjacent primary forest. The two Kaburusato men who elected this subsistence strategy secured a total of three wild pigs, all of which were taken in May and June, near the end of the harvest period. (These same two men also trapped four cassowaries.) All three pigs were relatively small with an estimated average weight of forty pounds each.[4] A fourth pig (of one hundred pounds) was shot at a sago stand (in September) when it was discovered partaking of the unworked portion of the palm by the work party arriving at the site. In all these instances the hunting and trapping were basically opportunistic and required virtually no extraordinary labor inputs. The strategy of cutting gardens at the margin of the primary forest expands the opportunities for taking large game but does not alter the characteristic nature of the endeavor. The Etoro rarely spend long hours tracking and stalking wild pigs in the bush.

---

4. These pigs were brought to the longhouse for distribution to community members in accordance with custom. It is not at all unlikely (indeed virtually a certainty) that other pigs were surreptitiously consumed by the hunters at their distant garden dwellings and the total take would thus be underestimated. The same caveat applies to other types of game listed in table 1.

Deadfall traps are also set for wild pigs. Two pigs were indeed procured by this method during the fieldwork period but both were domestic—a sow and a shoat.[5] These instances are indicative of a degree of conflict between pig husbandry on one hand and hunting and trapping on the other. It is evident that the Etoro favor the latter to the extent that they are willing to run the risk of accidentally culling valuable sows or immature pigs from their domestic herds.

Cassowaries are taken with snares which are set among the fruits and nuts on which they feed. This trapping activity is generally undertaken only when the maturation of particular cassowary foods creates the most favorable opportunities. I suspect that the cassowaries enter the margins of the secondary forest in large numbers several times during the year in order to feed on the fruits of certain trees specific to that floristic association. In any event, the two Kaburusato men gardening near the edge of the primary forest (at different locations) both snared the birds at about the same time (in second growth areas). The first pair of cassowaries was captured within a ten-day span in June and the second pair within an eleven-day period during November and December.[6]

Flying foxes are also hunted seasonally when optimal conditions are present. From late May to mid-June the animals feed on the fruits of a small (twenty to thirty feet) second growth tree (*fofononi*) which is prevalent along trails and in old gardens. The flying foxes arrive at these groves shortly after dark and by 10:30 are gorged and resting in the trees. The hunts take place between about 11:00 and 1:00 at night, being timed for maximum results. Parties of three or four men reconnoiter the groves using cane torches to light the understory of the trees. When a flying fox is spotted they rush to the base of the tree and shake it vigorously. If the animal attempts to take flight the oscillating branches knock it to the ground. More often, however, the flying fox will instinctively dig its talons into the branch to avoid being shaken loose. One man will then climb the swaying tree and dispatch the animal, either by

---

5. The individual who sets the trap keeps the pig but is obligated to replace it or otherwise compensate the owner. If the animal is a breeding sow with a litter both replacement and compensation are required.

6. Two of the birds were estimated to weigh 60 pounds apiece and the other two 30 pounds each. Several fledglings were also taken alive on other occasions and were kept for future exchange with the Huli. One of these died and was consumed at Kaburusato, adding the final 10 pounds to the total of 190 listed in table 1.

wrapping its wing around a branch and biting through the spinal cord at the back of the exposed neck or by ripping off a branch with a free hand and clubbing it. These hunts are undertaken nearly every night during the May to June season when the trees are in fruit. A sample of seven hunts totaling fifty-seven man-hours yielded a return of 163 ounces of game or 2.86 ounces per man-hour (not to mention the drama and excitement provided for participant and observer alike). The game included several frogs in addition to the five flying foxes (obtained on four of the seven hunts). Marsupials are sometimes procured on these occasions, although none of them are included in the sample.

The groves of trees which attract the flying foxes are, to some extent, a product of resource management. Although trees along the path to the longhouse and in adjacent old gardens are continually cut for firewood and construction, this particular species is left untouched. Over a period of time such selective cutting produces concentrations of these fruit trees, particularly bordering the paths which converge on longhouse sites.[7] Maintenance of the path also provides increased sunlight, which is evidently favorable to this species, and this in conjunction with the thinning of other trees augments their provenience in these locations. The overall effect is to widen the niche of the flying foxes and, more importantly, to create a convenient hunting ground close at hand where the animals may be procured with a minimum of effort. Rates of return on labor expenditure are thereby increased.

The Etoro maintain marsupial trap lines and associated hunting lodges in the primary forest on the upper slopes of Mt. Sisa for seasonal use. The trapping arrangement consists of a long picket fence about two to three feet high with deadfall traps placed along it at intervals of thirty to fifty feet. The fence line typically extends uphill from a fast-flowing stream to a steep cliff so as to block off a 200- to 300-yard section of the hillside. Any marsupials traversing this area are channeled into the deadfall traps. During the cloud season parties of two to five men spend several days at these sites. On arrival, the fence is repaired and the deadfall traps reconstructed in the vacant corridors along the line. This being completed, the men set out to search for bush hen eggs and to hunt for pythons and other game, returning at dusk to spend the night at the hunting lodge. In the morning the catch is collected, singed to

---

7. Longhouse sites are utilized for three to four years in a fairly regular process of rotation covering twenty-five years. The limited number of locations is a product of defensive considerations previously discussed.

remove the fur, gutted, and smoked for preservation. The traps are then reset and the procedure repeated for one or two more nights.

Patrilines whose territories are located in the northern sector of the tribal area maintain two or three of these traplines and each site may be utilized several times during the cloud season. The expeditions which took place while I was in the field yielded five to twenty marsupials weighing one to five pounds and averaging about two pounds apiece. (The smaller catch is usually obtained on the second utilization of the site.) Seventeen smoked marsupials are required for reciprocal exchanges between a betrothed man and his prospective wife's father so that catches of this order are apparently routine. In one case the required gift was accumulated by two men in two days. Isolated deadfall traps are scattered throughout the secondary forest and yield lesser quantities of game throughout the cloud season. Marsupials are also procured when their burrows and arboreal lairs are spotted in the course of daily activities.

Fish poisoning is undertaken at points where a river can be diverted from the main channel, making it possible to entrap the fish in an enclosed area and to reduce the quantity and velocity of water within it so as to allow for the buildup of a concentration of poison sufficient to kill the fish. (In open water, the poison is dissipated and swept downstream too rapidly to be effective.) Suitable sites occur naturally where a river divides around an island or large rock outcrop and are created at other locations by excavating a channel between the river and a smaller parallel-flowing tributary which empties into the main river one hundred yards or more downstream (see fig. 4). These diversion channels are said to have been constructed in the distant past. The first step in the fish poisoning operation is to build a series of breakwaters above the diversion point. These are placed at an oblique angle to the swift-flowing current so that they deflect it toward the side channel and reduce the force exerted against the main dam. Both are constructed by wedging logs between the boulders which protrude above the surface of the water. Stones are then piled against the logs and the holes are plugged with leaves and moss (pl. 7). While this work is in progress, a second, more loosely constructed dam is erected at the lower end of the 100- to 300-foot site to prevent the fish from escaping downstream. A woven, cone-shaped weir is lashed between the logs to provide an outlet which will accommodate the leakage of the upstream dam and the partial draining of the site. When the project is completed, the 20- to 30-foot wide main channel is reduced to a series of shallow, enclosed pools connected by a slowly flowing stream which exits through a weir only a foot in diameter. As the water drains from the enclosed area, the trapped fish become visible against the rocky bottom and the men attempt to stone them from positions atop the boulders along the shore. Generally missing, they leap into the shallow water to pursue the fish by hand. A period of pandemonium follows, while the men race through the small pools whooping, shouting, and falling over each other in their attempts to grab the elusive prey. The sport lasts for about an hour although some men tire of it earlier and wander off to collect derris from the adjacent forest. The roots and branches of these trees are tied in bundles, set on a rock at the upstream end of the site and pounded with a wooden club. The bundles are alternately beaten and washed in the water, being moved successively from pool to pool as each is saturated. Meanwhile sticks are used to prod under the large boulders and drive the fish from any areas where the poison may not effectively penetrate. The stunned fish are collected as they float to the surface, or are caught in the weir as they attempt to escape. After the poisoning is completed, the weir is emptied on the bank and then returned to its former position where it remains overnight. Any fish that expire during the night are carried into the weir by the current and are collected the following morning. The dams and breakwaters are left to be broken down by the force of the water and are constructed anew when the site is utilized again.

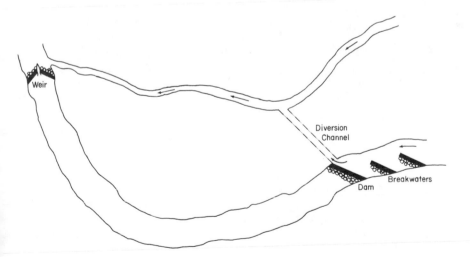

FIG. 4.   A Fish Poisoning Site

Fish poisoning expeditions yield eight to twenty-two pounds of fish (in observed cases)[8] or 3.5 to 11.0 ounces per man-hour. The latter figure is based on the total time spent at the site, including that devoted to the sport of attempting to stone and hand capture the trapped fish which will be killed by the poison in any event.[9] Omitting this, returns would be 4.6 to 14.3 ounces per man-hour. The number of participants ranges from two to six, depending on the size of the site. Nearly all the fish procured from the large rivers are a scaleless variety (called *abãso*) with feelers around the mouth, resembling a bullhead. The remainder are a smaller scaleless fish (*aĩ*) which lack feelers and are more prevalent in small streams. *Aĩ* are about the size of sardines while *abãso* may weigh a pound.

Aĩ are taken by a variety of methods which include stoning, hand capture, and poisoning. A bundle of unbeaten derris root is sometimes placed in a small stream near a deposit of frog eggs. The poison is gradually released and keeps the surrounding water sufficiently polluted to kill any fish which come to feed on the eggs. The derris is set out in the morning on the way to a garden or sago stand and on the return trip the fish are collected from a cone-shaped weir into which they are carried by the current. Small catches of three to twelve ounces are frequently obtained by this and other methods throughout the year. The bulk of these small fish are caught by children and are consumed by them.

Birds, lizards, snakes, bats, small rodents, and frogs are procured as the opportunity arises. Ground frogs are particularly abundant during certain periods of the cloud season when they are taken in large quantities (by hand) and smoked. The birds obtained are mostly juveniles hand captured from nests. Occasionally a snare will be placed around the edges of a nest which can be drawn tight from the ground in an attempt to catch nesting birds as well. None of these items are quantitatively important in the diet, with the exception of frogs (table 1).

Various greens, ferns, mushrooms, tree leaves, several varieties of wild nuts, a wild (*pandanus?*) fruit, and tuber are also col-

---

8. The Etoro maintain that very few fish are taken on some occasions, but I did not have the opportunity to weigh these minimal yields.

9. The derris "poison" kills fish by interfering with their oxygen intake and chasing the fish just before the poisoning begins may increase their oxygen requirements and therefore hasten their demise. However, it is doubtful that this makes a difference of more than five or ten minutes at most and would not alter the total take as the quantities of derris used are certainly sufficient to kill all the fish in the dammed area.

lected. All of these items are gathered as they are available in the course of daily activities, particularly while walking to and from gardens and sago stands. Tree ferns are regularly eaten and are also the object of special collecting expeditions (especially when meat is on hand to be cooked with them). Two kinds of wild nuts (*kisipe* and *morape*) are also specifically sought and are consumed in fair quantities. These are available during parts of the year when (cultivated) Tahitian chestnuts (*Edocarpus edius*) and breadfruit nuts are out of season and thus fill out a nearly year-round supply of nuts (table 4).

Etoro pigs are semidomesticated and spend most of their lives foraging in the bush unattended. When a sow produces a litter the owner will attempt to capture the piglets and bring them to the longhouse. They are then fed and fondled for three to six months, their ears are clipped to distinguish them from wild pigs, and the males are castrated. The rations provided for the animals are gradually decreased at the end of this period and the pigs forage for the majority of their food. They are permitted to wander unattended but generally stay within about a mile of the longhouse, sometimes appearing in the late afternoon to receive a few scraps of food (one sweet potato at most). Pigs also come to sago stands where a palm is being worked and are sometimes permitted to finish off part of the lower section of the trunk which contains tougher fibers and is more difficult to process. This sporadic feeding does not require any significant productive effort for maintenance of the pig herd but is usually sufficient to make the animals approachable when they are ready for slaughter. They sometimes elude their owners on specific occasions but are usually caught eventually.

Pigs are generally slaughtered to fulfill social obligations although they may also be killed simply because the owner is hungry for pork. A man who wishes to kill a pig must ask the permission of the *Sigisato*[10] spirits, channeling his request through a medium during a seance. It is said that these spirits will approve the request unless the pig is very small. The *Sigisatos* do not partake of any essence of the slaughtered animals nor are they spiritually connected with them in any way. Rather, the request is part of a general set of beliefs which involve these and other spirits in many human activities, including economic endeavors. One effect of the requirement is to socialize pork consumption. A pig cannot be killed unless

---

10. *Sigisato* spirits are nonancestral but are associated with particular lineages through the co-ownership of territory. Spirits and their relationship to subsistence activities are discussed in the concluding section of this chapter.

everyone knows about it and the pork must then be shared. Private slaughter and consumption would evoke the wrath of the *Sigisato* spirits, who would consequently withdraw the protection from witchcraft (and other disasters) which they normally provide.

Domestic pigs are killed for brideprice payments, customary exchanges with affines and cross-cousins, at mortuary ceremonies, and so that their hearts and livers may be employed in oracular procedures to determine the identity of a witch. These organs are steam-cooked to the name of an alleged witch suspected of being responsible for a death. If they come up raw, the man is guilty.[11] (The results are believed to be determined by the *Sigisato* spirits, but are rather easily manipulated.) The pork consumed at Kaburusato (table 1) was derived from eight different pigs, six of which were killed for the above reasons of social obligation. One was slaughtered because the owner was hungry for pork and one was accidentally killed in a deadfall trap.

Although pigs are occasionally fed, their rations are only a very small fraction of those consumed by their owners and do not begin to approach the 36 to 40 percent of total harvested root crops reported by Rappaport (1967:61) for the peak of the Tsembaga pig cycle. Pigs are regularly fed only during the first few months of their life and, perhaps, the last few months before anticipated slaughter.[12] Though no exact figures are available the rate of return on labor expenditure is undoubtedly quite high compared to the one-to-one ratio Rappaport reports. The yields of protein in hunting and collecting also appear to be reasonably favorable, ranging from 2.86 ounces per man-hour for flying fox hunts to approximately 7.0 ounces for the average fish poisoning expedition. Individuals evidence no signs of protein deficiency.

Consumption of domestic pork and wild game is governed by food taboos. The number and percentage of native taxa of game and collectibles available to various social categories is given in table 2. Although age is a factor, the same distinctions which are made concerning the occupation areas and symbolic architecture of

---

11. According to explicit Etoro belief, men are "raw" and witches are "cooked." Witches are particularly evil because they eat "raw" men. However, the latter may eat witches whom they have killed because witches are "cooked." This belief thus justifies doing unto witches precisely what witches are executed for for doing unto others. The intriguing oppositions will be analyzed on another occasion.

12. A pig might consider itself lucky to receive one small tuber and some garbage biweekly over the long midterm of its five-year life-span.

TABLE 2
Food Taboos and Social Categories

Type of Game	Total Number of Edible Native Taxa	Widows	Children of Deceased Men	Children of Living Men	Young Women Age 12–18	Mature Women Age 19 or Older	Unmarried Young Men Age 17 or Older	Married Men	Elderly Men
Birds	35	13	13	30	31	31	34	34	35
Marsupials	21	3	8	13	15	16	19	20	21
Lizards	3	2	3	3	3	3	3	3	3
Snakes	9			5	6	6	8	9	9
Frogs	6			6	6	6	6	6	6
Fish	2			2	2	2	2	2	2
Bats	1			1	1	1	1	1	1
Bush pig	2			2	2	2	2	2	2
Cassowary	1			1	1	1	1	1	1
Bush hen eggs	1	*					1	1	1
Flying fox	1					1	1	1	1
Eels	1					1	1	1	1
Total	83	18	24	63	67	70	78	81	83
Percentage of Total	100	21.7	28.9	75.9	80.7	84.3	94.0	97.6	100

*Available to widows beyond childbearing age.

43

the longhouse are also evident here as men are favored over women and both are favored over widows and the children of deceased men. These restrictions on the consumption of game are offset, to some extent, by the cultural rule that a man cannot consume domestic pork if one of his pigs (other than a shoat) has died of natural causes. This prohibition, which only affects married men and bachelors (over seventeen years of age), is lifted when the individual slaughters a domestic pig for general consumption. However, mortality among roaming quasi-domesticated pigs is rather high and five of nine males at Kaburusato (over the age of seventeen) were prohibited from consuming domestic pork. (One man distributed the entire bridal pork from his daughter's wedding without touching a morsel.) This rule has a number of effects: it encourages men to watch over their pigs, provides protein to those social categories of individuals most restricted with respect to the consumption of wild game, and stimulates men who cannot consume pork to hunt. The most avid hunters are often those who are debarred from partaking of domestic pork.

A calculation of game consumption according to the native taxa available to various social categories does not provide an entirely accurate representation of the distribution of total animal protein since some types of game are procured in larger quantities than others. Many of the taxa prohibited to widows, women, and children are rarely taken. To correct this deficiency, estimates of total animal protein available to various social categories are given in table 3. These estimates indicate that married women actually fare better than most adult men and bachelors (who frequently cannot eat domestic pork). Only (unremarried) widows and the children of deceased men (below age seventeen and twelve for males and females, respectively) are significantly disadvantaged, but this is a temporary condition for the individuals involved.

The seasonal availability of various types of game and collectibles, *Marita pandanus,* and nuts is illustrated in table 4.[13] It is clear that a substantial majority of game and eggs are consumed during the cloud season, particularly between May and August. This pattern is accentuated when the proportions of these items in the diet are taken into account. Only about 16 percent of the total wild animal protein is consumed during the *kahēo.* It is therefore

---

13. The availability of these selected items is not susceptible to human determination. The general pattern is quantitative rather than qualitative in some instances, i.e., *Marita pandanus* is consumed in all months, but only infrequently during the cloud season.

TABLE 3

Percentage of Total Animal Protein Available to
Various Social Categories

Social Category	Approximate Percentage of Total Animal Protein in the Diet Available for Each Category
Widows of childbearing age	35.0
Children of deceased men	35.5
Widows past childbearing age	53.2
Children of living men	73.8
Young women age 12–18	75.0
Mature women age 19 or older	97.0
Unmarried young men age 17 or older	99.0*
Married men	99.0*
Elderly men	100

*Includes domestic pork, 64.6 percent when this is prohibited.

not surprising that the Etoro generally elect to kill domestic pigs during this season. Most pigs are slaughtered for customary exchanges with affines and cross-cousins, typically during the latter half of the *pandanus* season.

Nuts are available in most months of the year, but in greatest quantity during the cloud season when breadfruit nuts and Tahitian chestnuts are bearing. On the other hand, *Marita pandanus,* which is rich in vegetable fats (as are nuts), is consumed throughout the *kahēo,* which is specifically named for this food.

The hunting, trapping, and collecting facet of the Etoro economy is much more affected by seasonal factors than are gardening and sago processing. Some items are obtainable only during the cloud season while others are most readily available (or most easily procured) during that period. In contrast, gardening may be undertaken at any time, as may sago processing. However, gardening tasks are generally scheduled so as to make time available for trapping and collecting, and horticultural activities consequently tend to conform to a seasonal pattern as well. The fact that large communal gardens account for most of the land in production gives an added impetus to this tendency. It is difficult to mobilize work parties for collective tasks such as fencing when, on any given day, some individuals prefer to check their dispersed deadfall traps, repair to the hunting lodges, or undertake egg collecting expeditions. The initiation of communal gardens requires a general consensus among the participants and such a consensus is unlikely to

TABLE 4
Seasonal Food Availability (Game and Tree Crops)

Prevailing Winds		Southeasterlies					Westerlies				Northeasterlies		
Etoro Seasons		Cloud Season (*Mugi*)					Marita Pandanus Season (*Kahẽo*)						
Months	Apr.	May	June	July	Aug.	Sept.	Oct.	Nov.	Dec.	Jan.	Feb.	Mar.	Apr.

Seasonal food availability:

Game and collectibles

- Bush hen eggs
- Wild pig
- Cassowary
- Marsupials
- Fish
- Frogs
- Flying foxes
- Grubs

Seasonal tree crops

- *Pandanus*
- Breadfruit nuts
- Tahitian chestnuts
- Wild *kisipe* nuts
- Wild *morape* nuts

Note: Solid and dashed lines distinguish continuous and intermittent availability.

46

emerge when there are competing activities. Thus the larger gardens are rarely initiated during the height of the cloud season, although the initial tasks are typically undertaken in August, toward the close of that period. The organization of concerted action is much simpler when a garden is made by one or two families, and the times of initiation of these smaller plots are also much more variable.

An estimated 78 percent of total annual garden acreage is planted in October and early November, with preparatory tasks being completed in August and September. As a result, the bulk of the harvested tubers is available during the same months (mid-February to mid-July). This in turn affects the scheduling of sago processing, as sago is not required when sweet potatoes are in abundant supply. Thus the seasonality of hunting, trapping, and collecting imparts a seasonal patterning to all subsistence activity, influencing the timing of garden starts and consequently the scheduling of sago working.[14] This pattern is quantitative rather than qualitative as gardening and sago processing occur throughout the year. However, there is considerable variation in the intensity of these activities.

The dominant agricultural cycle is illustrated in table 5. The larger communal gardens (of 1.5 to 6 acres or more) are generally initiated in early August (or the last week in July). The area is fenced by the men in August and September while the women clear the undergrowth from the area to be enclosed. These tasks are generally completed by October and the crops are planted during this month. In November, after the crops are securely rooted, the trees within the fenced area are felled on top of the garden. (The logic of this procedure is explained in a later section of this chapter.) Several smaller gardens (of 0.1 to 0.5 acres) are generally planted at the same time, although the preparatory tasks are compressed into a single month. All of these gardens planted in October are weeded once during January and begin to yield small sweet potatoes in the latter part of February (three and one-half months after planting). By mid-July weeds dominate the plot and the harvesting of tubers is essentially completed. Greens, sugar cane, etc., continue to be available and bananas are harvested in the twelfth and fifteenth months after planting (i.e., October through January). However, tubers are completely harvested before the

------

14. Although the observed timing of garden work might be due to climatic factors directly, the fact that some gardens are made throughout the year suggests that this is not the principal factor which governs the seasonal cycle. Nevertheless, the typical October planting does take advantage of a November dry spell.

new communal gardens are fenced in August. The sweet potato
supply from these large gardens is discontinuous, being available
for only about five months, i.e., mid-February to mid-July.

Smaller gardens accounting for 22 percent of the total annual
acreage in production tend to conform to an alternative cycle in
which gardens are planted at eight-month intervals so that three
plots are cultivated every two years. In this case planting takes
place in October, June, February, and again in October.[15] Initiation
of gardens planted at eight-month intervals in October of two successive years establishes two offset cultivation cycles in addition to
the dominant cycle discussed above so that gardens are planted
every four months and sweet potatoes are available on a continuous basis, but with definite periods of peak yields (table 5).

The articulation of these two cycles makes it possible for individual families to easily move from one to the other, switching over
from eight-month to twelve-month planting intervals when the two
cycles converge in October and thus participating in large communal gardens. There are a number of factors which influence an
individual family's decision to pursue one or the other of these
cycles at any given point in time, and I will only briefly outline
them here. First, individuals vary in dietary preference. Some prefer greater quantities of sago to sweet potatoes in their personal
diet and vice versa. Second, gardening generally requires that some
weeks be spent in small bush houses at the site but away from the
longhouse and the social center it represents (although this often
presents hunting opportunities). These absences from the longhouse may be regarded as advantageous or disadvantageous, depending upon the individual. Third, an individual family will have
variable quantities of mature sago palms which are ideal for processing in any given year. The palms must be cut before they
flower as the inflorescence utilizes the starch stored in the pith. On
the other hand, palms which are cut too early are low yielding,
more fibrous, and more difficult to process. Prior to depopulation I
believe that the availability of mature sago palms was the primary
factor which determined election of the eight- or twelve-month
gardening cycle. Fourth, male and female labor requirements are
significantly different in sago processing and gardening. Women do
76 percent of the work (in total hours of labor) in sago processing
and 62 percent of the work in gardening (since the introduction of

---

15. The 22 percent of total annual acreage in production refers to June
and February plantings. Small gardens planted in October are included in
the 78 percent total for the dominant cycle.

TABLE 5

Seasonal Gardening Cycles, Composite Yield Profiles, and Frequency of Sago Processing

Etoro Seasons	Cloud Season			Marita Pandanus Season									Cloud Season			Marita Pandanus Season									Cloud Season		
Months	July	Aug.	Sept.	Oct.	Nov.	Dec.	Jan.	Feb.	Mar.	Apr.	May	June	July	Aug.	Sept.	Oct.	Nov.	Dec.	Jan.	Feb.	Mar.	Apr.	May	June	July		
Dominant cycle (large communal gardens)	fence clear			plant	cut trees	weed		yielding tubers						fence clear		plant	cut trees	weed		yielding tubers							
Secondary cycle I (smaller gardens)	yielding tubers			fence clear plant	cut trees	weed		yielding tubers						fence clear plant		cut trees	weed		yielding tubers							
Secondary cycle II (smaller gardens)	cut trees	weed		yielding tubers			fence clear plant			yielding tubers				weed		fence clear plant			yielding tubers							
	Year 1												Year 2														
Annual tuber yields	15%			78%				7%	15%					78%						7%							
Annual banana yields	85%			15%										85%				15%									
Pandanus harvest*																											
Nuts*																											
Sago processing frequency																											

* These profiles are based on unquantified estimates.

49

steel tools).[16] The mix of starch staples in the family diet thus also reflects the familial division of labor. This is also influenced by the labor resources available, that is, the number of wives, daughters, sons, and widowed parents within or attached to the family or pair of families which normally garden and process sago together.[17] Fifth, sago processing is a more efficient form of production (in terms of returns on labor) than is gardening, even though steel tools have reduced labor expenditure in gardening but not in sago processing (cf. Townsend, 1969). The twelve-month gardening cycle thus requires less total labor output than the eight-month cycle. As a result of this, the added sago working entailed by the twelve-month gardening cycle does not increase female labor so much as it reduces male labor. It appears that, at least in some instances, men determine the election of the twelve-month cycle by the simple expedient of procrastination in fencing the garden and thus in initiating the project.

The fact that large gardens are not yielding tubers when new gardens are prepared means that everyone must work double-time during the August to January period in order to provide sago for food and also to complete gardening tasks (and most of this burden falls upon the women). To avoid this it would be necessary to plant gardens in June as these would yield during the period when the major (October-planted) gardens are made. However, June gardening interferes with hunting, trapping, and collecting and thus very little land is put into production at this time. Only two small gardens totaling 0.6 of an acre were planted in June (1968) as compared to 7.5 acres in October and 1.5 acres in February (1969).[18] In 1969, no June gardens were made.

---

16. Prior to the introduction of steel tools, the sexual division of labor was approximately equal as men did 58 percent of the total hours of work in gardening (vs. 38 percent currently), while women did 76 percent of the work in sago processing. (The latter is unaffected by steel technology; indeed stone adzes are still used to extract the pith.) In addition, housebuilding, hunting, trapping, egg and grub collecting, and splitting logs for firewood are male tasks. Both sexes gather wild greens, ferns, mushrooms, etc.

17. Widows, fatherless bachelors, and newlyweds thus tend to participate in the larger communal gardens where they can pool their labor.

18. This acreage accounts for most of the land utilized by members of the Kaburusato community (excepting one family) and these numbered twenty-seven to thirty-five individuals at different times during the year. However, residents had ten shares in the gardens of other communities throughout the year while only one nonresident had a section in the above

The frequency of sago processing generally varies inversely with sweet potato yields but is also affected by the availability of female labor time (table 5). Large quantities of sago are produced and stored in the last half of June and in July while tuber yields are maximal. This stored sago is utilized during the August to January period when individuals are engaged in making large communal gardens, thus easing labor requirements during these peak months. Sago processing frequency declines somewhat as female labor is diverted to clearing underbrush and planting, increases again between planting and weeding (in November and December) when female labor in the gardens is not required, drops off during weeding (in early January) and then declines markedly as sweet potatoes and taro become available.

The temporal articulation of gardening and sago processing within the seasonal cycle—in conjunction with defensive considerations—requires the spatial interdigitation of these two facets of the economy. This in turn affects both the selection of garden sites and the fallow period. It is convenient when sago palms (suitable for processing) are located near the garden site since substantial sago processing takes place during the same period that major gardens are prepared. This proximity facilitates the allocation of male and female labor during this period of peak demand, and also affords the women protection from enemy raiding parties. In the morning the men shred and extract the sago pith and then move to the adjacent garden to proceed with fencing or tree cutting while the women beat and wash the shredded sago fiber for the remainder of the day. Similarly, women may clear some of the undergrowth from the garden while the men cut and split the sago palm and construct the troughs (made from the fronds) in which the sago is beaten and washed and the starchy water collected. The proximity of the sago stand to the garden is thus essential in order to protect the women and, at the same time, allow the men to proceed with their required tasks. In the event of a raid the men are close at hand, yet they need not be away from their work in order to stand guard.

Defensive considerations and the effective utilization of labor in gardening and sago working therefore require adjacent sago resources. Conversely, sizable sago stands can be most conveniently

---

total of 9.6 acres of Kaburusato gardens. The latter figure represents annual utilization of about 0.3 acre per capita, and the shares in external gardens would probably increase this to 0.4 acre per capita. This range (0.3 to 0.4) may be taken as a rough estimate of land usage.

utilized when they are near current gardens (or the longhouse). The problem here is primarily one of timing. Distant sago would have to be worked when gardening labor is not required elsewhere. But with the exception of the June-July period, this occurs when tuber yields are maximal and substantial quantities of sago are not needed.

The availability of mature sago palms close to a prospective garden site is thus a major factor in site selection. It follows from this that garden fallows are regulated by the maturation period of sago, which is approximately twenty-five years (at these altitudes and temperatures). The sago must be cut before it flowers and goes to seed and this dictates a return to the same garden site when the palms are fully mature, or a few years before this. If there are two good garden locations near the sago stand they may be utilized at about fifty-year intervals, although the twenty-five year period is more typical. This pattern is explicitly recognized by the Etoro. They say that at about the time of his marriage,[19] a man will return to the garden land and sago stands utilized by his father when he was born.

The fact that proximate sago resources are considered by the Etoro to be one of the major factors in garden site selection indicates, indirectly, that a failure to prepare gardens in June is typical. It is because only a very few small gardens are planted at this time that sufficient tubers are not available during the major garden-making period, and this necessitates extensive sago processing during these months (and hence adjacent sago stands). The reluctance of the men to cut gardens in June is due to the fact that this is the height of the cloud season—the most favorable time for hunting, trapping, and collecting. The point that the seasonality of these activities determines the seasonal patterning of the entire economy bears reiteration.

The Etoro plant two types of gardens which are primarily distinguished by crop mix. Approximately 80 percent of the land in production (annually) is devoted to sweet potato gardens and 20 percent to taro-banana gardens. Sweet potato gardens are dominated by that crop, which accounts for 90 percent to 95 percent of plant cover. Small quantities of taro are planted in the wetter spots and particularly along small streams that run through these gardens. Bananas, New Guinea asparagus (*Setaria palmaefolia*), pit pit (*Saccharum edule*), and sugar cane (*Saccharum officinarum*) are all planted near piles of brush and undergrowth. *Rungia klossi*

---

19. Traditionally, men married when they were twenty to twenty-five years of age.

(a green) is typically interplanted with sweet potatoes. Other crops include hibiscus leaves (which are segregated), indigenous beans (*Psophocarpus tetragonuboles*), and cucumbers.[20] Pumpkins and pineapples have been recently introduced and are regularly grown. (Passion fruit, peanuts, and several other crops planted shortly before our arrival were regarded as curiosities.) All of these nontuberous vegetables are somewhat more prevalent in the garden surrounding the longhouse than in gardens farther afield. Similarly, the larger October-planted gardens contain a greater variety of crops than do smaller plots planted in February and May. Greens from the former gardens are harvestable throughout the year and the February and May gardens are consequently devoted more exclusively to sweet potatoes.

Taro-banana gardens are dominated by those two crops and contain relatively few sweet potatoes, generally confined to one portion of the plot. Short greens are omitted or segregated, while the taller New Guinea asparagus, pit pit, and sugar cane are interplanted. These crops are present in about the same proportion as in sweet potato gardens (i.e., 5 percent or less of plant cover).

I did not observe the planting of breadfruit trees or *Marita pandanus* groves. It is said that *pandanus* is planted in one section of a taro-banana garden and that a half-dozen or so breadfruit trees may be planted in either type of garden or near the longhouse.

As mentioned previously, the proximity of mature sago palms is a major consideration in site selection and this dictates a fallow period of about twenty-five years. The ease with which a plot can be fenced is also an important consideration. Nearly every garden is bordered on at least one side by a large river, deeply-cut stream, precipitous slope, or sheer cliff. Cliffside sites are prevalent due to the major fault lines which crosscut the slope of Mt. Sisa. Gardens are often located on old land slips or colluvial deposits which have a sheer cliff at the back and a steep slope over the front edge of the garden. These natural barriers require little or no fencing in order to preclude pig entry and labor expenditure is consequently reduced. For example, one garden of 1.55 acres with a total perimeter of 1,070 feet required only 354 feet of fence line. The unfenced 716 feet represented a saving of about eighty-four man-hours. These sites also simplify tree felling and conserve space in the garden that would otherwise be consumed by brush piles. The upper-story cover is generally comprised of seventy- to eighty-foot trees. Thus all the

---

20. The Etoro say they have always had cucumbers and regard them as a traditional food.

trees within sixty feet of the unfenced border can be felled so that the tops protrude over the edge of the steep slope. No trimming and stacking of branches is required and no garden area is lost to brush piles. There were four brush piles totaling 0.1 acre in the garden mentioned above and the conformation of the site obviated the need for an equivalent amount of unusable land.

Colluvial locations also tend to be relatively level and most of the enclosed area has a slope of 10° or less. Lighting conditions are favorable. The soils are probably deep and comparatively well drained—an important consideration when rainfall is over 260 inches a year. These favored sites are nearly always utilized for sweet potato gardens.

Proximity to the longhouse is not a major consideration in site selection. A site which is a half-hour's walk away will be preferred over much closer locations if it possesses the desirable characteristics noted above. The participants reside at the small dwelling in the garden during part of the period when daily labor is required and the treks made at other times often yield collectibles or information about game that is later utilized in hunting and trapping.[21]

Fences are constructed by stacking logs between pairs of poles which are driven in the ground and lashed together at the top or braced by forked supports placed at an angle against them. The base of the fence is often formed by large trees felled in a line. All the trees within an area about twenty to thirty feet wide on either side of the fence line are cut before the fence is begun. The cleared area outside the perimeter increases the amount of sunlight which the edge of the garden receives in the morning or evening. Most of the smaller trees on the garden side of the fence are incorporated in it, and the trimmed branches and tops are tossed over it. The finished product varies from two to six feet in height depending on the slope of the ground outside it and consequently the ease with which a pig might enter. On level ground, a fence four and one-half feet high is sufficient.

It is important to note that large communal gardens significantly reduce total labor expenditure in fencing. Twice as many running feet of fence line are needed to enclose eight half-acre plots as to enclose one four-acre garden. Communal gardening also provides

---

21. The presence of two types of trees and the absence of one other are considered to be indicative of favorable garden locations. Species identification of these trees is not available, although one of the two desirable trees is clearly an oak. Seventy- to eighty-foot oaks are generally the most prevalent upper-story trees on sites selected for gardening.

advantages of sociability, defense against enemy raiding parties, and adjustment of the labor supply to the sexual division of labor.

The area along the fence line of a large garden is sometimes planted before the interior of the garden is entirely cleared of underbrush in order to provide yields three or four weeks earlier. The remainder is planted after the removal of undergrowth is completed. A hole is poked in the ground with a digging stick and two or three sweet potato vines are pressed into it. Planting density is 4,940 sweet potato sets and 1,889 interplanted *Rungia* sets per acre in sweet potato gardens.

The trees within the garden are felled two or three weeks after planting when the sweet potato vines are securely rooted and have begun to put out new leaves. Procedures in cutting timber vary to some extent depending on the type and size of the garden. In multi-acre sweet potato gardens the trees within each hundred-foot square section of the garden are cut so that the tops converge on one central point while the trunks are arranged like the spokes of a wheel. Each successive tree top partially pulverizes the previous ones producing a compact brush pile measuring twenty by thirty feet in the center of this section. Most of the timber within such a section can be cut to fall in the desired manner and very little further work in trimming and stacking branches is required. However, in sweet potato gardens those trees felled across the basic astral pattern of trunks are usually trimmed and the branches are added to the brush pile. These clearing procedures are modified to take advantage of natural features. If the garden is bordered by a cliff, trees are cut so that the tops protrude over it; if there is a stream which runs through the garden, trees along both sides are cut so that the crowns fall into it.

Most of the trees rest on their tops a foot or so off the ground or on other trunks, and this clearing method thus does very little damage to the previously planted sweet potatoes. The vines are planted at densities of approximately one set per square yard so that very few are crushed by those trunks that do come in contact with the ground. After clearing, long-bearing crops such as bananas are planted around the edges of these large brush piles (see pl. 4).

Small sweet potato gardens of 0.5 acre or less are generally not more than one hundred feet wide and it is consequently possible to fell most of the trees outward from the center of the plot so that the tops are outside the enclosed area. However, this must be done before the fence is constructed so that it will not be crushed in the process. These small plots are thus cleared of most timber before fencing or during the course of fence construction. Only a thin tree cover is left to be cut after planting. These trees are felled in any manner which is convenient and the tops are usually trimmed and tossed over the fence. There are thus few or no brush piles and bananas and other long-bearing crops are frequently omitted from these gardens. In smaller plots, the entire garden-making sequence is often completed in four to six weeks.

In taro-banana gardens, no effort is made to create brush piles or to clear most of the garden of debris. Larger trees are felled first to form a network of trunks which will keep the bulk of the timber off the ground and prevent crop damage. The remaining trees are felled across these trunks in an irregular manner and are left un-trimmed. In overall appearance, the garden resembles a section of forest recently struck by a tornado. The leaves and twigs decompose providing a gradual release of nutrients and the taro and ba-nanas grow up through the debris.

Gardens are weeded in the third month after planting. About 95 percent of the weed cover which initially comes up in gardens consists of broadleaf plants, while grasses account for the remaining 5 percent. This facilitates weeding as the former are much more easily removed. The garden is thoroughly weeded only once.

Crops are harvested as they become available. Sweet potato vines are poked back in the ground after tubers are harvested and some weeds are removed in the process but little effort is made to replant and extend the productive period of the garden. The garden is almost completely harvested of tubers by the ninth month after planting and only a few small sweet potatoes are obtained after this. By this time the garden is generally overgrown with weeds which shade out the sweet potatoes and compete with them for nutrients. Grasses, which are more difficult to completely remove, are now more prevalent. Many cut trees have not died and new shoots which have sprouted from the trunk are already four or five feet high.[22] Soil fertility is reduced and rodents have multiplied in the garden and are beginning to consume a fair portion of the sweet potatoes. In short, an attempt to extend the productive period of the plot probably would not repay the effort. A complete weeding would be required and this is the most time-consuming task in making a garden—yet the expectable yields would be low or unpre-dictable at best. Only part of the garden adjacent to the longhouse is maintained for an extended period and this primarily as a source of greens rather than tubers.

---

22. Even cut poles used as fence supports sometimes take root and grow.

Succession of garden to forest is rapid and the grassy phase is brief, varying in different parts of the garden from about three to eight years. Brush piles and regrowth from tree stumps are particularly important in succession as they provide support for dense masses of fernlike vines which shade out the grasses. Small trees sprout under this vine cover and gradually extend it over the garden. This occurs at many points throughout the garden and after about five years there are only relatively small pockets of grass twenty or thirty feet across interspersed among groves of small trees. There are no permanent grasslands in Etoro territory and the only relatively persistent grassy areas are the sites of previous longhouses.

Etoro gardening procedures are adapted to the climatic conditions of the area and are also geared to the objective of obtaining high yields per unit of labor (rather than per unit of land). The high annual rainfall and the frequency of high intensity falls create problems of erosion, leaching, destruction of the soil structure, and disruption of the organic processes by which nutrients are formed.

The capacity of the Mt. Sisa soils to absorb water is quite limited. Experiments carried out in a cleared garden area indicated that one half-inch of rain can be absorbed in a little less than an hour, one inch in five hours and two inches in seventeen hours (after no rain the previous day).[23] During almost all days when two or more inches of rain was recorded (for twenty-four hours) the bulk of the precipitation occurred in the space of several hours and there was consequently extensive surface runoff. Daily falls in excess of two inches occurred nineteen times during a six-month

---

23. In another experiment, a hole 5 1/8 inches in diameter and 6 inches deep was filled with 2,000 ml. of water. This required ten hours to drain, although nothing prevented lateral flow. In the above experiment, lateral flow for the first 6 inches was prevented by a metal sleeve of the same dimensions as the above hole while infiltration capacity was measured by the declining level of 1,000 ml. of water in a graduated cylinder 3 5/16 inches in diameter. In this case, 108 ml. of water was absorbed in the first hour, 33 ml. in the second, 25 ml. in the third, and 17 ml. in each hour thereafter. Thus, five hours were required to absorb 200 ml., equal to one inch of rainfall. Comparison of the results of these two experiments reveals that capacity for lateral flow in the first six inches of soil is much greater than capacity for vertical flow. Both experiments were carried out in a garden adjacent to a newly constructed longhouse. The area had been cleared ten months before.

period for which complete daily records are available (June through December, omitting October) and probably occur about forty times annually.[24] In short, heavy rains which produce extensive surface runoff—and consequently erosion—are not uncommon.

The impact of high intensity rainfall breaks down the crumb structure of the soil, creating fine particles of clay which seep into the pores of the soil, thereby reducing infiltration capacity. This in turn increases surface runoff. It is clear from the preceding discussion that this reduced porosity was evident at the location where the experiment was conducted (which had been cleared ten months earlier). One may conclude that (1) the process occurs quite readily on Mt. Sisa soils which are unprotected by the forest canopy, and/or (2) that the soils of this region are of generally low infiltration capacity as a result of heavy rains experienced since their formation. Both conditions are probably applicable.

High annual rainfall also leaches the soil, washing nutrients into the deeper layers beyond the reach of crop roots. Available evidence indicates that leaching from heavy rains extending over a period of several days is sufficient to produce periodic nitrogen deficiency which retards plant growth early in the use period of the garden. Records of the leaf size and area of each new banana leaf were kept for seventeen plants (in a new garden adjacent to the longhouse). All plants experienced regressions in leaf size after planting as a consequence of nitrogen deficiency due to an initially poor rooting condition. However, after recovering from this, all plants experienced regressions in leaf size or reductions in the rate of increase on two subsequent occasions, eight and eleven weeks after planting. In both instances this took place about a week to ten days after particularly heavy rains extending over a period of several days (i.e., 8.24 inches in three days). It is probable that this precipitation leached a great deal of the available nitrogen from the soil curtailing the buildup of nitrogen in the meristem of the bananas and thereby triggering regressions in leaf size. The fact that this occurred so soon after planting indicates that the soil has a low initial fertility and that crops depend more on the continual production of nitrogen (and other nutrients) than upon residual quantities

---

24. One to 1.99 inches of rain may also be sufficient to produce surface runoff if the fall occurs in a short period. There were twenty days of precipitation in this range during the same six-month period. In addition there are probably no months during the year without at least two days of rainfall over two inches.

which accumulate during the fallow period.[25] In other words, the fallow period creates the preconditions for the production of nutrients rather than engendering an unutilized reservoir of them. Heavy rains disrupt the supply of nutrients available to the crops and produce periodic deficiencies. Similarly, it is not leaching of the soil per se that creates infertility over the term of the garden but rather depletion of the potential for the production of nutrients. Surface runoff is doubly detrimental inasmuch as it tends to wash away the humus layer and consequently reduces the potentiality for nitrification (as well as causing general erosion). This condition is probably the major reason why few tubers are harvested after the tenth month and also accounts for the failure of the Etoro to attempt to extend the use period of the garden. However, long-bearing crops are planted at those locations where eroded humus tends to accumulate.

The Etoro procedure of felling trees after the garden is planted minimizes the duration of the period during which the soil is directly exposed to destructive high intensity rainfall. The forest canopy protects the soil structure by breaking the impact of the rains. The trees are felled only after the sweet potatoes are securely rooted and the vines (and weeds) thus spread rapidly over the garden area providing a protective cover. The interval between tree cover and crop cover is thus brief (and minimal).

The forest canopy also holds a certain amount of precipitation and thus reduces the quantity reaching the soil. This decreases the possibility that infiltration capacity will be exceeded and hence

---

25. Soil analysis carried out in the field supports this interpretation. A composite sample of the first 8 inches of soil was taken several feet from the base of the banana plant which evidenced the greatest rate of growth (leaf area had increased from 89 square inches to 5,328 square inches in six months and three weeks since planting). The soil was analyzed immediately after extraction and twenty-four hours later in order to measure the production of nutrients and change in pH levels. Soil pH levels for the initial analysis and the later analysis were 4 and 5 respectively. The results for the nutrients were:

Nutrient	Initial (ppm)	After 24 Hours (ppm)
P	0.5–1.0	2.5
K	<5.0	<5.0
NH_4	<2.0	2.0–10.0 (closer to 10.0)
NO_3	0.0	2.0

reduces the chances that surface runoff and erosion will occur during this particularly vulnerable period (before crop roots are sufficient to hold the soil). In addition, there is usually a dry spell of about a week's duration in November,[26] and tree felling in October-planted gardens is timed to take advantage of this. The garden is initially exposed during a period when rainfall is least likely. The chance that heavy rains will wash out plant roots and cause reduced infiltration capacity and reduced potential for the production of nutrients by washing away the humus layer is thus minimized by both timing and procedures.

The delay in cutting trees also has a beneficial effect on weed germination. Although the shade conditions do not appear to inhibit the rooting of sweet potato vines, they tend to promote the germination of shade plants rather than sun plants (particularly grasses). Ferns and broadleaf plants generally come up initially in the areas between sweet potato sets. However, many of these do not thrive in the full sun conditions presented after tree felling and the sweet potatoes spread easily at their expense while the germination of grasses is delayed. This facilitates weeding. (This probably also explains the fact that grasses do not become prevalent in the garden until several months after weeding.)

Felling the timber on top of the garden provides erosion control since anything which impedes the flow of water reduces erosion. This point is nicely illustrated by erosion in the old gardens adjacent to the longhouse. Over a period of years, many of the cut trees in these gardens are removed for firewood. After heavy rains, entire sections of one of these old gardens washed out although this was never observed in current gardens.

The manner in which trees are felled also provides for utilization of humus which is washed away during the cultivation period. This is directed toward brush piles where long-bearing crops are planted by the astral pattern of tree trunks which converge on this point. The products of erosion thus end up where they will do the most good. In addition, the leaves and twigs from cut timber replenish the humus layer of the soil, particularly in taro-banana gardens where trees are evenly dispersed over the garden area. In sweet potato gardens, undergrowth piles and brush piles also provide a gradual release of nutrients which can be taken up by the

---

26. Such a dry spell occurred while I was in the field and is mentioned in patrol reports. This period is typified by a superabundance of flies which the Etoro say occurs yearly at this time.

plants as they are produced. In this rainfall regime burning would not be advantageous since most of the nutrients provided would be leached out of the soil or washed away before they could be utilized by the crops. (Burning is probably possible even under these wet conditions but would require considerable labor expenditure.)

Etoro gardening procedures are designed to minimize labor expenditure. Sites which require the least effort in fencing and cutting timber are preferred. Large communal gardens also reduce fencing labor. Clearing time is decreased by felling tree crowns on top of each other and thus allowing the energy released by the falling trees to do the work of removing branches. Cutting the trees six weeks or so after clearing undergrowth provides for the initial germination of weeds which do not flourish in full sun and later reduces labor expenditure in weeding since few grasses are present. Time consuming tasks of burning, mounding, and soil preparation are avoided. These procedures tend to maximize yields per unit of labor (cf. Clark, 1966). Yields per unit of land are probably comparatively low.[27]

Supernatural Aspects of Subsistence Activity

Supernatural agencies impinge upon many subsistence activities, according to Etoro belief, and the success or failure of these endeavors therefore conveys important information concerning the relations between man and spirits. Fish poisoning is particularly significant in this respect. The fish (*abãso*) which the Etoro poison are the corporeal abode of the spirits of the dead and their spirit progeny (collectively, the *Kesame* spirits). Fish poisoning can thus only be initiated at times and places designated by these spirits (which occupy the bodies of hornbills for the duration). The *Kesames* communicate this information to a medium in the course of a seance and the medium directs the operation at the specified location the following day.

These beliefs invest fish poisoning with supernatural signifi-

---

27. Although no figures on yields are available, comparatively low yields per acre can be inferred from the annual quantity of land in production. The Etoro utilize between 0.3 and 0.4 of an acre of garden land per capita per year (excluding *pandanus* groves) even though sweet potato and taro-banana gardens provide only about half of the food consumed. (Sago accounts for 55 percent to 60 percent of the starch in the diet and *Marita pandanus* is the most important nonstarchy food.) In the Highlands where garden produce provides nearly all the food consumed, 0.2 of an acre of land per capita is commonly utilized.

cance and the size of the catch is meaningful in a number of ways. It reveals the state of a medium's relation to his particular spirit (or spirits)[28] and the condition of the community's relation to the spirit world. A bountiful catch signifies the cooperation and general goodwill of the *Kesame* spirits toward the community. Moreover, the medium's ability to enlist spirit aid is clearly demonstrated. A poor catch has the opposite connotations but is open to a variety of causal interpretations. A seance is conducted to determine the reason for the failure and the explanations range from capriciousness of the spirits to faulty procedures (e.g., the poison was brought to the site before it was sealed off and the fish smelled it and fled).

No matter what the interpretation, it is difficult to avoid the conclusion that the medium is at fault—particularly since he directs the empirical operation and therefore bears the responsibility for procedural errors (as well as for supernatural failings). If the medium does not confess to being inept in his organizational role then he must tacitly admit that his spirit (or the spirits in general) have played him false. In the latter event his ability to command the cooperation of the spirits in every context will be open to question. In short, he appears as a medium who cannot mediate. Indeed this point will be made by other mediums in the form of snide allusions to his shortcomings, as there is a considerable degree of competition among mediums (and this is particularly manifested in fish poisoning). A medium's professional reputation thus hinges on his empirical success at timing and directing these operations. Fish poisoning then, is not merely an economic endeavor but also an event of supernatural significance, and one which has an important bearing on the professional careers of mediums and their attainment of positions of leadership within the community.[29]

The *Sigisato* spirits inhabit the bodies of cassowaries during the daylight hours and subsist on the fruits and nuts they consume

---

28. A medium acquires a spirit wife from among the *Kesames* (specifically from the progeny of the spirits of the dead) and has a child (or children) by her. This spirit wife and spirit child (particularly a spirit son) provide a medium's links to the *Kesames* in general. It is not without structural significance that the spirits of the dead are affinally related to the living.

29. Leadership will be discussed in a separate publication. However, it may be noted here that whereas there are customary procedures which specify a course of action in nearly every situation, only mediums have the ability to define the essential nature of a situation effectively (through spirit pronouncements) and this is the basis of their considerable power.

during this period. These spirits tell men when and where traps are to be set and also direct the cassowaries to these particular locations. (However, the spirits change into human form and return to the sky before the birds are caught.) This information may be communicated directly to any man in a dream by the *Sigisatos* of his lineage or may be related through a medium. I suspect that favorable opportunities for cassowary trapping are presented by the fruiting of certain trees (as mentioned earlier) and in this instance, as in many others, mediums merely foretell the seasonal cycle. In any event, the successful capture of a cassowary is a manifestation of the general goodwill of these spirits toward the community and particularly the members of the lineage with which they are associated. A seance is generally conducted during the night following capture of the bird and the community thus celebrates the renewed closeness of its relation to these spirits while the cassowary is cooked and eaten.

Almost every routine event or activity which takes place in an Etoro community is foretold in advance by the spirits during the course of seances and the spirits are, to this extent, involved in nearly all subsistence activity. However, the degree to which spirits dictate procedures and influence the outcome is quite variable. It is only in the two preceding instances that the objects of the hunt are the corporeal abode of spirits so that the time, place, and results are directly controlled by them. Although the *Sigisato* spirits tell the crops in the garden to "come up bountifully" and instruct the sago palms being processed to "have much starch" they do not specify in advance the garden sites or sago palms that are to be selected. The Etoro say that, irrespective of spirit injunctions, the crops will not come up bountifully if the site is insufficiently fallowed, or the soil is inferior. Thus unfavorable yields do not necessarily imply a breach in the relation of men and spirits, although they may be interpreted in this way. The *Sigisatos* may instruct the crops not to flourish if they are angered by inappropriate human behavior, specifically by violation of the taboo against heterosexual relations in the garden,[30] by bickering among the participants in the communal garden, or by the blasphemous utterance of their names.

---

30. Etoro myths contain the paradigm homosexuality:life::heterosexuality:death which succinctly summarizes important aspects of their belief system. The belief that heterosexual relations in the garden will cause the crops to wither and die (through the intervention of displeased spirits) is one expression of this. Conversely, homosexual relations in the garden cause the crops to flourish (see Kelly, 1974).

Neither the *Sigisato* nor *Kesame* spirits can be influenced or placated with offerings and they receive none. Rather it is the spirits which offer their "flesh" to the community—or withhold it. The *Sigisatos* are protective and beneficent by inclination and act negatively only in reponse to improper or immoral human behavior. The *Kesames* are sometimes capricious and unreliable but never maliciously so. Witchcraft is the root cause of all evil and both types of spirits aid men in counteracting its effects through curing, while the *Sigisatos* may also protect men against acts of witchcraft.

Plate 1. A man with his brother's daughter in a newly cut communal garden at the close of a day's work. He is the younger of two mediums of the Kaburusato lineage.

Plate 2. Center, Kaburusato longhouse as seen from a current longhouse garden on an adjacent ridge. *Foreground,* sago palms line the course of a small stream and are scattered throughout the second growth forest which covers the ridge.

Plate 3. Women perform the opening dances at a ceremony marking a betrothal. The prospective bride's kinsmen (and their allies) are gathered at the entrance to the longhouse. *Below left,* the future groom's party is assembled at the opposite side of the cleared area. Note the steep-sided ridge on which the longhouse is constructed.

Plate 4. The forest canopy has just been felled atop this newly planted garden. The crowns of the large trees converge on a stream which runs horizontally across the center of the area. *Left center,* bananas are planted by the brush pile while clumps of sweet potato vines are barely visible *below.*

Plate 5. A garden approximately eight months after planting. Most of the sweet potatoes have been harvested and the plot is now overrun with weeds. *Left,* sugar cane is still available and the banana plants, *to the right,* will bear fruit in four to six months.

Plate 6. The wives of cross-cousins jointly process a sago palm. The white pith extracted from the trunk is placed in troughs constructed from the palm's fronds, where it is beaten and washed. The starch is thereby separated from the fiber and settles out in the bottom of the water-filled collecting trough.

Plate 7. The author with a group of young men constructing dams in preparation for fish poisoning. The river divides into two channels which flow around a small island at this location. *Upper left*, the breakwater diverts the main flow of water into one of these channels. The breakwater will seal the channel in which the fish are to be poisoned.

a

Plate 8. A widow (*a*) and her daughter (*b*) await the outcome of a fish poisoning operation. A proud and happy hunter (*c*) displays a flying fox he has brought as a gift for the author.

c

b

CHAPTER 3

The Patrilineage

The nature of the relationship between structural principles constitutes one of the major foci of the analysis of Etoro social structure presented herein, and this chapter is designed to serve as both prelude and preliminary to that analysis. In the latter respect I will be concerned to describe the salient characteristics of the lineage: genealogical form, demographic dimensions, corporate characteristics, internal pattern of segmentation, and modes of external relationship. The processes of fission and genealogical revision by which lineage boundaries are delineated will also be examined. However, consideration of these various aspects of lineage structure will consistently indicate the same general conclusion—that descent operates in conjunction with other principles. The focal issues of the precise nature of the relationship between such principles and the character of their interaction in the social field are thus implicitly raised. These issues will be specifically addressed in the concluding chapter. However, it may be noted here that Etoro social structure is founded upon a fundamental contradiction between the principles of siblingship and descent and that it is the dynamic interplay between these countervailing forces which orders Etoro social relations.

GENEALOGICAL STRUCTURE

Etoro lineage genealogies are characteristically unbranched at the upper levels and the descent group is consequently of greater genealogical depth than is required to encompass the constituent membership. The nearest common ancestor of the patrilineage is generally the grandfather or great-grandfather of the current generation of adult (ever-married) male members and the descent group thus seldom contains agnates more distantly related than FFBSS.[1] Forty-five percent (9/20) of the patrilines are exclusively

---

1. Kin relationships are abbreviated as follows: F—father, M—mother, S—son, D—daughter, B—brother, Z—sister, H—husband, W—wife. FFBSS designates father's father's brother's son's son, etc.

composed of brothers and FBSons while an additional 40 percent
(8/20) included FFBSSons as well; only 10 percent (2/20) encompass more distant agnates (and one lineage, accounting for the
remaining 5 percent, currently contains only true brothers—see
table 6). The restricted genealogical span of the Etoro lineage
reflects a structural emphasis on close consanguineal relationships
which will be discussed more fully in a subsequent section of this
chapter.

TABLE 6

Genealogical Span of the Lineage

Relation of nearest common ancestor to adult men	F	FF	FFF	FFFF	FFFFF	Total
Number of cases (lineages)	1	9	8	1	1	20*

*This sample excludes Nemisato, Somosato, and Kudulubisato for which genealogi-
cal data above the level of recent generations are not available.

The nearest common ancestor of the lineage is himself the
descendant of more remote patrilineal forebears who constitute a
line of brotherless sons extending indefinitely into the past. This
extensive but indeterminate genealogical depth is attained by repeating the names of two ancestors in an alternating sequence ad
infinitum. Thus if Y is the nearest common ancestor and X is his
father, the order of ancestral names in ascending generations would
be Y, X, Y, X, etc. This repetition may begin with the FF, FFF,
FFFF, or FFFFF of the nearest common ancestor, although the
first of these possibilities (exemplified above) is the most typical.
Alternatively, the lineage genealogy may culminate in a totemic
ancestor who is the FF or FFF of the nearest common ancestor.[2]
But in either event, the antecedents of the patriline are projected
into the distant mythological past. Although of narrow span, the
Etoro lineage is therefore not genealogically "shallow" in terms of
ancestry, generational time, or the Etoro conception of its history.
This conception also expresses the view that lineage history repeats itself, as indeed it does: past external relations are reduplicated in current generations by continuity in the exchange of

---

2. Totemic ancestors cap the genealogies of three of the twenty-three
patrilines while some of the others possess associated totems which are
nonancestral. The reason for this variation will be explained when the role
of these totemic figures is discussed in chapters 4 and 5.

women between patrilines. (For convenience in exposition I will use the term "apical ancestor" to refer to the most distant ancestor who bears a distinctive name, this designation encompassing totemic and nontotemic ancestors alike. These ancestral figures are important in providing points of linkage between pairs of patrilines. More remote ancestors do not enter into such relationships and are principally a vehicle for projecting lineage history into the distant past.)

The single-stranded line of patrilineal ancestors which characteristically surmounts the lineage genealogy similarly reflects the fact that external relationships are based on marriage, and the kin and affinal relationships which follow from it, rather than descent. The antecedents of the nearest common ancestor lack brothers who would serve to convey descent relationships with other lineages. They are, of course, superfluous to relationships within the lineage as well (since these are defined with respect to the nearest common ancestor). The structural significance of these more distant ancestral figures follows from their marriages, which are recorded in lineage mythology. One type of myth relates a sequence of events whereby the widow of one lineage's apical ancestor is selected as a wife by a totemic snake who then founds a second lineage through the progeny of this union. Such myths express and encode "brother" relationships between pairs of patrilines which stand in a relationship of matrilateral half-siblingship as a consequence of this transfer of a widow between apical ancestors (fig. 5). Brother lines derive their wives from the same exchange group (or groups) and are therefore matrilateral siblings (i.e., the sons of "sisters") by virtue of contemporary unions as well. They share a common source of wives, mothers, and matrilateral filiation and occupy homologous structural positions in the marriage system. The nature of these "brother" relationships and the processes by which they are established are discussed in chapter 4.

A second type of myth encodes and expresses exchange relationships between pairs of lineages. These myths record a totemic python's selection of an unmarried young woman as a wife, the transformation of the snake into a handsome young man of the totemically designated patriline, and the marriage of a daughter of this union to a man of her mother's natal line. A supernaturally sanctioned bilateral exchange relationship between lineages (as units) is specified by these legendary events which, at the same time, merge myth and genealogical history: the wife of the totemic python-man is the putative sister or FZ of the nearest common ancestor of the patriline and her daughter is the true FM or FFM of

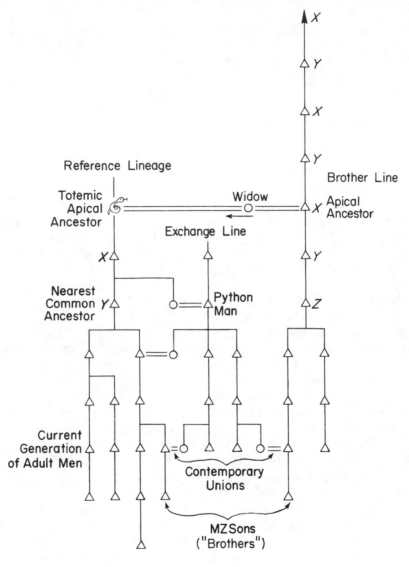

△ Male
○ Female
= Marriage
| Parent–child relationship
— Sibling relationship

FIG. 5. Internal Genealogical Structure and External Relationships of the Lineage

living men. The python-man is the nearest common ancestor of the exchange line, or his F, B, or S. Exchange relationships between lineages are discussed in chapter 5. The elements of the genealogical structure of the lineage and the points of external connection considered thus far are illustrated in figure 5.

Genealogical Knowledge

The range and pathways of genealogical reckoning are consistent with (and circumscribed by) lineage form, and are also strongly influenced by Etoro belief concerning the contemporary reduplication of past relationships. Having accepted the premise that history repeats itself,[3] the Etoro are relieved of the burden of remembering the genealogical details of it—since they are not significantly different from those of the present (conceived as the two prior generations). The vertical range of genealogical knowledge is consequently rather limited and kin relationships established through linking relatives in the third ascending generation frequently cannot be traced.[4] Although every individual can trace his relationship to the nearest common ancestor of the lineage and to his fellow agnates, about half the men cannot recall the name of the apical ancestor without prompting. However, they are well appraised of the "brother" and exchange relationships which are encoded in the myths concerning ancestral unions and are well versed in the kin and affinal bonds based on the contemporary counterparts of these mythical marriages. Lateral genealogical knowledge is very extensive and most men can provide complete genealogies of several "brother" and exchange lines. A few experts in this field are able to trace the relationships of nearly every individual and lineage within the tribe.[5]

---

3. This view is nicely illustrated by the fact that a single Etoro word means both yesterday and tomorrow. (The difference can, of course, be indicated by the tense of the accompanying verb.)

4. In these instances terminological designations are based on lineage relationships (as discussed in chapter 7) or parental usage, i.e., "he is my x because my father called his father y."

5. The most notable of these is a young man in his early twenties who was my principal informant. He is also a repository of myth and a medium-designate who is widely expected to emerge eventually as a tribal leader. Sharing this expectation himself, he considered it his business to know everything about the Etoro and I was extremely fortunate to have his friendship and assistance.

THE DEFINITION OF LINEAGE BOUNDARIES

A lineage which contains only brothers, FBSons, and FFBSSons at a given point in time will, in subsequent generations, encompass more distant agnates as a consequence of the natural process of genealogical aging. The fact that the Etoro lineage rarely includes such agnates therefore requires explication. As one might logically infer, the maintenance of lineages of such narrow span necessitates both extensive genealogical revision and frequent fission so that distant agnates are either converted into close agnates or excluded from the lineage. These two processes of revision and fission also represent alternative solutions which are necessarily in complementary distribution (in the sense that one obviates the need for the other) and this poses a second question concerning the conditioning factors which predispose the occurrence of each.

Before exploring these interrelated questions it will be useful to register several orienting observations. The central issue is one of the definition and maintenance of lineage boundaries over genealogical time which, in broader terms, concerns the cultural partition of genealogical space. An examination of the descent group from this point of view places it in a perspective entirely different from that which flows from a synchronic analysis of lineage form as presented at any given point in time. This is due to the fact that lineage boundaries are not defined by descent alone, but by additional principles which group or segregate descendants. An example will clarify this: two men related as FFBSS are included within a single lineage while their sons are either segregated into different lineages (by fission) or must revise the terms of their relationship. However, these two generations are not differentiated by descent per se as the FFFBSSSons share the same common ancestor shared by their fathers. Descent does not instigate the alternative processes of fission or revision by which lineage boundaries are maintained within a specified range of relationship. At any point in time, the lineage presents itself as if it were constituted exclusively by a rule of patrilineal recruitment although, viewed diachronically, it is a product of other processes governed by other principles.

Descent, then, is a constant rather than a variable with respect to the process of fission. Indeed this is always the case. Classic segmentary organization is formulated on the condition that two lineages which are the products of fission will maintain a unit to unit relationship by appeal to common ancestry. This common ancestry therefore cannot be a source of the internal division instru-

mental to the process by which they split. Although the lines of
cleavage may be specified by descent, the separation is dictated by
other factors. Recourse to more proximate ancestors which are the
axes of cleavage must also be effected on grounds other than those
of descent.

The event of fission also constitutes an explicit breach of agnatic solidarity which proceeds in accordance with principles
which are subversive of the general organization of the social system. One may readily perceive that a thorough and unconstrained
application of the principles that instigate and implement such a
division would decompose the entire segmentary structure. Thus a
lineage constituted in terms of descent fissions as a consequence of
processes which are guided by antithetical principles. The structural form which the lineage presents to us at any given point in
time is, then, an explicit denial of the processes by which it emerges as a distinct, bounded unit—inasmuch as this emergence entails
the severance of the same sibling bonds which form the basis of its
organization. In this sense form is a denial of process not a reflection of it. Indeed it is precisely because of this that the second law
of thermodynamics does not apply to social systems; fission engenders higher order relationships rather than entropy.

It follows that a processual account of the Etoro lineage places
it in an entirely different perspective than that derived from a synchronic or ideological account. It would consequently be a misap-
prehension to infer a diminution of the structural role of the principle of descent in Etoro society from the following discussion of the
nondescent principles which govern the definition of lineage boundaries. The operation of such principles is part of the nature of the
lineage, including the African variety. The similarities and differences between the two will be discussed in the concluding chapter.
Consideration of the interplay of antithetical or contradictory structural principles, which has been broached in the preceding discussion, will also be resumed there.

Having outlined the general orientation of the inquiry I return
to the specific problem at hand, employing a degree of repetition in
order to reestablish the continuity of discussion.

Recruitment to lineage membership is governed by the principle of patrilineal descent. Reaffiliation is rare to nonexistent (for
reasons discussed in a subsequent section of this chapter), and
virtually all lineage members are therefore the true descendants of
a patrilineal ancestor. However, fission occurs relatively frequently
so that not all the descendants of a given common ancestor are
necessarily included within the same lineage. Descent, then, does

not exhaustively specify the boundaries of the lineage as these develop over genealogical time. The passage of generations increases the span of the lineage engendering FFFBSSS relationships between lineage members. These distant relationships are either converted into closer ones by genealogical revision or the individuals are excluded from the lineage through fission. These two processes are in complementary distribution such that fission occurs when the criteria for a redefinition of relationships are not met. Lineage boundaries are thus effectively demarcated by these criteria, operating within a general context of descent (as a constant).

Genealogical Revision

A lineage incorporates agnates who are also close consanguineal kinsmen. Although the agnatic bonds are genuine, the requisite degree of consanguinity may be established through either matrilateral or patrilateral parallel relationship (e.g., via MZS as well as FBS). The true patrilineal descendants of a great-grandfather may be conceived, for analytical purposes, as constituting the primary consanguineal "core" of the lineage. Agnates related to this "core" group by a more distant patrilateral connection (i.e., as FFFBSSS) are generally not included within the lineage unless they possess a closer matrilateral relationship to one or more of its members. Such matrilateral bonds are established through agnatic parallel marriage[6] and the levirate. A FFFBSSS (x in fig. 6) who is also a matrilateral half-sibling as a consequence of his father's leviratic union will be included within the lineage, as will his son. A FFFBSSS (y in fig. 6) who is additionally the MZS of a member of the lineage "core" as a result of his father's agnatic parallel marriage is likewise included. The same applies to other distant agnates who are related to the "core" group as MBSD, MFZS, FMZSS, FMBDS, or MFZSS due to agnatic parallel marriage.[7]

Relations of matrilateral siblingship between lineage members are converted into agnatic relationships in the following generation by genealogical revision. The sons of MZSons become FFBSSons and the sons of matrilateral half-siblings become FBSons (see fig.

---

6. I will use the term parallel marriage to designate the marriage of a pair of women of the same descent group by any two men. If the latter are of the same descent group, I will refer to this as agnatic parallel marriage (when this is not otherwise clear from context).

7. The son of any woman of mother's natal patrilineage, in her or adjacent generations, is classified as a "brother." All the relationships designated above are thus relations of classificatory matrilateral siblingship.

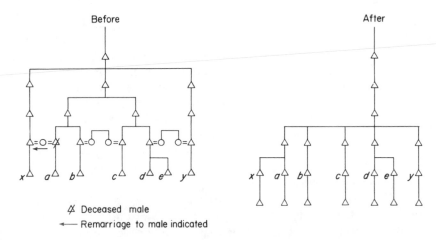

Before   After

⚤ Deceased male

◄— Remarriage to male indicated

FIG. 6.   Genealogical Revision

6). These revisions restate matrilateral consanguinity in agnatic terms without altering the degree of relationship.[8] Although the lineage is empirically composed of small patrilineal segments linked by close matrilateral consanguinity (and distant patrilineal ties), this actual constitution is perpetually reformulated as one of close agnatic connection. Both the agnatic bonds and the degree of consanguinity accurately reflect the genealogical facts of the matter, yet the latter is not based on the former. The purely agnatic form which the lineage presents thus *conceals* and *denies* the matrilateral means by which this is attained. However, it is equally important to emphasize that the Etoro delineate the *filo* (patrilineage) through processes of genealogical revision which are conceptually based on the principle of patrilineal descent. This is demonstrated by the following facts: (1) matrilateral consanguinity is recast in patrilineal terms, (2) kin relationships are reformulated in terms of ancestry, and (3) the (relocated) nearest common ancestor of the *filo* becomes the reference point for the calculation of interrelationship between and among the constituent members of the group.

In summary, a lineage is composed of a "core" of close consanguineal agnates and all those more distant agnates whose

---

8. Although the degree of consanguinity between *x* and *a* and *e* and *y* (respectively) is accurately restated, that between *x* and *y* is not (fig. 6). Such discrepancies are sometimes expressed in multiple versions of the lineage genealogy which themselves reveal the processes of revision. They do not portend fission since the lineage lacks discrete segments (as discussed in the following section of this chapter).

mothers (or FMothers) are of the same natal patriline as the mothers (or FMothers) of the men of this "core" group. However, inasmuch as patrilineal consanguinity is necessarily diluted by the passage of generations, it is only agnatic parallel marriage (and the levirate) which can provide the requisite degree of consanguinity over time and these ultimately define the boundaries of the descent group.[9] The lineage is ideologically and synchronically defined by patrilineal descent and processually and diachronically bounded by its enduring exchange relations with other descent groups. Marriages outside of these exchange relations institute the internal divisions which precipitate fission.

The role of true consanguineal relationships as a criterion and basis for genealogical revision is related to Etoro conceptions concerning witchcraft. It is believed that witchcraft will not take place between first cousins or persons more closely related than first cousins. Suspicion of witchcraft increases with genealogical distance beyond this point.[10] The conversion of a FFFBSSS to a FFBSS by genealogical revision does not alleviate this suspicion unless he is, in fact, more closely related. Etoro ideology concerning the relationship between consanguinity and witchcraft is thus an expression of the solidarity vested in close consanguineal kinship. Witchcraft allegations and the fear of witchcraft are instrumental to the process of fission and symptomatic of the structural weakness of descent relationships which are not underwritten by close consanguinity.

Fission

The natural process of genealogical aging of the lineage constitutes an impetus to fission insofar as the succession of generations increases the consanguineal distance between agnates until this eventually exceeds the degree of relationship within which lineage boundaries are maintained. In the absence of countervailing measures the passage of time would divide the lineage into discrete segments (delineated with respect to the sons of the nearest common ancestor) whose relationship to each other would become pro-

---

9. Similarly, the "core" of close consanguineal agnates is a product of genealogical revision and an analytical device for explaining the processes thereof. In the revised genealogy in figure 6, the entire lineage is the "core" as is characteristically the case.

10. There is a definite structural boundary between relationships at the first cousin level and more distant relationships. Marriage with first cousins is incestuous while marriage with FZSD is preferred.

gressively more distant and, accordingly, more susceptible to the witchcraft accusations which precipitate fission. However, this inherent impetus to fission is countered by the consanguineal consolidation of the lineage, achieved through leviratic and parallel marriages, and by the genealogical revision which follows from this consolidation. Fission may thus be viewed as the fruition of natural processes of genealogical aging, an event which occurs in due course when lineage members fail to arrange the marriages which would prevent it. In order to answer the question of why fission occurs in certain instances but not in others, it will therefore be necessary to designate the conditions which interfere with the arrangement of the leviratic and agnatic parallel marriages that are generally sought. This inquiry will be pursued following a consideration of the structural principles and social rules which govern segmentation and define the internal division realized in fission.

Lineage segments are differentiated in terms of congruence in the external kin and affinal relations of lineage members. Congruence in individual kin networks refers to the condition whereby two (or more) persons have relatives in common and are related to them in the same or similar ways, i.e., as "brother," "father," or "son" on one hand, or as "cross-cousin," "MB," "ZS," or affine on the other.[11] Such points of correspondence in individual kin networks are an inherent aspect of all close consanguineal relationships. True FBSons have the same FZ (FZS, FFZ, FMB, etc.) while matrilateral half-siblings and MZSons have the same MB (MBS, MBDS, MFZS, etc.). Classificatory sister exchanges also produce congruence such that, for example, the FZSons of the former (i.e., FBSons mentioned above) may also be the MBSons of the latter (i.e., the MZSons) as is illustrated in figure 7. (The degree of congruence is always less than complete and I use the term with the adjective "partial" omitted but understood.)

The differentiation of lineage segments creates an internal division within the descent group which constitutes the line of cleavage in fission, developing as a prelude to it.[12] This fissure is revealed by

---

11. This dual division corresponds to the Etoro distinction between brother and exchange relations at the lineage level. The external "brothers" I refer to are MZS (MBDS, MFZS, etc.), relationships which are a consequence of (nonagnatic) parallel marriage.

12. It should be recalled that a lineage which has achieved consanguineal consolidation and translated this into agnatic relationships through genealogical revision does not contain discrete segments. In the terms of the preceding analysis, the entire lineage is the "core."

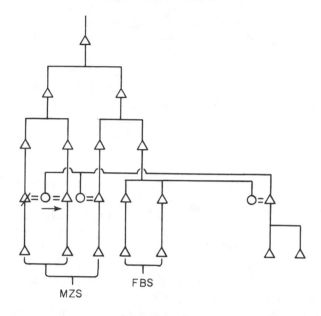

FIG. 7.　Congruence in the Individual Kin Networks of Lineage Members

the alignment of donors and recipients of witchcraft (death) compensation in a series of internal witchcraft accusations[13] which typically precede and precipitate fission. The accumulation and redistribution of compensation has the effect of sorting agnates into two groups which are, at the same time, made conscious of their internal unity and their opposition to each other. The characteristic pattern of donor-recipient alignment (and consequently the composition of segments) is very strongly conditioned by the jural rule that a woman's husband and brother are each responsible for accumulating half of the required compensation in the event that she is named as a witch. It is this rule which produces a differentiation of segments in terms of congruence.

The jural stipulation of divided liability for a woman's witchcraft activities operates like a magnet in establishing major lines of force in the field of Etoro social relations. The rule has a number of important ramifications which both impinge on and extend beyond

---

13. Witchcraft accusations are publicly lodged (or expressed) only in the event of a death and in conjunction with a demand for compensation. Since all deaths which are not the instantaneous result of humanly-caused bodily injury are believed to be caused by witchcraft, death compensation is typically witchcraft compensation.

the question at hand. These may usefully be outlined here (and subsequently introduced into the discussion of fission at the points where they become relevant). First, the rule of divided liability augments the number of situations in which the lineage is internally divided by the payment of witchcraft compensation (and these events effectively define lineage segments). Second, it aligns affines in the accumulation and redistribution of compensatory payments. Third, it segregates agnates in relation to their affinal and cross-cousin relationships (such that segments are delineated on the basis of congruence). Fourth, it influences the composition of the net-work of relatives that an individual draws on for support so that affinal bonds are favored over those between distant agnates. In short, the divided liability for a woman's witchcraft compensation divides the lineage and promotes the solidarity of affinal relationships.[14]

A lineage is internally divided into donors and recipients of witchcraft compensation whenever the witch named as responsible for a death is related to the victim in one of the following ways, illustrated in figure 8:

1. as a man's male agnate (four of forty-three cases),
2. as a man's male agnate's spouse (six of forty-three cases),
3. as a woman's husband's male agnate (one of forty-three cases),
4. as a woman's husband's male agnate's spouse (two of forty-three cases).

The internal division follows from a husband's responsibility to compensate the kin of a victim of his wife's witchcraft in (2) and (4) (where an agnate's spouse is the witch). The stipulation that a man is also responsible for half the compensation when his married sister is named as a witch adds two additional situations[15] in which the lineage is internally divided by these payments, namely, when the witch is:

5. a man's married female agnate (one of forty-three cases),
6. a woman's husband's married female agnate (two of forty-three cases).

---

14. Afficionados of comparative social structure may find it interesting to contrast this with Fortune's classic analysis of lineage and affinal relationships in Dobu (Fortune, 1963[1932]; also see Kelly, 1968a).

15. Several additional situations, for which there are no observed cases, arise when the witch is:

7. a married woman's male agnate,
8. a married woman's male agnate's spouse.

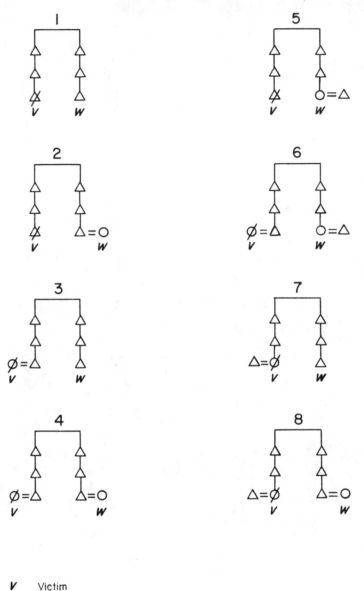

V	Victim
W	Witch
⚤	Deceased male
∅	Deceased female

FIG. 8.   Genealogical Relationships between Witch and Victim in Which Compensation Divides the Lineage

78

If the husband alone were responsible for a woman's witchcraft, lineage members would be compensated by their lineage sister's husband (and his close agnates and kinsmen) on these occasions. This would introduce divisiveness into affinal (and exchange) relationships since a lineage would be required to pay compensation to the patriline that had given them a witch as a wife. The stipulation of sibling responsibility alleviates the potential divisiveness inherent in this situation by requiring that the woman's brother bear half of the burden of compensation. This aligns affines but at the same time sets one segment of a lineage against another. Affinal bonds are reinforced at the expense of lineage solidarity.

The conflict which witchcraft accusations engender occurs largely within rather than between the major social groups of Etoro society (thereby preserving a tribal unity). Witch and victim are residents of the same community in 72 percent (31/43) of the recorded cases and the men who are principally engaged in the accumulation and redistribution of compensation (or the request and denial) are agnates in 37.2 percent (16/43) of these instances. The agnates who are placed in opposition are typically FFBSSons (or more distantly related)[16] and the event publicly defines and exposes the divisions within the lineage. Compensation was paid in half of these cases, refused in one-fourth, and not requested by the closest relative of the victim in the remaining fourth. The brother or husband of the deceased may forego compensation if the witch is the spouse of a close kinsman or in response to requests from individuals closely related to both sides. (However, ill feelings and grudges frequently result from such forbearance as noted in subsequent discussion.) Finally, the aggrieved kin may elect vengeance rather than compensation.

The line of cleavage in fission is defined in terms of congruence in the external kin and affinal relations of lineage members.

---

16. All five cases where witch and victim themselves were agnates involved FFBSchild or FFFBSSchild. More closely related men are engaged as accumulator and recipient of compensation only when an agnate's spouse is either the witch or victim. None of the cases involve close consanguineal kin or immediate affines (WB, ZH, WF, DH) as witch and victim. The witch was the victim's deceased BW, patrilateral 1/2 BW, SW, HBSW, and HFBSW in five cases while the agnates who were principals in the event were FFBSS or more distantly related in eleven cases. All of the women named in the first five instances were witches who had been previously accused, and the same woman was the witch in three of these. No compensation is paid when BW is accused since the surviving B (and spouse of the witch) would be both compensator and recipient. However, a claim for compensation can be made by FBSons when the wife of a deceased brother is named (both H and HB of the witch then being deceased).

These external (nonagnatic) relationships are necessarily a major factor in the alignment of lineage segments because such relationships determine an individual's allegiance in the internal witchcraft accusations which precede fission. In four of the six situations in which agnates are principals in these events—(2), (4), (5), and (6) —and in eleven of the sixteen cases, the brother and husband of a female witch are jointly responsible for the payment of compensation. The group accumulating compensation therefore includes agnates (of the victim) and their affines. Any man whose W, M, D, DH, ZH, or FZH is of the same lineage as the affinal line responsible for half the compensation tends to be recruited as a supporter of the witch's brother—in (2) and (4)—or husband—(5) and (6)—on the basis of his relation as affine, cross-cousin, MB, or ZS to this exchange group. In other words, agnates which have congruent kin networks with respect to the external (affinal) lineage involved in the compensation payment will tend to comprise both a group of donors and a lineage segment. These individuals will be related to each other as full brothers and FBSons (who have the same FZ and FZSons), as matrilateral half-brothers and MZSons (who have the same MB and MBSons), and as the agnatic parties to a classificatory sister exchange (who have the same affines). In short, the segment is delineated by the principle of congruence as a result of the rule which stipulates divided liability for a woman's witchcraft.

Internal witchcraft accusations (or those in which agnates are principals) are incapable of dividing the lineage into discrete segments when leviratic and parallel marriages have established matrilateral bonds between the descendants of two FFBrothers (who are sons of the nearest common ancestor). Such consolidating unions provide that some individuals will be close patrilateral kin (FBS) of the victim's brother and, at the same time, close matrilateral kin (MZS) of the witch (and vice versa). In such instances the differentiation of lineage segments is incomplete and fission will not occur.[17] Conversely, fission is imminent when an internal witch-

---

17. Agnates who are closely related to both the witch and victim will generally attempt to minimize the strife and hostility produced by internal witchcraft accusations in one of two ways. First, they may promote an amicable payment of compensation. They will then contribute (sometimes substantially) to the compensation and also receive in redistribution, reaffirming their ties to both sides. Second, they may seek to convince the aggrieved kin to forego compensation altogether in the name of brotherly solidarity. Although this is sometimes done it tends to produce unresolved grievances which are later expressed in subsequent accusation or in a failure to contribute to the brideprice of those who should have paid but did not.

craft accusation segregates lineage members into discrete segments, i.e., when the agnatic divisions which follow from genealogical aging are not consolidated by matrilateral consanguinity. Lineage boundaries are thus effectively delineated by this criterion[18] (descent being a constant rather than a variable). Moreover, the two segments which represent emergent lineages will be externally defined by the different lines with which they have respectively exchanged women.

Etoro social structure is not "segmentary" in the usual sense of the word and it is therefore important to provide a concise definition of the term "segment" as it is employed herein. Segmentation entails group formation and the required definition may thus be most readily established by describing the sequence of events by which a group of agnates develops a unity apart from that of the lineage as a whole. First, a division is initially created within a lineage when two groups of agnates who are the descendants of a pair of FFBrothers fail to establish co-affinal relationships through agnatic parallel marriage, participation in classificatory sister exchange, or the passage of a widow between them. Although the men of these two groups may be more closely related by matrilateral ties, the absence of co-affinal relations ensures that their sons will lack the close consanguineal (first cousin) relationships which preclude witchcraft accusations. Second, this division is significantly deepened when these two groups internally manifest the characteristics of consolidation absent in the lineage as a whole, i.e., when co-affinal relationships have been established within each (see fig. 9). I designate such groups as segments on the formal grounds that they have established all the necessary preconditions for the emergence of discrete segments in the following generation.[19] The marriages contracted are themselves indicative of a

---

18. Co-affinity is also an important criterion and I focus on matrilateral consanguinity in my phrasing here principally because it serves as a basis for genealogical revision. Co-affinal bonds based on agnatic parallel marriage engender matrilateral consanguinity in the following generation which is then translated into agnatic consanguinity in the next. Co-affinity based on cooperation in effecting a classificatory sister exchange produces congruence but not matrilateral consanguinity. The relationship between the descendants of agnates who are parties to such a transaction (as wife-giver and wife-receiver) is not revised on that account.

19. I will employ the term "branch" in order to refer to the purely agnatic internal divisions of the lineage (irrespective of current matrilateral and co-affinal ties). A branch of the lineage may be defined as the (putative) patrilineal descendants of an ancestor in the second ascending generation (i.e., FF).

tendency to function as independent units (particularly with respect to rights of disposal over widows). It should be recalled that most lineages lack this dual pattern of internal consolidation which is here employed as the criterion of segmentation.

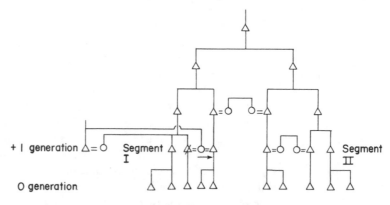

FIG. 9.   Segmentation

Segmentation normally leads to fission in the next generation. The formal separation (signified by the offshoot segment's adoption of a lineage name) follows from a series of internal witchcraft accusations as previously discussed. One may readily perceive the alignment of donors and recipients of witchcraft compensation which would result from an accusation spanning the cleavage in figure 9. Such accusations usually commence upon the death of the men and women of the senior (+1) generation, but before most of the men of the junior (0) generation have married. A momentum toward fission is thus established before consolidation can be effected. By the time all the men of the senior generation have died the separation will normally be complete. Occasionally, a discrete segment will be reabsorbed in the generation following its emergence (as is discussed in chapter 3). But in either event a discrete pattern of segmentation does not persist for more than one generation.

Demographic growth creates a predisposition to fission since it inhibits the ability of the lineage to contract the agnatic parallel marriages which would provide a general consolidation. Although the arrangement of the necessary leviratic unions is ideally within the control of the lineage,[20] its success in arranging the requisite

---

20. The extent to which the lineage successfully exercises its jurally mandated control over widow remarriage is consequently an important question and one which is considered in detail in chapter 8.

parallel marriages rests with exchange groups. Fission thus tends to occur when a patriline increases in size to the point where its internal concentration of marriages is impaired by the inability of smaller exchange groups to provide sufficient wives. A decrease in agnatic parallel marriage (relative to lineage size) leads to a dilution of the internal bonds of matrilateral siblingship which hold the lineage together as it ages genealogically.

At the same time, numerical growth forces some lineage members to marry outside of traditional exchange relations in order to secure a spouse. This in itself creates opposition between agnates in the following generation as the kin relationships which follow from these "wrong" marriages weaken the kin-based claims of lineage members to women of traditional exchange lines vis-à-vis the claims of other lineages (as explained in chapter 4). Finally, demographic increase engenders competition among agnates for the women who are readily available from exchange groups at a time when increased cooperation is needed in order to arrange consolidating unions for maximum effect. Sisters tend to be deployed in accordance with personal rather than lineage objectives, particularly in direct exchange with descent groups which are not normally a source of wives and would not otherwise provide them. This problem is further aggravated when lineage growth results from an imbalance of male over female births in a particular generation and consequently entails a shortage of sisters available for exchange. All these considerations promote segmentation and hence fission.

Internal witchcraft accusations are also most common within the larger lineages, a tendency exemplified by the largest—Kaburusato with thirty-seven members. Such accusations have been lodged in five of the last six deaths of Kaburusato lineage members and their wives; the attempted execution of a witch related as the victim's FFFBSSS occurred on one of these occasions. This witch subsequently reciprocated the accusation when his mother died, naming the brother of the man he had bewitched (i.e., the individual who had previously accused him). The father of the witch (and husband of the deceased woman) denied that this reciprocal allegation was valid[21] and did not request compensation, although he had

---

21. The credibility of the accusation was questionable, since witch and victim were not co-resident as Etoro belief normally requires (see chapter 5). The validity of it was also dubious as a consequence of the fact that neither of the two mediums of the lineage would endorse it through spirit pronouncements. One outside medium (the accuser's MB) did attest to the occurrence of the alleged witchcraft but another specifically denied it.

paid it when his son was named. The restraint of this and other older men has forestalled a split which will very likely occur after their passing, instigated by the naming of the witches responsible for their deaths. If this does occur, it will be the second time Kaburusato has split in the four generations since the lineage was founded (through fission) by three brothers. Fission in every other generation represents the maximum recorded frequency, applicable only to the most rapidly expanding lines.

An increase in lineage size relative to exchange lines creates conditions which promote segmentation and the internal witchcraft accusations which accompany increased size impel a segmented patriline toward fission. At another level, however, fission involves a rupture of agnatic solidarity that permits demographically induced difficulties to be translated into conditions which render the descent group vulnerable to witchcraft accusations. Explication of this aspect of fission focuses on the character of the relationship between FFBSSons and the structural factors which impinge upon it. By seeking agnatic parallel marriages and by cooperation in arranging classificatory sister exchanges and widow remarriages, FFBSSons can prevent segmentation. Alternatively, by eschewing these, they may ensure segmentation and hence fission. Several factors are conducive to cooperation. The lineage as a group holds jurally mandated control over the disposition of women, and agnates therefore possess grounds for objecting to the marriage of a "sister," "daughter," or widow which does not benefit the descent group. Moreover, terminological prohibition and strong disapproval of the true brother levirate creates a structural predisposition toward consolidating leviratic unions. Finally, the publicly expressed ideology of agnatic solidarity urges cooperation and unity. In short, all the appropriate structural and ideological machinery is in place. However, the reality of FFBSS relations is often a somewhat pale reflection of agnatic solidarity as a consequence of strong countervailing forces. These are predominantly a product of the jural stipulation of divided liability for a woman's witchcraft (and, in more general terms, a result of the structural emphasis on siblingship[22] which the rule expresses). Given this rule, the structure of the situation is such that FFBSSons (who are not otherwise more closely related) may perceive and clearly envision their eventual division. There is a definite expectation that such agnates will

---

22. As evidenced, for example, by the 65 percent frequency of violation of the terminologically prohibited and strongly disapproved true brother levirate (discussed in later chapters).

be aligned in opposition to ego in internal witchcraft accusations[23] and they therefore cannot be depended upon to render material aid and assistance in these crucial situations of an individual's life. Their affinal and matrilateral connections dictate other allegiances, predictable in advance. Under these circumstances men are often disinclined to follow a course of action which would enhance the solidarity of these relationships and their failure to do so further weakens the bond, promoting fulfillment of the envisioned opposition. The disinclination is clearly reflected in contributions to brideprice: FFBSSons who are not also matrilateral siblings of the groom provided only 2.4 percent of the total value of brideprice in a sample of fourteen cases.

The joint responsibility of husband and brother for a woman's witchcraft also creates expectations of mutual assistance and support among brothers, FBSons, and agnates who are also matrilateral siblings, and among affines and cross-cousins. As past or potential contributors to witchcraft compensation, they are favored in the redistribution of these payments and others as well. Such relationships are enhanced by the same factors which debilitate those between distant agnates. This joint responsibility thus significantly influences the composition of an individual's effective network of personal allies and supporters.

There is a significant difference in the solidarity vested in close (first cousin) and distant agnatic relationships, respectively, as a direct consequence of the differential effects of the rule of divided liability which reinforces the former and weakens the latter. The FFBSS relationship evidences a certain fragility and, given this, the strains introduced by an increase in lineage size are readily translated into the failure to cooperate in arranging marriages which produces segmentation. These strains are, moreover, manifested in witchcraft accusations at the same time that segmentation renders the lineage vulnerable to fission. Such accusations themselves impose additional stress on FFBSS relationships which do not readily bear it and these bonds ultimately give way under repeated (and reciprocal) allegations. The lineage then divides along a line of cleavage which has been publicly formulated and revealed in the alignment of donors and recipients of compensation payments arising from these same witchcraft accusations.

---

23. Such accusations are themselves expectable since a witch is named for nearly every death and will normally be a co-resident more distantly related than first cousin. FFBSSons and their wives are likely candidates simply by virtue of their representation within the category of potential suspects.

Witchcraft also provides the rationalization for the rupture of agnatic solidarity which fission entails: they—members of the other segment—are "false" brothers because "true" brothers will not bewitch one another.[24] The ideology of the solidarity of brothers is thus reaffirmed, by definition, even as it is denied by events—since those who do not manifest it are labeled as something else. The manner in which these terms are employed is itself significant. The designation "true brother" (*neto tofā*) may be restricted to full and half-siblings in some contexts but in general usage refers to FBS and MZS as well, including a MZS of another lineage (whose mother was a full or half-sister of ego's mother). The attribute of "trueness" is thus associated with close consanguinity. The term "false brother" (*neto-fani*) is formed by adding a suffix common to several rather uncomplimentary words, namely, *wāfani*—a lie, *hōnofani*—small in size, stingy, ungenerous. This designation is applied to any more distant matrilateral or patrilateral sibling who has violated the norms of brotherhood.

Reaffiliation

Changes in lineage affiliation occur very infrequently and nearly always entail a concurrent change in tribal affiliation. The individuals involved are characteristically witches who have relocated in order to avoid vengeance. In all recorded instances matrilateral siblingship provided the basis for reaffiliation, i.e., ego was related as MZS to the patriline into which he and his descendants were incorporated. Such incorporation is effected through the normal processes of genealogical revision by which the sons of (agnatic) MZSons become FFBSSons. However, several factors militate against reaffiliation effected on this basis, especially within the tribe. Of particular importance is the fact that MZS and matrilateral half-sibling bonds between individuals of different lineages are utilized as a mechanism for establishing and maintaining "brother" relationships between entire descent groups. These bonds constitute the points of linkage through which classificatory brother

---

24. An act of witchcraft is a psychic act which does not involve the potions or incantations usually associated with sorcery. However, the performance of witchcraft and the selection of a victim are entirely within the control of the witch so that such acts are conceived of as totally malicious —perhaps akin to murder preceded by torture (corresponding to the duration of the illness). Witchcraft within the lineage is all the more devastating due to its intentionality and the hostility engendered is also augmented by this.

terms are extended. A patriline has little to gain and much to lose by internalizing such linking relationships through assimilation of a MZS to lineage membership.

Reaffiliation raises thorny issues concerning rights of disposal over daughters which may lead to bloodshed. External widow remarriages best exemplify the ambiguities which arise. A widow may be given to a "brother" line (without payment of brideprice) in order to consolidate the bond between the two groups and, less frequently, may be remarried for brideprice to a potential exchange group.[25] In either case, the deceased husband's lineage most emphatically claims rights of disposal over the widow's daughters by her first marriage. Such daughters are held to be members of their deceased father's line by the principle of patrilineal descent, even though they may have been raised from infancy by a man of another lineage. The agnates of a girl in this situation will thus insist upon their right to determine her marital destination, to deploy her in a bilateral exchange, and to collect brideprice. If necessary, they will employ force of arms to ensure their claims.[26]

Rights over women form an important part of the corporate estate of the descent group and these rights are guaranteed only by strict adherence to a rule of recruitment based on patrilineal descent. Thus, the rule which applies to the daughters of an externally remarried widow applies equally to her sons (who are related to their MHusband's line as matrilateral half-siblings). Reaffiliation

---

25. Both of these alternatives to leviratic remarriage are discussed in detail in subsequent chapters.

26. In one rather interesting case a man attempted to marry his deceased wife's daughter by a previous marriage. The deceased wife was a widow given by a "brother" line and the girl was therefore a classificatory daughter who, moreover, had been betrothed to another man by her natal lineage. In order to secure his wife's daughter as a spouse for himself, the man had intercourse with her (although she was not physically mature). He refused brideprice on the grounds that he had fed and raised the girl and, as her "father," was himself entitled to receive it. On the other hand, he claimed she was only a classificatory daughter, not a consanguine, and that his marriage was no worse than anyone else's in that respect. One might say his case rested on the distinction between pater and genitor. However, the party of men from the girl's natal line and the lineage of her betrothed which came to seek redress found it unconvincing and killed the man, delivering his "daughter" to her intended husband. No one came to his assistance at the time and everyone roundly condemned his actions after the fact, stressing the point that he had stolen the girl from his "brothers."

in such cases would establish a most undesirable precedent and it is strongly disapproved.[27] Moreover, the same fundamental issue is involved irrespective of the nature of the relationship through which membership in another descent group is established. A patriline which accepts a nonagnate as a member and incorporates his descendants has "stolen" his daughter from her natal lineage— undoubtedly an allied "brother" or "exchange" group (except in the unlikely event that the reaffiliate is not a close kinsman of the line in which he seeks membership). Such a course of action holds advantages only for a lineage of another tribe.

Reaffiliation also offers no significant advantages to an individual unless he is seeking to avoid vengeance by moving to another tribe. There is little to be gained by lineage membership that is not obtainable on the basis of consanguineal or affinal relationships through which it might be effected. This follows from the fact that an individual's personal network of allies and supporters is not primarily or exclusively agnatic. One need not become a member of a MZSon's, affine's, or cross-cousin's lineage in order to be assured of the unqualified assistance of these kinsmen. Access to economic resources is also readily acquired and nonagnatic residents suffer no disability in this respect vis-à-vis agnates with the single exception of hunting rights. On the other hand, rights to women (of exchange lines) cannot be obtained simply by a declaration of allegiance to a nonnatal descent group. The protection of the *Sigisato* spirits associated with a lineage is similarly unavailable.

The Etoro acknowledge only one current generation change in lineage affiliation. The man involved has become a member of his MZSon's patrilineage of the neighboring Petamini tribe. Branches of two other Petamini lineages are the descendants of such reaffiliates. There are no recognized cases of reaffiliation within the tribe, although it may be suspected in a few instances. The most striking evidence of the rarity of changes in lineage affiliation is the fact that six lineages contain only one adult male member. Only one of these six men is attempting to establish membership in another lineage, i.e., the individual discussed above.

The narrow genealogical span of Etoro lineages, their propensity to fission, and the rarity of reaffiliation all have a pronounced affect on lineage size. The average lineage contains only seventeen

---

27. There is also a distinction drawn in kinship terminology between father and mother's husband by a second marriage. The term employed for the latter is also applied to the husbands of classificatory mothers, i.e., MBDH and MZH.

members, including approximately four adult (ever-married) men, five out-married female agnates, two young men between the ages of sixteen and thirty, one young woman between the ages of twelve and seventeen, and five children. The largest lineage contains thirty-seven individuals and the smallest two. (The age and sex composition of each lineage is shown in table 7.)

The small average size of these descent groups is partly a result of depopulation. More important, however, is the fact that the members of depleted lineages do not reaffiliate. Lineage identity is maintained to the last man—and in one case to the last two female agnates. Reaffiliation would considerably augment average lineage size by incorporating the same population in a smaller number of lineages. If all the members of lineages with one (or zero) adult males were to reaffiliate, the average lineage would contain twenty-four individuals, including about six adult males.

THE LINEAGE AS A CORPORATE GROUP

Each Etoro lineage customarily maintains well-defined exchange relationships with a limited number of other lineages in regard to giving and receiving wives. These relationships are conceived as permanent and obligate the lineages involved to provide each other with wives on a continuing basis. Although the exchanges should be equivalent over a period of generations, women are to be given in accordance with the needs of the receiving lineage irrespective of the immediate prospects of obtaining a woman in return. The obligation to give and the right to receive women are held in common by all lineage members, as are rights of disposal over sisters, daughters, and widows. These rights and obligations are among the most important corporate possessions of the descent group. A branch of the lineage which consistently marries outside established channels of exchange will ultimately exclude its descendants from the patriline by failing to maintain consanguineal (MZS) ties to the main body of the descent group.

Each lineage possesses a number of *Sigisato* spirits which are said to "belong to" the members of the agnatic group. These spirits are nonancestral and their antecedents and descendants are *Sigisatos*, not men. All the *Sigisatos* of a particular lineage are brothers to each other although the exact genealogical connections between them are not known. The descent group and its associate group of spirits are co-owners of the lineage territory from which both draw their sustenance. These spirits assist and protect lineage members. Their assistance is particularly important in warfare and

TABLE 7

Lineage Composition and Size

Lineage	Adult Males	Adult (Out-Married) Female Agnates	Young Men Age 16–35	Young Women Age 12–17	Male Children	Female Children	Total
Nagefi	1	4	2	0	2	2	11
Turusato	9☆	7	5☆☆☆	1	5	2☆	29
Alamafi	1☆	0	2	0	0	2	5
Salubisato	2☆	4	0	4☆☆	5☆☆☆	1☆	16
Kobifi	3	11☆☆	6☆	1	4	1	26
Gemisato	4	5☆	3	0	0	0	12
Haũasato	1	6☆☆	2	0	2	1	12
Sarado	8☆	11	2	1	6	7	35
Poboleifi	5☆	7☆	5	4	5	1	27
Masianifi	2	5	2	1	4	1	15
Somosato	1	1	0	0	1	1	4
Kaburusato	9	7☆☆	4	1	8	8	37
Ingiribisato	10	6	6☆	1	8	4	35
Haifi	5	9	4	0	7	1	26
Tifanafi	0	2	0	0	0	0	2
Owaibifi	2	2	0	0	0	0	4
Katiefi	6	8	3	2	6	1	26
Hilisato	1	1	2	0	2	0	6
Somadabe	3	2	1	0	2	0	8
Kasayasato	3	2	1☆	0	3	2	11
Waysato	9	5	1	1	7	0	23
Kudulubisato	1	2	0	1	0	0	4
Nemisato	4	3	5	0	3	1	16
Total	90	110	56	18	80	36	390
Average	3.91	4.78	2.43	.78	3.48	1.57	16.96

Note: Each ☆ represents one person living outside Etoro tribal territory.

in some aspects of subsistence such as cassowary trapping. Through mediums they convey warnings of impending witchcraft, foretell success in trading, reveal the whereabouts of lost pigs, and so forth. Acting through a medium, a *Sigisato* cures individuals who are sick as a result of witchcraft.[28] When a man dies, the spirits confirm the identity of the witch responsible and may say of him, "I give you this man to kill." A *Sigisato* may also appear in dreams to lineage members (other than mediums) in order, for example, to inform a man of his wife's adultery.

---

28. The *Kesames* perform some of these same functions, such as curing. A medium's most important *Kesame* spirit is his son— the product of a union with his spirit wife. These spirits consequently are associated with individual mediums and do not "belong to" the lineage.

Lineages generally have two names, one of which is derived from the name of one of its *Sigisatos*. Kaburusato, for example, is named for the spirit Kaburu who is associated with a named section of the lineage's territory (Giãnipia). *Sigisatos* live in the sky but come to earth by day to feed on nuts and fruits while occupying the bodies of cassowaries. Each *Sigisato* is associated with the named section of the bush where he usually feeds (although not every section is the abode of a spirit). A lineage's second name is formed by adding the suffix -*fi* (from *filo,* the term for lineage) to the name of an ancestor or to the name of a major river running through the lineage territory.

The lineage and its *Sigisatos* are the co-owners of a territory of one to two square miles which includes ten or so named sections. (Each of these sections is divided in half with the higher or upstream portion designated by the suffix -*mia* and the lower or downstream portion by the suffix -*pia*.) Individual rights in lineage lands will be discussed in detail subsequently. However, it should be noted here that no member of the lineage holds exclusive rights of stewardship over any portion of the territory. Although most individuals follow the use patterns of their fathers, any agnate— including female agnates—may make a garden or plant sago or other tree crops in any part of the territory at his or her discretion. Sago palms, *Marita pandanus,* breadfruit, and Tahitian chestnut trees (*Edocarpus edius*) are individually owned and may be transmitted, as gifts or inheritance, to individuals outside of as well as within the lineage. The sons of female agnates may acquire these crops although they cannot acquire the land on which they grow. Rights in the land are not divided and are consequently not partible. In view of the equivalent rights of female agnates this indivisibility of the lineage territory effectively prevents the transmission of land to individuals outside the lineage. Moreover, land cannot be alienated from the lineage without alienating the protective *Sigisato* spirits who are co-owners and who reside upon it.

The members of a lineage share common substance. A child is the product of a union of semen and menstrual blood. His flesh, blood, and skin are derived from his mother; his bone and hair from his father.[29] The soul is implanted in the child's body at birth by a *Sigisato*. Sex, which is an aspect of the soul, is also deter-

---

29. Semen contains both bone substance and a life-growth force. This latter element is acquired by boys in homosexual initiation before puberty and comes from individuals outside the lineage (see Kelly, 1974). Bone substance, present from birth, is the exclusive property of the lineage.

mined by the *Sigisato*. Members of the patrilineage share both
bone substance, inherited in the male line, and souls, which are
derived from a common set of spirits who are themselves brothers.
Lineage members also share maternal flesh as a result of parallel
marriage and the levirate. (There are, however, no matrilateral
spirits.)

The definition of the lineage as those descendants of a common patrilineal ancestor who are closely related through agnatic
and matrilateral consanguinity is symbolized by the Etoro three-
part burial. The body of the deceased is initially placed on a platform near the longhouse. The maternal flesh soon rots away (consumed by the witch reponsible for the death) and the patrilineal
bones which remain are placed in a net bag and hung from the
rafters of a small house constructed in the bush near the deceased's
last garden. After three years have passed the bones are placed in a
lineage-owned burial cave with the bones of the ancestors from
whom they are derived. At this time the spirit of the deceased
passes into the realm of the remote dead and can no longer communicate through mediums with his wife and relatives. The final placement of the bones is carried out by a classificatory mother, e.g.,
MBD. Although the maternal flesh lasts only a lifetime, the
"mother" who brings forth the child also commends the patrilineal
bones to the ancestors and assures the passage of the spirit to its
final abode. The union of a man's bone and spirit with those of his
patrilineal ancestors is dependent upon matrilateral consanguinity.

CHAPTER 4

"Brother" Relationships between Lineages

Every lineage regards a number of other descent groups as "brother" patrilines. Such "brother" lines assist each other in the accumulation of brideprice and witchcraft compensation, in intra-tribal fights and disputes, and in external warfare.[1] Brother groups provide mutual aid in all areas where the typically small Etoro lineage lacks sufficient personnel to function effectively. The relationship is functionally comparable to that between sub-clans of the same clan in segmentary systems, but is based on matrilateral sib-lingship rather than descent.

Sibling relationships between lineages are processually based on the development of congruence and closure in the individual matrilateral sibling relationships of lineage members. An ac-knowledged "brother" relationship between patrilines is estab-lished when all (or nearly all) the men of two respective lineages can trace classificatory sibling relationships to each other. "Brotherhood" is a projection of individual kinship to the lineage level. An analysis of the formation of such lineage-level brother relationships will thus necessarily begin with a consideration of the rules governing the classificatory extension of sibling terms.

Matrilateral sibling ties follow from parallel marriage and the transfer of widows between patrilines. Closure (or saturation) in the individual brother ties between two patrilines is largely a pro-duct of concentrated parallel marriages. Multiple sibling ties result whenever two lineages receive a number of wives from the same third lineage.

---

1. Lineages which exchange women extensively also cooperate in these endeavors. Exchange relationships will be discussed in the following chapter.

The transfer of widows between lineages is particularly important in establishing congruence in agnatic kin networks. A widow may be given in exchange for a wife received in the past. This satisfies the requirements of reciprocity while at the same time transforming the relationship between the descendants of the individuals involved in the previous marriage into one of matrilateral half-siblingship. Lineages which have intermarried in the past, but which subsequently become engaged in parallel marriage, establish sibling relationships by eliminating conflicting ties in this way. (This will be explained more fully in subsequent discussion.)

The gift of a widow, without brideprice payment, is patterned after the levirate and constitutes a formal expression of "brotherhood" between lineages. The donor line has residual rights in the widow, as a descent group, and the transfer is thus a transaction at the lineage level. In a few cases, brother relationships between lineages are formally expressed in myths which record the remarriage of the widow of one line's apical ancestor to the totemic founder of a second line. Such mythologically based siblingship is the culmination of the aforementioned developmental processes through which lineage-level "brother" relationships come into being.

CLASSIFICATORY MATRILATERAL SIBLINGSHIP

Every woman of ego's mother's lineage, in her generation or adjacent generations, is equivalent to mother as a linking relative.[2] The children of all these women are siblings. The Etoro themselves

---

2. Women of mother's lineage, in M and MBD generations, are called "mother" (*neme*) while women of MFZ generation are addressed by a grandparental term (*naye*). However, MFZ is nevertheless equivalent to mother as a linking relative since her son (MFZS) is a "brother" (*neto*) to ego (MFZS being the reciprocal of MBDS).

Although Etoro kinship terminology will be more fully discussed in a later chapter it may be noted here that the terminology can be considered a partial Omaha system. Cross-cousins are distinct from siblings and parallel cousins. Patrilateral cross-cousins are distinguished from matrilateral cross-cousins. The female matrilateral cross-cousin (MBD) is classed with members of the first ascending generation, but the male matrilateral cross-cousin (MBS) term is distinct from those applied to ascending generation males. Patrilateral cross-cousins are not classed with members of a descending generation in the men's terminology. In other words, M, MZ, and MBD are all called "mother" (*neme*), while MBS (*sago*) is distinct from MB (*nebabo*), and FZS and FZD (*nesago*) are distinct from ZS and ZD (*nemano*) respectively (man speaking).

explain such relationships by saying, "my mother and his mother are of the same lineage, therefore we are brothers." The sons of these "brothers" are also "brothers" and the relationship may be continued by their sons in turn. Sibling relationships established through a linking female of father's mother's lineage (in FMother's or adjacent generations) can be traced genealogically, while more distant sibling relationships usually cannot. The Etoro explain these nongenealogical relationships by saying, "I call x 'brother' because my father called his father 'brother.'"

Parallel marriages generate sibling relationships at an appreciable rate. The sons of any pair of men who marry women of the same lineage (in the same or adjacent generations) are "brothers." A typical lineage contains four out-married female agnates per generation. Mother's lineage would then contain about eleven women equivalent to mother as linking relatives. The sons (and daughters) of all these women are ego's siblings. The sons' sons of an equal number of women of father's mother's lineage are also ego's "brothers," while some relationships established at the FFMother's level continue to be maintained as well.

Sibling relationships are further multiplied by the classification of FBW and FFBSW as "mother," and by the stipulation that the sons of women of these classificatory mother's lineages are also "brothers." All men of the same lineage and generation are thus "brothers" to the sons of all women of the lineages from which their collective "fathers" received wives. The members of a typical lineage which had taken four wives in the previous generation would be able to trace sibling relationships through forty-four linking relatives equivalent to mother. (This number would be reduced, however, by the extent to which agnates contract parallel marriages.)

"Brother" relationships are further extended by the reciprocals of relationships traceable through FBW and FFBSW. All of ego's MZSon's lineage brothers, for example, will consider ego to be their "brother" since he is the son of a woman of "father's" wife's lineage. In other words, ego will be a sibling not only to the sons of the women of his true mother's lineage, but to all the lineage brothers of each of these men as well. The sibling relationships between the members of two lineages linked by a single parallel marriage are shown in figure 10.

All men of the same lineage and generation are "brothers" to the sons of all women of the lineages from which their collective "fathers" received wives. Thus a, b, c, and d of lineage X are all brothers of e (of lineage Z). Each of these lineage brothers is also a

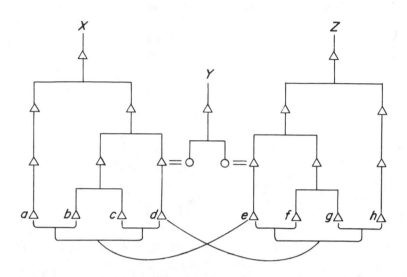

Brother Relationships (+)

Men of Lineage *Z*

Men of Lineage *X*

	e	f	g	h
a	+			
b	+			
c	+			
d	+	+	+	+

FIG. 10.   Brother Relationships Resulting from a Single Parallel Marriage

sibling of all the same generation agnates of the sons of women of his true mother's lineage. Thus *d* (of *X*) is a "brother" to *e*, *f*, *g*, and *h*, while *d*'s agnates are siblings only to *e* of this line.

As is evident from the grid, the percentage concentration of sibling relationships is a function of lineage size. There are seven dyadic brother relationships out of a possible sixteen (43.75 percent) when each lineage contains four members in the relevant generation. As lineage size is expanded, the percentage declines.

The figure can be determined for any lineage size by the formula

$$\frac{N_x + N_y - 1}{N_x \times N_y}$$

where N_x and N_y are the number of same generation agnates in the two respective lineages.

Since lineage-level brother relationships are based on the development of a high concentration of individual sibling relationships, the small size of Etoro patrilines[3] is an integral aspect of the social organization. Frequent fission maintains appropriate numerical size and fission itself is promoted by growth as this dilutes the degree of matrilateral consanguinity within the lineage.

LINEAGE-LEVEL SIBLINGSHIP: THE DEVELOPMENT OF CONGRUENCE AND CLOSURE

Etoro kinship terminology generates very extensive classificatory sibling relationships between individuals of different lineages. These "brother" ties follow from parallel marriages and are thus in complementary distribution with respect to relationships based on the exchange of women. Any pair of individuals who are not otherwise related through marriage in the present or past generations (as affines, cross-cousins, etc.) will be able to trace a sibling relationship via a classificatory mother or father's mother.

The individual kin relationships of lineage members are partially congruent as a consequence of the rule that FBW and FFBSW are classified with mother. Ego is a "brother" to his MZS and ego's agnates are likewise "brothers" to this man. This congruence is not complete because ego is also the "brother" of his MZSon's agnates (same generation), while ego's agnates are not.

The partial congruence in the kin relationships of lineage members tends to develop, and to be developed, toward complete congruence and closure. This projects kinship to the lineage level where it provides the organizational basis of interlineage relationships. The latter are defined in terms of the complementary categories of matrilateral siblingship and exchange. Each lineage thus

---

3. The average lineage contains about four living, ever-married men, but these may not all be of the same generation as shown in the diagram (fig. 10). The average sum of $N_x + N_y$ is seven rather than eight, and the average percentage concentration of brother ties is 50 percent (6/12) as opposed to 43.8 percent (7/16).

regards every other lineage either as a "brother" line or as a descent group with which it exchanges women.

When individual sibling relationships encompass all, or nearly all, the members of two patrilines, brotherhood is conceived as a relationship between lineages and is expressed in these terms. The development of both closure and congruence in the matrilateral sibling relationships of agnates is largely a product of the concentration of marriages and the continuity of relationships involving the exchange of women. Any two lineages (*B* and *D*) which consistently exchange women with the same other patrilines (*A, C*, etc.) will be "brothers" to each other as a consequence of the repetition of parallel marriages. New sibling relationships are continually generated while previous ones are maintained and renewed. After a few generations these individual relationships extend throughout both lineages and provide a basis for the establishment of a lineage-level "brother" relationship.

Parallel marriages contracted by agnates are particularly conducive to the development of sibling relationships which encompass the entire membership of two lineages as they provide multiple points of linkage in a single generation. When two men of a particular lineage marry sisters, almost complete siblingship is created between that lineage and any other patriline which receives a single wife from the sisters' natal patriline. This is illustrated in figure 11. A small number of marriages is thus sufficient to produce a dense concentration of sibling relationships between lineages when parallel marriages are contracted by agnates. As noted earlier, such marriages also provide a means of maintaining close consanguinity within the lineage as it ages genealogically, and are specifically sought.

Each Etoro lineage contracts an average of 56 percent of its unions with only three other patrilines over a period of two to three generations. At least three pairs of agnates (in the same or adjacent generations) will have married lineage sisters (or women related as FZ/BD) of these three major woman-exchange groups. As a result of such agnatic parallel marriages, the lineage will possess multiple sibling relationships with individuals of all the other patrilines which have also received wives from these three descent groups. Brother relationships will be particularly dense between pairs of lineages which exchange women extensively with the same other descent group (or groups). As shown in figure 12, any given lineage (*B*) can therefore be expected to have all-encompassing sibling ties to about four to six patrilines (*D, F, H, J, L*) which have corresponding concentrations of marriages, i.e., which have at least one

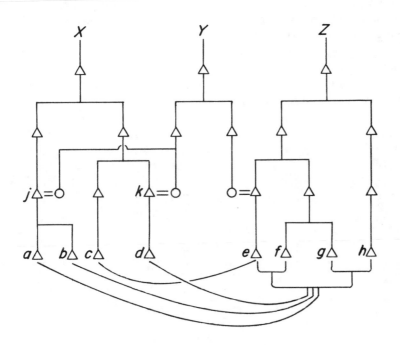

Brother Relationships (+)

Men of Lineage Z

	e	f	g	h
a	+	+	+	+
b	+	+	+	+
c	+			
d	+	+	+	+

Men of Lineage X

FIG. 11. Brother Relationships Resulting from a Combination of Agnatic
Parallel Marriage and Parallel Marriage

major wife-supplier (*C, E, G*) in common with *B*. Lineage *B* will also have substantial individual sibling relationships (like those shown in figure 12) with members of a second group of four to six patrilines which have received only an occasional wife from *B*'s major wife suppliers (and which account for the remaining 44 percent of *C, E,* and *G*'s unions). In other words, each lineage has complete or substantial brother relationships to about half of the twenty-two lineages in the tribe traced through "mothers" of its major wife-providing lines alone.

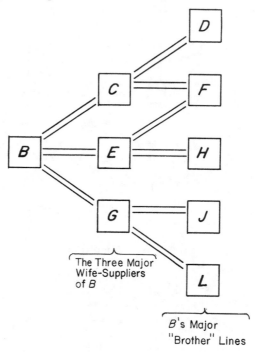

FIG. 12. Brother Relationships Established through Major Exchange Groups

When individual sibling relationships encompass all the members of two patrilines (in any particular generation) intermarriage cannot take place as the Etoro do not marry women whom they acknowledge to be their "sisters." The recognition of encompassing sibling ties thus entails a commitment to exogamy and at the same time establishes a lineage-level "brother" relationship. The absence of intermarriage contributes to the perpetuation of this relationship by excluding conflicting kin ties and by ensuring that the two patrilines will seek wives from the same external group of lineages and therefore will be likely to contract additional parallel marriages.

A failure to renew such "brother" relationships through subsequent parallel marriages—providing some close consanguineal MZS (MBDS, etc.) ties between individuals of the two lines—will eventually lead to dissolution of acknowledged lineage-level siblingship. Should this occur, the erstwhile "brother" lines may begin to exchange women. Matrilateral siblingship is the direct product of parallel marriage and does not persist in its absence. Lineage-level "brother" relationships are necessarily generated by the concentration of marriages, but do not necessarily involve the same pairs of lineages in each generation. Continuity is contingent upon the persistence of the exchange relationships through which the sibling ties are traced.

Siblingship and Exogamy

Sibling relationships which involve some, but not all, of the individual members of a pair of lineages have the effect of discouraging any intermarriage between the two. Marriages contracted with women of patrilines which contain one or more "brothers" are disadvantageous because they introduce ambiguity into the contracting lineage's relationships with its exchange groups. Whenever a patriline receives a woman from a descent group containing a "brother," it creates a sibling relationship with the "mother's" lineage through which the original brother relationship was traced. This may be most easily explained with respect to a diagram (fig. 13).

The woman a is a sister to x's agnate (the son of y), but need not be classified as a "sister" by x himself (cf. fig. 10). Although the marriage between x and a would not itself violate any rules it has the effect of decreasing the possibilities of marriage between lineages B and C in the next generation. Ego (the son of x and a) is now the MBDS of f and the FFBSWBDS ($=$"MBDS") of e so that both these men would call ego "brother." The daughters of these two men would be ego's classificatory daughters. The woman h would also be a "daughter" to ego's agnates (t, for example). These relationships are not so extensive as to preclude intermarriage (t and g being an acceptable union, for example) but they reduce the possibilities of arranging an exchange in which the parties are suitably related and also meet requirements of age and so forth.

The question arises as to whether these classificatory father-daughter ties do, in fact, constitute a significant impediment to the marriage of individuals so related. Couldn't they simply be

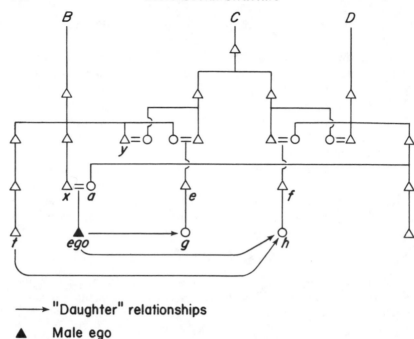

———➤ "Daughter" relationships

▲　　Male ego

FIG. 13.　Marriage Possibilities between Partial Brother Lines

ignored? In theory they might, but in practice this seldom occurs due to the intervention of third parties who also have claims to the women involved.

Wives are very competitively sought—indeed men of marriageable age outnumber girls in the same social category by 1.8 to 1. In this situation a man's chances of obtaining a wife depend on the strength of the claim he can advance with respect to a particular woman. Such claims are based on women given in the past and are defined in terms of kinship (i.e., FZSD, FFZSD). A secondary "sister" or "daughter" relationship does not nullify a claim but does weaken it vis-à-vis the claims of other men—and they will not fail to point this out. A potential wife-giver would find it difficult to reject a second suitor with an equivalent claim and no overlapping "father" or "brother" relationship. To do so would constitute a blatant disregard for the exchange relationship with the lineage of the pedigreed claimant. Rejection would clearly imply that the latter patriline could not expect fair treatment in obtaining wives for women given in the past—that it was regarded as a "least favored nation." On the other hand, a secondary "father" relationship provides a convenient excuse for rejecting an otherwise acceptable claim and delaying reciprocity for a generation.

The extent to which a patriline's claims to women are weakened by contracting a marriage with a lineage containing "brothers" is directly proportional to the number of sibling ties between the two. If both B and D (fig. 13) have also married women of a fourth lineage A, then the same difficulties previously noted also apply with respect to B's claims to women of A.

The agnates of x are likely to disapprove of his marriage to a partial "brother" line unless they do not expect to receive any further wives from C (due to depletion of that line, for example). If x contracts the marriage against his agnates' wishes he may well initiate the process of fission. Indeed, the main body of the lineage may deny that x and his son are members. This is particularly likely should a dispute arise over claims to women. For example, the man t can refute the allegation that he is a "father" to the woman h (of C) by denying that x and his descendants are members of lineage B. Since there is only a single marriage between B and D, x's descendants will necessarily lack MZS ties to their agnates. If the patrilineal relationship between these lineage branches were distant as well, a split would be almost certain. Fission is the likely result whenever two distantly related lineage branches contract marriages which respectively weaken each other's claims to women and at the same time fail to establish close consanguineal ties within the descent group. The splitting-off of a lineage segment which has contracted one or more marriages with a partial "brother" line also reestablishes the exogamous relationship between the original "brother" lineages.

Marriage between partial "brother" lines is also discouraged by the fact that there is little to be gained by giving a woman to such a group. If lineage D were to obtain a woman in exchange for the one (a) given to B, it would incur all of the problems noted above. Moreover, D might well expect to have difficulty obtaining a wife from B if the majority of the men of that line disapproved of the initial union. Since there is little advantage in giving a woman when the prospect of obtaining one in return is unlikely—or undesirable—patrilines are generally unwilling to provide a wife for a lineage which contains "brothers." Such a marriage would be likely to occur primarily when both descent groups (D and B) anticipated no further exchanges with the lineage (C) through which the sibling ties were established.

The incomplete sibling ties which follow from a single parallel marriage thus discourage intermarriage between partial brother lines while at the same time allowing for flexibility in the establishment of new exchange relationships. There is a tendency toward the development of an exogamous "brother" relationship when present exchange patterns are stable. If they are not, however, the incompleteness of partial "brother" ties leaves open the option of converting such relationships.

Each lineage attempts to develop and maintain unambiguous relationships with every other patriline, that is, relationships based exclusively on either siblingship or exchange. These external relationships are particularly important because lineages are of insufficient size to carry out many necessary functions internally. Ambiguous external relationships are inherently lacking in dependability with respect to claims to women and in other respects as well. The lineage seeks not only brides, but also a substantial portion of the brideprice from nonagnates. Both cannot be obtained from the same group.

Clear-cut external relationships are also important to the internal organization of the lineage as they entail agnatic parallel marriage, close consanguineal ties of matrilateral siblingship within the lineage, and congruence in agnatic kin networks. This provides that the lineage will be composed of close kinsmen whose obligations and self-interest are largely isomorphic.

The avoidance of marriage with partial brother lines maintains unambiguous relationships not only for the lineages involved, but also for the exchange groups through which the sibling tie is traced. This is particularly important because any given lineage lacks control over the location of its matrilateral sibling relationships. A man cannot dictate who his MZ, MBD, or WZ will marry and thus cannot determine the descent group affiliation of his (or his son's) "brothers."[4] Consistency would be difficult to achieve if a man's MB married his agnates' MZ (fig. 14). However, marriages of this type rarely occur because they create the same problems for contracting parties as the marriage of "brother" lines.

As a consequence of his father's marriage (fig. 14), ego's FZSD and her lineage sisters are also classificatory (or true) MZSD. While this marriage creates a problem of ambiguous relationships for lineage *C*, it is much more damaging to ego's lineage and particularly to ego himself. Due to the problems discussed

---

4. Although men of different lineages may seek to establish a "brother" relationship by marrying a pair of sisters, the success of this endeavor lies with the wife-givers.

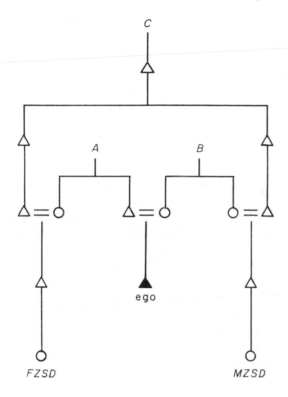

FIG. 14.   Consequences of Intermarriage with Partial Brother Lines

earlier, it will be extremely difficult for ego to obtain a "FZSD" from *C*, and this would normally be his strongest claim.

In order to prevent this situation from arising, a lineage will generally avoid giving a woman to any agnate's WZHusband's line, that is, to a patriline that will contain "brothers" in the next generation. To do so is to provide a wife with little expectation of reciprocity. Similarly, a lineage will attempt to obtain women from descent groups that have not contracted marriages with a ZHusband's agnates. (In other words, either ego's father's marriage or ego's father's sister's marriage would be avoided.)

A patriline which avoids these types of marriages can establish unambiguous claims to women for its descendants. In so doing, it also contributes to the development of congruence in the agnatic kin networks of the lineages with which it exchanges women. From the standpoint of the latter, this provides that one man's MB will not marry his agnate's MZ. Although a lineage cannot determine whom its mothers' sisters will marry, it can refuse wives to the sons of MBrothers who contract marriages with these women. This introduces a degree of indirect control over the location of matrilateral sibling ties.

The strategy of exchange thus dictates the avoidance of those unions which are deleterious to the development of both unambiguous external relationships and congruence in agnatic kin networks. As a result sibling and exchange relationships tend to be mutually exclusive and in complementary distribution at the lineage level.

Widow Transfers

Sibling ties engendered by parallel marriage are supplemented and expanded by the transfer of widows between patrilines. Such widow transfers are employed to consolidate a warfare alliance, to renew and extend previous "brother" relationships, and particularly to redefine ambiguous relationships between patrilines which are partially related as brothers but which have also intermarried in the past. The gift of a widow is particularly suited to these objectives because the donor lineage has direct control over the location of the resultant sibling relationships.

Widows are given to men of "brother" lines without payment of brideprice, and the Etoro conceive of the transfer in terms of the idiom of the levirate. The transaction is an ideological statement of relationship affirming that the two lineages are "like" brothers. Siblingship is a consequence of the transfer, not a precondition; the widow is given as a gift rather than in satisfaction of a claim based on the jural rights of matrilateral siblings.

The relationship between the two lineages involved in such a widow transfer is strengthened by the fact that the donor patriline —as a corporate group—has residual rights in the widow according to the ideology of the levirate.[5] The gift of a widow is thus a transaction between corporate groups, and is similar in this respect to a first marriage. Widows create sibling ties in the same way that out-married daughters create ties of affinity.

The widow-gift creates matrilateral sibling relationships between the donor and recipient lines similar to those which follow from parallel marriage. The half-sibling tie is stronger than a MZS

---

5. The levirate accounts for 47.2 percent (17/36) of all widow remarriage and the widow-gift for 30.6 percent (11/36). In 22.2 percent (8/36) of the cases the woman was given to an exchange group for brideprice. The destination of a widow should be determined by the lineage membership with the deceased's brother having a leading role in the decision. The extent to which lineage rights are effectively exercised is considered in chapter 8.

tie due to the closer degree of consanguinity, but the classificatory relationships are identical. The widow is regarded as a linking relative equivalent to mother by both groups. Half-siblings retain their affiliation with their father's lineage, and the same generation agnates of each set of half-siblings are classificatory brothers to the opposite set.

A lineage which has enlisted assistance in warfare from "brother" lines should, after the completion of the hostilities, award the widows of agnates killed in battle to men of these allied patrilines. The latter may reciprocate if they have lost men as well. This transfer of widows consolidates the alliance and ensures the continuity of the sibling relationships on which it is based.[6] In the event that no widows are available, a polygynist of the recruiting patriline may even donate one of his wives in order to cement an important alliance. In one well-remembered case, a Nagefi man gave his second wife to a member of a Petamini lineage (Sesimato) which had aided Nagefi in a fight. The alliance is particularly important to these lineages, which share a common border between tribal territories, because it blocks off the major access route of raiding parties moving in either direction. The man who gave his wife and the man who received her are now the nearest common ancestors of their respective patrilines, and all their descendants are consequently "brothers."

The gift of a widow or second wife is particularly effective in consolidating an alliance in that it engenders multiple relationships. In addition to the sibling ties created between donor and recipient, the latter also acquires consanguineal (MB) ties to the woman's natal line and sibling relationships traced through females of that line (these ties being retained by the donor lineage as well). The receiving group is thus brought into relationship with the widow-giver's other allies, including both affinal lineages and "brother" lines. Postwarfare widow-gifts to allied brother lines account for three of the eleven recorded cases of widow transfers (without brideprice).

The widow-gift is also particularly effective in redefining ambiguous relationships between lineages which are "brothers" as a consequence of recent parallel marriages, but which have also intermarried occasionally in the past. A widow given in exchange for a woman previously received satisfies reciprocity, but does so in a way that terminates the exchange relationship. Existing claims to women are fulfilled while no new claims are generated.

---

6. Similarly, an alliance based on an exchange relationship is reaffirmed by further exchange of women.

A widow transfer in this context forges a dependable sibling relationship between the two lineages involved. Since reciprocity in the exchange of women is honored, reciprocity may be expected in the areas of mutual assistance appropriate to "brother" lines. This affirmation of equivalent reciprocity and mutuality is important in establishing a firm ideological basis for the sibling relationship.

The clarification of an ambiguous relationship offers other advantages as well. Sibling relationships are aligned with current exchange patterns so as to strengthen each of the two patrilines' claims to women. The widow-receiving lineage, for example, avoids acquiring matrilateral sibling ties to the lineages from which it currently receives wives by avoiding marriage with a "brother" line.[7] However, it need not forgo a wife to achieve this. In addition, the two lineages each gain a greater degree of congruence in their respective agnatic kin networks.

The following case provides a good example of how the widow-gift is employed to redefine both internal and external relationships.

A generation ago, two segments of Hauasato related as FFFBSSS were beginning to split into separate lineages. Each segment had contracted marriages with different groups and widows had been remarried by close agnates or given to men outside the lineage. There were consequently no close consanguineal ties of matrilateral siblingship (resulting from parallel marriage or the levirate) which bridged the genealogical fissure. The external relationships of the two branches were also inconsistent, particularly with respect to Kobifi. One segment of Hauasato had established multiple sibling relationships with Kobifi while the other had given a woman in marriage to this group.

In the following generation declining numbers led to an attempt to reverse the process of fission. A single widow donated by Kobifi provided the basis for both the internal consolidation of Hauasato and the redefinition of its ambiguous external relationships. This transaction is diagramed in figure 15.

The Hauasato segment (*B*) which had previously supplied a FZ to Kobifi received a (deceased) "FZSon's" wife instead of a FZSD. This widow transfer not only terminated the exchange relationship by preventing the establishment of any new claims to

---

7. Since the widow is not natally of the donor (brother) line, the women of that group do not become "mothers." Exchange groups, through which the current sibling ties to the widow-giver are traced, thus do not become siblings themselves.

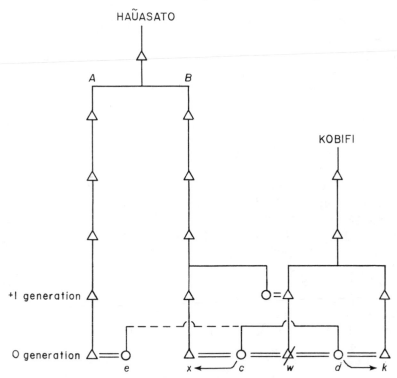

FIG. 15.   The Widow-Gift as a Means of Redefining Relationships

women but also created multiple ties of matrilateral siblingship in the −1 generation both within Haũasato and between Haũasato and Kobifi. The woman involved was one of two true sisters (*c* and *d*) married by a Kobifi man. While one widowed sister was given to Haũasato, the other was married by the deceased's FBS of Kobifi. This established a parallel marriage between the two lineages in addition to the widow link. The sons of *x* of Haũasato *B* would then be matrilateral half-siblings to one branch of Kobifi (*w*'s sons) and true MZSons to a second branch (*k*'s sons). These two segments of Kobifi would also be matrilateral half-siblings in addition to being FFBSSons.

The two true sisters (*c* and *d*) were also lineage "sisters" (FFBSD) to the wife (*e*) of another Haũasato man of the "brother" segment (*A*) of that lineage. The transfer of one of these true sisters to the wife-giving segment of Haũasato (*B*) thus created a parallel marriage between the two segments of that lineage. The sons of the *A* and *B* branches would thus be matrilateral siblings in addition to being FFFFFBSSSSS. The consanguineal relationship traced through these women would still not be particularly close (MFFBSDS), but nevertheless an improvement. Of perhaps more importance was the fact that lineage members now possessed congruent kin networks, having common ties to the same "brother" and "mother" patrilines. These isomorphic external relationships are themselves conducive to future agnatic parallel marriages.

Over the next few years an additional parallel marriage was contracted by men of Kobifi and Haũasato and a second widow transferred. The matrilateral half-brother and FBS of *x* (Haũasato *B*) and the brother of *w* (Kobifi) married women who were true sisters. The brother of *k* (Kobifi) died and his widow was given to the same half-brother of *x* (Haũasato *B*).

Prior to the initial widow transfer there had also been three sets of parallel marriages (in the 0 and +1 generations) contracted by men of Haũasato *A* and Kobifi, respectively. One of these involved a pair of true sisters (of a Petamini line) and the other two involved women related as true FZ/BD.

As a result of all these parallel marriages and widow transfers, the (−1 generation) sons of each lineage could trace sibling relationships to each other in ten different ways. Every son of Kobifi was a brother of his counterparts in Haũasato and vice versa. Moreover, nearly all the ties were based on close consanguinity as the linking females were themselves closely related.

This case illustrates the way in which the widow-gift is employed to redefine ambiguous relationships between partial "brother" lines. In four additional cases, a widow was given in delayed exchange for a wife previously received. There were no prior marriages between the donor and recipient lineages in the five remaining cases. However, the latter include one instance in which brother lines exchanged widows. Reciprocity was thus evident in eight of the eleven recorded widow transfers to "brother" lines.

This case also illustrates how widow transfers are used, in conjunction with parallel marriage, to achieve closure in the individual sibling relationships between two lineages. The gift of a widow is most effective in increasing the density of brother relationships between lineages when it does not duplicate existing ties based on parallel marriage, that is, when the woman's first and second husbands are not consanguineally related matrilateral siblings or WZH. The Etoro themselves maintain that it is preferable to give a widow to the deceased's MZSon's (or WZHusband's) agnate, rather than to the MZS (or WZH) himself. This preference is largely realized in practice, and in only one case was a widow given to a WZH. In a second instance (previously described) a widow went to the deceased's true brother's WZH. The remainder all involved more distantly related first and second husbands and, like the Haũasato-Kobifi example, were quite effective in increasing and extending existing ties based on parallel marriage.

Interlineage relationships which are based on kinship, rather than descent, require considerable ingenuity in the positioning of women—since women are the points of linkage in all relationships outside the patrilineage. The Kobifi widow transfers are a good illustration of some of the fine points in this art of positioning women to maximum effect. The flexibility of kinship-based external relationships is also exemplified by the utilization of widow transfers to redefine ambiguous relationships.

Mythologically Validated Siblingship

In a few cases, exogamous "brother" relationships between lineages are formally expressed in myths which record the remarriage of the widow of one line's apical ancestor to the totemic founder of a second line. The sequence of events in each of these myths is the same, and a single example will thus suffice.

> There was a big longhouse where many men lived. One of the men died. He died and his wife became a widow. She remained a widow and yet she saw that she had become pregnant. Wo! Her belly was very large.
>
> So a man asked her, "Who ate[8] you?" ["Who made you pregnant?"]
>
> "Ah! I didn't see, I didn't see who made me like this," she replied.
>
> Here, beside her, some dead marsupials. It is night. Over there are more dead marsupials. All around her are dead marsupials. He watches her. Mother! under the sleeping platform she sees, watching her—Mother! a huge snake. A *faitilo,* a large black python, was there. Mother! he lies watching her, the *faitilo.* When night came he went out and later returned to see her. He placed many marsupials he had killed there, beside her. Others he put there, on the other side. (This is our custom—for a husband to bring his wife who has just borne a child freshly killed marsupials. Thus, she knew that the snake was the father of her child.) They slept. They lived on together. The child grew to manhood. The child and the snake slept there one night, two nights, three nights, four nights. They lived on there together.

---

8. "To eat someone" is a euphemism for sexual intercourse.

Mother! the *faitilo* had brought marsupials. He had stayed with her,
he had taken the woman as his wife. He did not become a man, he
remained a snake.[9]

The *faitilo*'s child was Sekea. Sekea fathered Faia, Faia fathered
Pimo, and Pimo's sons were Nage and my grandfather Yero. The
woman, the mother of Sekea, was Afoti.[10] Her deceased husband,
Toene, is the ancestor of the Turusato men, my brothers.

The events described in this myth are understood by the Etoro as
follows: the totemic python *Faitilo* wishes to take a wife. There are
many single and married women to choose from, but *Faitilo* selects
Afoti, the widow of a Turusato man. According to the idiom of the
levirate, the totemic python thus reveals himself to be a "brother"
to that patriline. If this were not the case he would have chosen a
different woman.

Faitilo's choice does not create a "brother" relationship ex
nihilo but is rather a revelation of preexisting siblingship that is
inherent in the nature of things.[11] Turusato and Nagefi are not
brother lines merely as a consequence of a single half-sibling tie
which diminishes in significance with each passing generation but
are inherently and thus permanently "brothers."

Although the Etoro understanding of these myths emphasizes
the timeless, ahistorical nature of the relationship between the two
lineages, mythologically based siblingship appears, in fact, to be a
formalization of exogamous brother relationships which come into
being through parallel marriage and widow transfers and which are
subsequently maintained and renewed over a period of generations.
In the last three generations 51.7 percent (16/28) of the women
received as wives by Nagefi and Turusato have been of the same
natal patrilines. All the members of Nagefi and Turusato can trace
recent matrilateral sibling relationships to each other. Poboleifi and
Masianifi, which possess a similar myth, evidence 41.7 percent
(5/12) parallel marriage.[12] Mythologically validated siblingship is

---

9. In myths which delineate exchange relationships, the totemic python becomes a man.

10. No one was able to recall the lineage affiliation of Afoti.

11. The concept of revelation by performance of a customary act
(e.g., widow remarriage) is also evident in the way in which *Faitilo* makes
known his paternal role to Afoti—by presenting marsupials. The myth thus
formulates, by analogy, the key to the Etoro interpretation.

12. In the final case (Tifanafi and Arafi), one of the lineages is extinct
and no marriage data are available.

thus present only when the two lineages involved are also related as "brother" lines through recent parallel marriages.

Only six of more than forty dyadic "brother" relationships between lineages are phrased in terms of mythological widow remarriage, and only three of twenty-three lineages possess totemic ancestors. However, three additional lineages have genealogies which include the wife of a distant ancestor but omit the wife of his son. These women are extraneous to the patriline and with respect to current claims to women (since their natal line is not remembered). Their genealogical presence suggests that they once served as widow-links to other lineages, and that mythologically validated siblingship was more prevalent in the past. There has been a considerable degree of realignment of exchange and sibling relationships as a consequence of depopulation, and it may thus be suggested that past sibling relationships which became inconvenient were forgotten, while recent brother ties have not persisted long enough to be mythologized.

Both Nagefi and Poboleifi possess the same totemic animal, the black python (*faitilo*). Although the two lineages regard each other as brother lines they explain this relationship in terms of kin ties of matrilateral siblingship. On formal grounds they might be regarded as a totemic clan, but the members of the two patrilines specifically deny belonging to any higher order group. They emphasize the fact that their respective ancestors were different individual snakes. I asked one informant if the two snakes might be brothers. He said that might be so, but "the myths don't say so."

Nagefi, Poboleifi, Masianifi, and Turusato—the four lines included in the myths—are all "brother" lines and are related as matrilateral siblings through parallel marriages (table 8). There is one recent marriage between Poboleifi and Masianifi, while the other five dyadic brother relationships are exogamous.

Tifanafi's totemic ancestor is also a snake—the death adder or *saiabe*. Although no other lineages possess totemic ancestors, totemism is present in the mythology in other contexts, e.g., the Etoro themselves are the descendants of a marsupial and a primeval woman. It seems probable that totemic relationships were previously more prevalent and perhaps the entire system of interlineage relationships was once defined in these terms. However, this is not presently the case and speculation along these lines, although intriguing, cannot adequately account for current relationships.

Mythological widow remarriage is structurally significant as an expression of the principles of relationship which are appropriate both within and between lineages. These myths codify patrilineal

TABLE 8

Percentage of Parallel Marriages between
Mythologically Related Lineages

| Lineage | Percentage of Parallel Marriages | | | |
	Nagefi	*Turusato*	*Poboleifi*	*Masianifi*
Nagefi		57.1 (16/28)	60.0 (12/20)	21.4 (3/14)
Turusato			34.6 (9/26)	15.0 (3/20)
Poboleifi				41.7 (5/12)
Masianifi				

descent as the principle which defines the lineage internally and specify women as the points of linkage in relationships between lineages. Although the Nagefi and Turusato lines are both composed of the patrilineal descendants of a common female ancestor (Afoti), this ancestor is not a member of either descent group by birth. The consistent application of the principle of patrilineal descent thus excludes the only ancestor which these two lineages have in common. If the myth is to be interpreted as formulating a descent relationship between Nagefi and Turusato, it can only be concluded that this relationship is stipulated in the most awkward manner one can conceive. Indeed, the myth appears to be designed as a specific denial of descent as a principle of relationship in the external field.

The Etoro conception of the nature of the "brother" relationship between Nagefi and Turusato is grounded in the rules for classifying the descendants of matrilateral kinswomen. Pairs of individuals explain their brotherhood by stating that "our mothers are of the same lineage." Similarly, pairs of patrilines are "brothers" because their lineages are of the same mother. The relationship is conceived as matrilateral siblingship at the lineage level.

The low incidence of mythologically validated siblingship thus does not indicate a lack of homogeneity in the structure of external relationships. Relations between lineages are consistently phrased in terms of the complementary categories of matrilateral siblingship and the exchange of women. These relationships are always based on current ties, while some are based on mythological ties as well. The form, however, is invariable.

Postfission Relationships

Although fission occurs frequently, it does not lead to the formation of higher order descent groups because the agnatic ties between the resultant lineages are either excised from their respective genealogies or denied. A case in point: it is general knowledge that Alamafi recently split from Turusato and formed a separate lineage. Hasuãn is the nearest common ancestor and FF of adult men in the genealogies of each of these patrilines. It is maintained, however, that this is coincidental. Informants of these lineages state that "many men have the same name." I pointed out that in both cases, Hasuãn had married Sinaya of Katiefi. It was then further explained that "many women also have the same name."

These two lineages are "brother" lines, but phrase this in terms of matrilateral siblingship. A very high percentage (88.9 percent) of their wives have come from the same groups in the past two generations. However, Alamafi has recently contracted unions with former "brother" lines of both lineages.

Lineages are reluctant to acknowledge past fission partly because this recalls witchcraft accusations and disputes which were instrumental in the process, but which are inappropriate to the establishment of amicable relationships after the event. More importantly, phrasing their relationship in terms of matrilateral siblingship creates the possibility of intermarriage after a period of one or two generations, as sibling relationships expire if not renewed by parallel marriage. Since fission is usually the result of a divergence in the exchange relationships of lineage segments, the two newly formed patrilines frequently gravitate toward opposite exchange networks and eventually intermarry. Maintaining a history of common descent would necessitate the continued use of sibling terms and this would preclude marriage as the Etoro do not marry women whom they acknowledge to be their sisters.

In the interim between fission and intermarriage, the maintenance of a "brother" relationship is useful as it may provide the basis for limited mutual assistance. The event of fission often alleviates the sources of tension which brought it about and an attempt to establish a congenial relationship follows. Distant classificatory ties of matrilateral siblingship which are insufficient to hold the lineage together—due to the absence of close consanguinity—are adequate for the purpose of maintaining limited siblingship. Such ties do not preclude intermarriage in succeeding generations if an exchange relationship is sought. If not, these sibling ties may be renewed.

GROUPS OF "BROTHER" LINES AND DE FACTO MOIETIES

The development of "brother" relationships between lineages has been described primarily in dyadic terms. There are, however,

larger groups of lineages which are all "brother" lines to each
other. Etoroi is a grouping of this type, and the only one which is
named. Nagefi, Turusato, Alamafi, Salubisato, and Kobifi are generally included as the constituent lineages of this group. The exact
composition is not a matter on which there is general agreement.
Kobifi is sometimes omitted and Haũasato is sometimes included.
This ambiguity in delineating the membership of Etoroi is a consequence of the fact that membership is based on matrilateral siblingship. Different evaluations of these ties are made by different informants, depending on their position in the network of exchange
relationships.

Etoroi is a group of patrilines which do not themselves intermarry, but which exchange women with the same other lineages.
Of the fifteen dyadic relationships between these six lineages, there
is only one instance of intermarriage, that between Haũasato and
Kobifi. This single union and the kin ties resulting from it were
nullified by the widow-transfers discussed in an earlier section of
this chapter.

The four lines which are always included in Etoroi all receive 60
to 81 percent of their wives from Kaburusato, Ingiribisato, Haifi,
and Katiefi. Each of these lineages thus has at least two major wife-
suppliers in common. Kobifi, however, only obtained 27.3 percent
of its wives from these groups. While Kobifi has some additional
parallel marriages through minor wife-suppliers of these Etoroi
lines, its marginal position in Etoroi is a product of this lower density of matrilateral sibling relationships. Haũasato has received 50
percent of its wives from these four lines, but is excluded by informants who omit Kobifi, its major "brother" line. The recent ambiguity of its external relationships may be a factor as well.[13]

The Etoroi lineages are a potent political force in Etoro society. Each of these patrilines can depend not only on the others, but
on the four groups to which all are affinally related. These ten
lineages together include over 50 percent of the adult male members of the tribe. Individuals of these ten lines which cannot be
mobilized in a dispute, due to conflicting ties, can at least be im-
mobilized. An Etoroi line can draw twice the support of any lineage outside of its alliance network.

---

13. There have been no widow transfers between Etoroi lineages other
than those between Kobifi and Haũasato. This is in keeping with the fact
that such transfers are generally employed to redefine ambiguous relationships, while none of the brother relationships between the four major
Etoroi lineages are at all ambiguous.

There is no other acknowledged group of brother lines comparable in size to Etoroi. However, there is also no other large group of lineages which evidences both exogamy and such extensive parallel marriage. The fact that Etoroi is the only named group of this type is therefore not surprising. Indeed, this group is sufficiently inclusive that it would be difficult for another similar group to be formed outside its purview.

Etoro kinship terminology dictates a complementary opposition between the categories of siblingship and exchange and this fundamental duality imposes itself at every organizational level. At the tribal level this duality generates a division of the society into two largely exogamous groups of "brother" lineages which constitute de facto moieties. These "moieties"[14] are 80 percent exogamous although they are neither named nor recognized by the Etoro as distinct social groups. They do not form part of the Etoro conceptualization of their society and are not employed in the regulation of marriage or the organization of relationships between lineages. The Etoro are not aware of this major structural division within their society.

These moieties exist everywhere but in the minds of the Etoro. They constitute a glaring statistical reality. They correspond to the ideal structure stipulated by the marriage system, and they are inherent in the complementary opposition between siblingship and exchange dictated by the system of kinship terminology. The reasons for this lack of recognition will be investigated subsequently. Our immediate concern is to explain their presence.

Each lineage regards every other as a "brother" line or as a group with which it exchanges women. Every lineage has about three major wife-supplying lines and can trace sibling relationships to all, or nearly all, the individual members of four to six other lineages with which it has major wife-suppliers in common. In addition, each lineage has partial sibling relationships with another four to six descent groups which receive some women from its major wife-suppliers. Any given lineage also exchanges women less intensively with another six to eight descent groups (and these will constitute the major wife-suppliers of its partial brother lines). In short, every lineage has sibling relationships with about half of the

---

14. For convenience in exposition I will refer to these two predominantly exogamous groups as moieties. However, it should be kept in mind that they are de facto groupings whose membership is not recruited by the principle of descent.

patrilines in the society and exchange relationships with the other half.

The society is thus divided into two sets of descent groups—sibling and exchange lines—from the standpoint of any particular lineage. This moiety division will become sociocentric to the extent that all lineages arrive at corresponding categorizations—and this is implicit in the classificatory kinship system. The four to six major "brother" lines of the reference lineage are so related by virtue of occupying the same position in the exchange system. That "brother" lineages regard the same set of descent groups as sources of women is the definition of siblingship.

The four to six partial brother lines of the reference lineage will be similarly related to the latter's four to six major "brother" lines, since these relationships are traced through women of the same three major wife-suppliers. Thus, all the lineages which are partial or complete sibling lines to any particular lineage will be related in this same way to each other. Since any degree of siblingship discourages intermarriage, these ten to eleven patrilines will seek wives externally—from the other half of the tribe—and in so doing will generate further ties of matrilateral siblingship as a consequence of parallel marriage. These additional sibling ties increase the difficulties of marriage within the moiety, requiring further parallel marriages.

Etoro moieties, then, are the product of a set of generative rules. Of primary importance are the rules governing the extension of classificatory sibling terms and the prohibition of marriage with sisters. Given these stipulations every union creates sibling ties which foreclose a large number of marriage possibilities and directs future marriages to the same location as past marriages. Any group of patrilines which receives women from the same set of descent groups cannot easily intermarry. In seeking wives externally they can hardly avoid contracting further parallel marriages, thereby increasing the density of their sibling ties and decreasing the possibilities of intermarriage. This tendency toward the development of exogamous groups of "brother" lines is further reinforced by marriage preferences. Preferred unions are those which are based on kin relationships established through previous exchange. This promotes the recurrence of parallel marriages and the consolidation of siblingship.

Marriage within the moiety—to partial brother lines—prevents the attainment of 100 percent exogamy but cannot prevent the emergence of a moiety division. The basic precept of the kinship system, and of Etoro social organization in general, is that relationships are defined and redefined in terms of the realities of exchange. Both the lineage's internal composition and its external relationships are finally delineated by the marriages it contracts. Continual exchange with a partial "brother" line redefines the relation as exchange. Sibling ties traced through "mothers" of the former brother line automatically place the wife-receiver in the opposite moiety. In the process, marriages which were previously endogamous with respect to moiety become exogamous. Errors thus have no cumulative effect on the moiety division.

Intermarriage between partial brother lines is necessary for the maintenance of a balance in the supply of women both between lineages and between moieties. A large lineage which cannot obtain sufficient wives from established exchange groups contracts a few marriages with those partial brother lines which contain available women who are not sisters. If the supply of women is sufficient in following generations, widow transfers may be employed to reestablish siblingship. If not, the continuation of such marriages will generally initiate the processes of fission as lineage segments will be at cross-purposes with respect to claims to women. The completion of fission reestablishes a balance in the supply of women in this segment of the exchange network since the offshoot line switches moieties by establishing exchange relationships with former brother lines. Endogamous marriages continually occur in response to short term fluctuations in the supply of women available to any particular lineage through its exchange networks.[15] However, these marriages are an integral part of the process of fission through which lineage size is maintained within the range at which the kinship system is effective and through which a balance in the supply of women is reestablished.

Although Etoro moieties are necessarily present as the product of a set of generative rules, they do not necessarily contain the same descent groups in each generation—since they are defined by exchange rather than descent. The rules specify only that the society will be divided into two groups of exogamous "brother" lines, but not which lineages will be found on either side of the division. This confers both a continuity of structural form and a flexibility in the relation of particular lineages to this form.

---

15. The percentage of exogamy would be substantially higher if a correction were made for those lineages currently in the process of fission. For example, 53 percent of the endogamous marriages in Moiety I (see table 39) involve members of Sarado. Sarado is and has been the largest lineage in this moiety, and the wives received by it in the past two to three generations account for 20 percent of all women married by the eleven patrilines of Moiety I.

CHAPTER 5

Exchange Relationships

Each lineage maintains enduring exchange relationships with two to four other patrilines with regard to giving and receiving wives. These major exchange relationships are designated by statements such as "we marry women of *X* patriline," and in some cases are also stipulated by a totemic myth such as the following.

A long time ago, a woman lived with her brother and his wife at Ofesebia.[1] They are living there together when her brother says, "I am going to the ceremony [*nolo*] just over there at Kaburusato's longhouse." He set out leaving the young woman to stay there, alone.

Mother! she is there when she hears a rustling in the thatch. She sees, Mother! a huge snake. A huge *somodo* [a python] is there. It came into the house and began to entwine itself around the young woman. She fled, she ran away down the path toward Kaburusato. She ran and ran and ran until she came to Wadieme bush. Mother! like this she looks over her shoulder and sees the *somodo*—coming after her. She runs on down the path. As she runs, she calls out "A *somodo* is coming, I saw it."

She came to the longhouse where the ceremony was in progress. Many people were there. Quietly, she slipped into the women's section of the house.

The *somodo*—the huge *somodo*—followed her. He followed her into the women's section and like this, like a vine, he entwined himself around her chest. The young woman threw the snake off. Again the *somodo* wrapped himself around her and again she threw him off and yet again he entwined himself around her chest.

They were returning to Ofesebia—the young woman, her brother, and the *somodo*. The woman carried the snake in her net bag. As the woman was carrying the *somodo* it said to her "shut your eyes." The woman shut her eyes and then she saw before her, Mother! a very handsome young man. The *somodo* who had become a man took the woman as his wife.

---

1. A section of the territory of Nagefi lineage.

120

The woman's name was Nuba.[2] The man's name was Hŏnteseta. Hŏnteseta's child was Tate. Tate's husband was Nage, the namesake of Nagefi. Hŏnteseta was a Katiefi man.

This myth stipulates an exchange relationship between Nagefi and Katiefi. As in the *Faitilo* myth, the theme of wife-selection by a totemic snake is the vehicle for stating the relationship between patrilines. The totemic python *Somodo* could choose any number of women as his wife but he selects Nuba of the Nagefi line. The totemic snake's choice thus establishes the inherent appropriateness of the exchange of women between Nagefi and Katiefi. The exchange relationship is embedded in the supernatural order.

The events of the myth which reveal *Somodo*'s preference for a Nagefi wife take place in an appropriate setting. The python is insistent in his choice and presses his suit in the context of a ceremony—the context in which preferences for mates are expressed and in which marriage itself is validated. Nuba's brother is present and his consent to the union is implicit in the story.

Reciprocity in the exchange of women is mythologically specified by the subsequent marriage of Hŏnteseta's daughter, Tate, to Nage. This second marriage is also part of a sister-exchange although this is not mentioned in the myth (fig. 16). The omission places an emphasis on delayed reciprocity which is balanced over a period of generations—an emphasis which is consistent with the Etoro ideology of exchange relationships.

Major exchange relationships entail a mutual obligation to provide wives as they are available and in accordance with the needs of the other lineage. Although these transactions should be equivalent over a period of generations, the obligation to supply wives takes precedence over considerations of immediate reciprocity. A major exchange group may be given as many as four women in one generation while none are received in return.

Delayed reciprocity is appropriate to the continuity of exchange relationships and is also to some extent necessitated by the Etoro preference for agnatic parallel marriage. A single sister-exchange does not provide that agnates will have "mothers" of the same natal lineage. A double sister-exchange (fig. 17) is highly desirable but requires that each patriline simultaneously contain four individuals of the appropriate age and relationship. These conditions cannot easily be met by lineages of this size and it is often necessary to forgo immediate reciprocity in order to accommodate

2. Also the generic term for "snake."

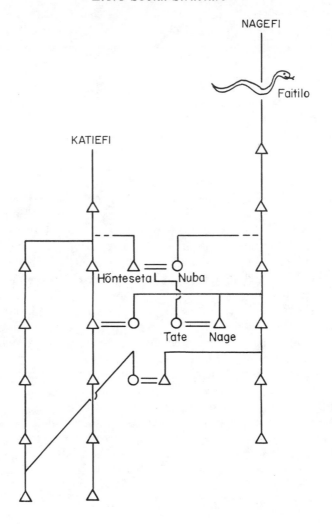

FIG. 16.   Mythic and Subsequent Unions between Nagefi and Katiefi Lineages

agnatic parallel marriage. The ideological emphasis on the mutual obligation to provide wives promotes this accommodation.

A nonequivalent exchange of women which occurs in one generation cannot be balanced in the next if the rule prohibiting classificatory FZD marriage is followed. All +1 generation women of ego's lineage are "FZ" (*nawisi*) and their daughters are "FZD" (*nesago*). All women of the same lineage and generation as these "FZDaughters" are also *nesago* and individuals in this kin cate-

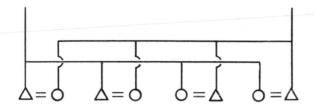

FIG. 17.   Double Sister Exchange

gory should not be married.[3] Although not always followed, this rule generally has the effect of extending delayed reciprocity an additional generation. As a result the balance of exchange between intermarrying patrilines generally favors one line or the other at any particular point in time.

Table 9 shows the balance of exchange between all intermarrying pairs of lineages with each pairing representing one case. The table presents the distribution of these cases with respect to the number of women given and received. Table 10 indicates the percentage of total cases—and the percentage of total marriages these represent—for each point on the balance-of-exchange continuum.[4]

---

3. Women who could be classified as *nesago* according to the above rules may be married if an alternative genealogical relationship can be traced. In practice, marriage with potential "FZDaughters" occurs rather frequently because it does fulfill reciprocity and is consistent with the obligation to supply wives to major exchange groups. This will be discussed further in chapter 7.

4. These tables are based on a total of 219 intratribal unions of the past two to three generations. (Widow remarriage and two incestuous unions are excluded.) It should be emphasized that the data represent the balance of exchange at a particular point in time. Unions in the middle (+1) generation may constitute reciprocity for unbalanced exchanges in the +3 generation—for which no data are available. Marriages of the current (0) generation generally cannot redress imbalances of exchange in the +1 generation due to the prohibition of "FZD" unions. Moreover, middle (+1) generation unions represent a little more than half of the total since not all men of the current (0) generation have married and some unions of the +2 generation are deleted from genealogies in the process of genealogical revision. On the other hand genealogical revision reduces the number of parallel marriages (which contribute to unbalanced reciprocity) because the son's sons of lineage sisters are given as the son's sons of one man with one wife.

TABLE 9

Balance of Exchange: Distribution of Cases with Respect to Number of Women Given and Received by Each Pair of Intermarrying Patrilines

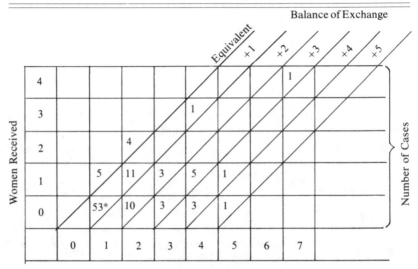

*Twenty-four of the 53 cases (45.1 percent) where the balance of exchange is one to zero are marriages to partial "brother" lines within the same moiety. These 24 unions account for 57 percent of all marriages within the moiety. In other words, most marriages within the moiety are nonrecurring, nonreciprocal unions (see chapter 4).

TABLE 10

Balance of Exchange between Intermarrying Patrilines: Percentage of Cases and Marriages at Each Point on the Balance of Exchange Continuum

Balance of Exchange	Number of Cases	Percentage of Total Cases	Number of Marriages	Percentage of Total Marriages
Equivalent	9	8.9	26	11.9
+ 1	65	64.4	93	42.5
+ 2	13	12.8	32	14.6
+ 3	9	8.9	45	20.5
+ 4	4	4.0	18	8.2
+ 5	1	1.0	5	2.3
Total	101	100.0	219	100.0

There are 101 pairs of lineages between which one or more marriages have occurred in the last two to three generations.[5] An equal number of women have been given and received in only nine of these dyadic relationships (representing 11.9 percent of the total number of intratribal unions). A state of perfectly balanced reciprocity in the exchange of women—at any particular point in time—is thus a relatively infrequent occurrence. On the other hand, the deviation from balanced reciprocity is generally small. One partner to the marriage transactions is favored by two women or less in 87 percent of the dyadic relationships (accounting for 69.0 percent of all unions).

Relationships which evidence an imbalance of three or more women tend to produce dissatisfactions concerning reciprocity which are frequently expressed in witchcraft accusations. Table 11 shows the relationship between the incidence of witchcraft accusations and the number of marriages between the patrilines of the witch and victim respectively. The distribution of cases is bimodal. Witchcraft allegations occur when the lineages of witch and victim have not intermarried or have only a single union between them. Such allegations also occur when there are five unions between the two lineages—but rarely when there are two, three, or four unions.

TABLE 11

Distribution of Witchcraft Accusations in Relation to Number of
Marriages between Patrilines of Witch and Victim

Number of marriages between lineages of witch and victim	0	1	2	3	4	5
Number of cases of witchcraft accusations	7	4	0	1	0	5

Note: Only the cases in which both witch and victim are adult males are included. In addition, four cases of witchcraft within the exogamous lineage are excluded.

The balance of exchange favors one lineage by three women (four to one) in all five cases where there are five unions between the patrilines of witch and victim. In every case the witchcraft

5. There are 181 pairs of lineages which have not intermarried in the last two to three generations. These represent 64.5 percent of the (282) total pairings.

accusation was directed at a member of the lineage which owed three women. Recorded witchcraft accusations between major exchange groups are thus always associated with substantially unbalanced reciprocity and are always directed at the delinquent wife-giver.[6]

These recorded instances of witchcraft between lineages which evidence substantially unbalanced reciprocity in the exchange of women account for a significant proportion of all such relationships. The five cases involved four pairs of lineages (one delinquent wife-giving line being named twice), and there are a total of fourteen dyadic relationships in which one lineage has received three, four, or five more wives than it has given (table 10). Witchcraft accusations are thus *known* to have occurred in 28.5 percent (4/14) of all exchange relationships in which reciprocity is significantly unbalanced. This figure is remarkably high considering that recorded witchcraft accusations represent only a sample of the total incidence of such accusations.

There is no conscious design in naming the member of a wife-owning line as a witch. The direction of these accusations is rather due to the fact that a failure to reciprocate is the sine qua non of a witch, the outward sign by which his (or her) evil inner nature may be known.[7] A failure to honor the requirements of reciprocity (and generosity) does not make an individual a witch but constitutes the behavioral correlate of that condition. The members of a lineage owing many women are thus suspected of being witches as a consequence of their observed failure to comply with these norms. Such suspicions apparently come to mind when a dying man "sees" the witch who has come to devour his heart and liver (thus causing his final demise). An act of witchcraft is a supernatural event and the Etoro themselves recognize no explicit connection between the naming of a witch and the balance of exchange between the lineages of witch and victim. They conceive of witchcraft accusations in supernatural rather than social terms.

The payment of witchcraft compensation by a delinquent wife-

---

6. The balance of exchange is one to zero (four cases) and two to one (one case) in the additional instances where witchcraft allegations involved (with the exception of the latter case) minor exchange groups or partial brother lines which have one union between them. A member of the line owing a woman was named in four of the five cases, a one to zero instance being the exception.

7. A witch possesses an evil spirit entity (*tohorora*) absent in normal individuals. For further discussion of witchcraft beliefs see Kelly, 1974.

giver does not in any way reduce the inequivalence of the exchange relationship as marriage and witchcraft compensation are transactions in entirely distinct domains. Women are still owed and the "debtors" may continue to be subject to the suspicion of being witches as long as reciprocity is unfulfilled. In spite of this, the exchange relationship continues. In one case a marriage was arranged about a year after the payment of witchcraft compensation. A girl of the wife-owing line was betrothed to a man of the patriline which had given three unreciprocated women. Witchcraft accusations rarely lead to the termination of a major exchange relationship. On the contrary they constitute a sanction which is conducive to the restoration of balanced reciprocity.

The ideology of exchange relationships emphasizes the mutual obligation to supply wives over a period of generations, generosity in wife-giving, and delayed reciprocity. But albeit delayed, reciprocity must be fulfilled when the obligation comes due; generosity in giving wives creates the expectation of an equally generous return. Witchcraft accusations enforce equivalence in the exchange of women over the long term and sustain the ideological requirement of generosity.[8]

---

8. The association of witchcraft with the absence of reciprocity also has the effect of suppressing a structural tendency toward generalized exchange. This tendency is a product of the emphasis on agnatic parallel marriage and delayed reciprocity.

CHAPTER 6

Residence and the Organization of Local Groups

The complementary opposition between the categories of sibling-ship and exchange which is inherent in Etoro kinship terminology provides a single structural master plan for the organization of social groups at every level. Longhouse communities necessarily replicate the moiety organization of the society as a whole because the kin-ship terminology which generates this dual division operates in the same manner in both contexts. Any pair of individuals who are not otherwise related through marriage in the present or past genera-tions will be able to trace a sibling relationship via a classificatory mother or father's mother. When two men who are affinally related co-reside, a third man who joins them will therefore be a "brother" to one of the two while the third man's wife will be a "sister" to the other. Every community is thus composed of two groups of "sib-lings" who have married each other's "sisters" and "brothers."[1] Any aggregation of individuals selected at random from the tribe is necessarily related in this way. The structure is therefore capable of providing an organizational framework for whatever happens "on the ground" (and is similar to an Australian section system in this respect). This is not to say that any random aggregation of individu-als constitutes a potential local group since other factors, such as access to resources and the spatial distribution of kinsmen and affines, impose some limits on an individual's choice of residence. It is important to note, however, that these constraints are not organ-izational. One longhouse community consists of nine adult male

---

1. The parties to these "sister-marriages" are not necessarily affines because the sibling pairs are not of the same lineage and affinity follows from the transfer of a woman between lineages.

members who belong to six different lineages—a composition which is the result of *a* going to live with *b* who is residing with *c*. The kinship structure brings order to such arrangements.

The Etoro do not express an ideological preference for patrilocal residence or for the maintenance of the lineage as a local group. They say that brothers and sisters should live together and that it is good to reside with affines and close kinsmen of all types. One longhouse community (Arigadabo), composed of the parties to a true sister exchange and additional true full and half-siblings of the exchange group, was consistently pointed out as an example of the ideal arrangement. (A genealogical diagram of this community is presented in figure 18.) The component relationships which are emphasized by expressed residential preferences, and by the idealization of this particular community, are those between true same- and cross-sex siblings and between affines and the parties to an exchange of women.

A residential group composed of the parties to a true sister exchange and the true siblings of the exchange group represents a conjunction of the principles of siblingship, consanguinity, affinity, and exchange. It is not only an ideal but also an ideal type and, as such, stands in direct opposition to the descent-based compromise kin group defined by Murdock (1949:66). Murdock argues that the imperatives of lineage exogamy and the co-residence of husband and wife preclude the localization of the lineage in its entirety, and that an approximation may be achieved only by excluding adult agnates of one sex and including the spouses of those of the opposite sex. This resolution of the problem compromises cross-sex siblingship and affinity at the expense of descent while the Etoro ideal envisions a reversal of these priorities. Sets of true siblings of both sexes and their spouses are included in the residential group while other agnatically related sibling sets are drawn to other longhouses. A compromise is effected but it is one which favors siblingship, close consanguinity, and affinity at the expense of descent.

The Etoro compromise comes at the expense of descent because it fails to assemble those members of the descent group through whom descent is traced and therefore fails to provide for the continuity of the lineage as a residential unit. The children of a local group composed of the parties to a true sister exchange and their true siblings reside from infancy with their MB, FZ, FB, and MZ and all first cousins. This residence pattern reinforces relationships with all close consanguineal kin and, at the same time, frequently entails the separation of FFBSSons and more distant agnates. Such dispersed lineages are deprived of the prerogative of agnatic socialization.

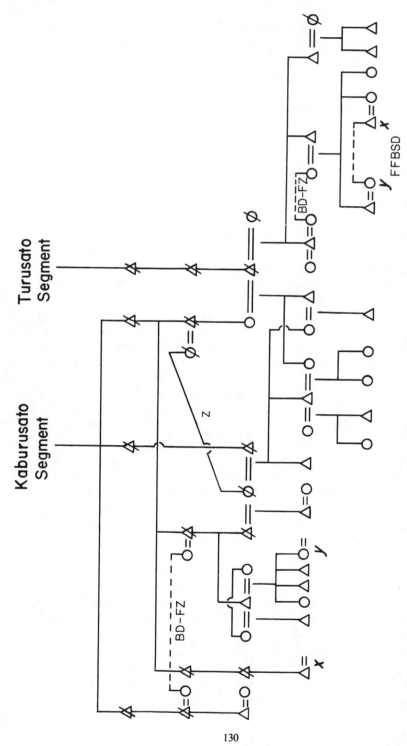

FIG. 18. Genealogical Relationships among Members of Arigadabo Longhouse Community. *Note:* x and y are lineal descendants at left and relatives by marriage at right.

It has been argued by Reo Fortune in his classic ethnography of Dobu (1963:6) that the strength of the descent group is enhanced by the lack of kinship relationships among "those-resulting-from-marriage." The Etoro residential ideal, on the other hand, provides for an equal degree of relatedness among both the agnatic hosts and their in-married spouses. "Those-resulting-from-marriage" are ideally related to each other as true siblings and necessarily related as classificatory siblings as a consequence of the kinship system. Realization of the Etoro preference for the co-residence of brothers and sisters is, in the classificatory sense, unavoidable.

The structural form of the Etoro local group is thus immutable; the residential ideal is to actuality as true relations are to their classificatory counterparts. The ideal community is composed of the parties to a true sister exchange and the true full and half-siblings of the exchange group, while every longhouse community is constituted as two sets of "siblings" who have married each other's "sisters" and "brothers." The idealized condition differs from the inevitable one only in terms of the degree of consanguinity within each of the two sibling sets and the directness of the ties of affinity and exchange between them.

True sister exchange is the enabling precondition for the aggregation of all the close kinsmen and affines encompassed by Etoro residential preferences. However, such exchanges are rarely possible due to demographic limitations and individuals must therefore choose between a number of longhouse communities which each contain a different array of relatives. The remainder of the chapter is devoted to an examination of the factors which enter into these decisions and an analysis of the resultant residential configurations. The fact that residential groups are less than 50 percent agnatic in (adult male) composition raises questions concerning the nature of the longhouse community and the relationship between the lineage and the local group which will also be considered.

The Longhouse Community

Both the location and composition of the longhouse community are subject to frequent change. The community is neither a place nor the membership of a corporate group but rather an assemblage of kinsmen who function as a social, economic, and ceremonial unit. The residents of the longhouse cooperate in gardening, sago processing, fish poisoning, hunting, and other economic endeavors. Food is freely shared among all members. Indeed it is expressly required that any available pork or game be divided among all persons present at the longhouse during the communal late afternoon meal, provided they are not in a social category to which consumption of the item is forbidden. Residents, visitors, and anthropologists are alike included in this general distribution. In the evening the people gather in the communal section of the longhouse to talk, sing, and relate myths and stories. At least once a week there is a seance which usually lasts until dawn. The most important spirits, the *Sigisatos,* will come to a medium only at the longhouse.

Etoro longhouses are traditionally located on the spur of one of the many narrow, saddle-backed ridges which fan out from the twin peaks of Mt. Sisa. The front of the house is at ground level while the back rests on piles some twenty-five feet above the slope of the ridge—a form of construction which facilitates defense against raiding parties. Several other longhouses are usually in view on an adjacent ridge, or within earshot, so that assistance can be quickly marshaled in the event of a Kaluli or Petamini raid.

Every lineage territory contains about seven or eight named longhouse sites which are generally located on prominent ridges or cliffs. Each site is marked by a stand of tall black palms rising eighty feet or more above the second growth. In the evening these palms are often frequented by a red bird of paradise, the corporeal abode of a particular *Kesame* spirit—the spirit wife of a resident medium. These exceptionally tall black palms link the community with the spirit world and thus are never cut. They are the signposts of every house site.

The seven or eight house sites within each lineage territory are utilized for three- to four-year periods. The total cycle of longhouse rotation covers approximately twenty-five years and is governed by the maturation period of the sago palm. Convenient sago resources, a visible and easily defended location, and a nearby spring are the primary factors governing the selection of house sites. Although a garden is always made on the steep slopes surrounding the longhouse, the better gardening sites are usually located some distance away on more gently sloping ground.

Longhouse communities are not restricted to the territory of a single lineage. The members of the community may utilize a house site on the lineage territory of any of the constituent sibling sets. A community such as Arigadabo (fig. 18) is likely to move between Kaburusato's and Turusato's lands and to occupy house sites along the border between the two adjacent territories. The border itself is not clearly defined. The named section of the bush (Efelebomia) which separates the two territories is said to be the joint property of both patrilines (which are major wife-suppliers to each other). Sago processing and gardening activity are similarly unrestricted by boundaries. An individual may work sago or garden on the lands of one lineage while he resides in a longhouse located on the territory of another. (In tabulations presented later in the chapter I have defined each individual's residence as the longhouse community where he or she brings food, sleeps, and participates in the social and ceremonial life.)

The abandonment of one longhouse and the construction of another often occasions a substantial change in community membership. Some sibling sets move to established longhouses which are more convenient to their sago resources or the areas where they customarily hunt and trap. New members are drawn to the freshly constructed longhouse for the same reasons. A desire to live with other relatives and a new set of faces also enters into these changes of residence. Pairs of true sibling sets linked by one or more affinal ties tend to move as a group during such residential shifts. These units of close consanguines and affines often form the organizational "core" of a longhouse community—the nexus of the complex kin and affinal network which interrelates the membership.

The residents of the longhouse maintain one large communal garden and several smaller ones at any given time. The large garden is generally not more than fifteen or twenty minutes' walk from the longhouse while the smaller gardens may be as much as an hour's walk away, sometimes within other lineage territories. Most adults have shares in two to four gardens so that there is overlapping membership between gardening groups while at the same time each group is composed of a different set of individuals. A few persons also have shares in the gardens of other longhouse communities.

Each garden contains a small bush house. The residents of the community divide their time between the longhouse and these garden dwellings according to distance, labor requirements of the gardening cycle, interest in hunting, personal preferences, and social circumstances. Widows and bachelors generally concentrate their efforts in the largest communal garden nearby and rarely spend the night at a bush house. Married men more frequently have gardens some distance afield and may live in their garden dwelling (with their families) during the peak period of gardening activity, visiting the longhouse only once or twice a week for several months.

Married men can be divided into two groups in terms of their attendance at the longhouse. The members of one of these groups spend 50 to 60 percent of their nights there and the members of the other group 85 to 90 percent. Interest in hunting and trapping is the primary factor which differentiates these two residence patterns. The avid hunters make gardens far from the longhouse, but close to the primary forest which lies above three thousand feet on Mt. Sisa. There are favorable areas for trapping marsupials and cassowaries close at hand and the maturing sweet potatoes attract wild pigs. Married men who are less interested in hunting make their gardens fifteen to thirty minutes from the longhouse and spend more time at the communal dwelling. These men outnumber the hunters by a ratio of about two to one. The time spent by both groups walking from the longhouse to gardens and sago stands provides an opportunity to gather mushrooms, frogs, tree ferns, and other collectibles. Fish traps, snares, and deadfall traps may also be set along the way and checked on the return trip in the afternoon, or the following day. These treks nearly always yield something edible.

The way in which an individual divides his time between the longhouse and his garden dwelling nearly always conforms to one of the patterns described above. The only exception involved a man whose son had been named as a witch on several recent occasions. The members of this family lived in virtual exile at their garden for almost a year, seldom visiting the longhouse. The witch never slept at the longhouse during this period although he occasionally visited his kinsmen in the daytime. During these visits he was sometimes tormented by the children of the village who threw dirt clods at him and ripped off his tanket leaf tail-feathers as they ran past. Nevertheless, he participated as a member of the community in all ceremonies. The protracted garden dwelling residence of this family is unusual and only occurs in exceptional circumstances. The case at hand involved not only several witchcraft accusations but also an unsuccessful attempt to execute the witch.

The Demographic Characteristics of Local Groups

The continued existence of any particular longhouse community is not assured by the structural foundation upon which it is constituted. The local group is not organized by lineality nor is the lineage necessarily localized or aggregated. The community is therefore subject to the possibility of complete dissolution with the membership being absorbed into other longhouses. The size and number of local groups cannot be taken as given. However, the prevailing demographic characteristics can be explained as the resolution of several centrifugal and centripetal forces. The aggregating influences of warfare and residential preferences are countered by the dispersive effects of witchcraft beliefs and accusations. These countervailing forces are at the same time the instrumentalities of social process, the proximate causes which impel ego from one longhouse and attract him to another.

The value which the Etoro place on the co-residence of true siblings, affines, and close kinsmen is integrally related to two central elements of witchcraft belief: that ego will not suffer bewitchment at the hands of close relatives and that the witch responsible for death or serious illness will very likely be a resident of the victim's longhouse. The possibility of witchcraft at a distance is formally acknowledged in ideology but discounted in practice. Suspicions invariably focus on members of the community. The reasons for this are beyond the scope of the present discussion. It is sufficient to note here that witch and victim were co-resident in 72 percent (31/43) of the recorded instances and, more importantly, that the Etoro are acutely aware of this pattern.

An individual thus has good cause to fear bewitchment at the hands of his fellow residents and this enters into a family's selection of a place of residence. The Etoro believe that a witch will not attack his close kinsmen (first cousin or closer) or his spouse or spouse's true siblings. A longhouse composed exclusively of individuals related in this way offers security and peace of mind that is not available elsewhere. There is usually no community which completely meets these specifications for any particular ego. However, the closest approximation is the most desirable place to live.

Every individual's suspicions concerning witchcraft activity thus focus on co-residents who are not close kinsmen or affines. At each death these fears are translated into a witchcraft accusation and this is usually followed by change of residence. In 51.6 percent (16/31) of the cases where witch and victim co-resided the alleged witch moved to another longhouse accompanied by his (or her spouse's) true siblings and, in some cases, by other kin and affines as well. In another 22.5 percent (7/31) of these cases (involving seven victims and four witches) the witch was executed. The witch remained at the same longhouse following accusation in only 26 percent (8/31) of the instances. Witchcraft beliefs and accusations therefore have a twofold effect on residence patterns: close relatives are assembled by the definite advantage of a reduced possibility of witchcraft while distant kin are periodically named as witches and subsequently depart from the community (or are killed). This process continually operates so as to aggregate siblings, close kinsmen, and affines. (It is also clear that localized lineages would be difficult to sustain under this ideological regime unless the lineage contained no agnates more distant than FBS.)

Witchcraft beliefs and accusations also have a pronounced centrifugal effect on Etoro residential units in that a group composed only of individuals who are so closely related as to preclude internal witchcraft is necessarily quite small. Such a group can generally contain only two sets of true siblings linked by one or more current marriages.

Several countervailing forces offset this centrifugal tendency. A large community offers definite defensive advantages of which the Etoro are well aware. In times of warfare pairs of longhouses traditionally combined into a single local group. More important, however, are the augmentative effects of the Etoro preference for residing with as many close kinsmen and affines as possible. In the absence of true sister exchange, the co-residence of a male ego and his true sister and ZH entails the separation of ego's wife and ego's ZH from *their* respective true brother and sister (fig. 19).

This dilemma can be resolved if ego is also joined by his WB and his ZHZ and her spouse. But then ego's WBW is separated from her brother and ego's ZHZH from his sister and so on. The point I wish to make is that every ego can live with *all* his close kinsmen and affines only if the entire tribe is lodged in a single longhouse. The stated preference for living with as many of these relatives as possible thus constitutes a definite centripetal tendency —and one that is clearly effective inasmuch as there are only half as many longhouses as there are lineages (a point considered more fully in a subsequent section of this chapter).

Etoro residential preferences thus have the effect of continually attracting marriage-linked sibling sets (and their close kinsmen) into the local group. Cluster *C* joins *B* which is residing with *A* and is in turn joined by *D*. However, this process of aggregation is subject to reversal by a witchcraft accusation between (for example) *A* and *D*, which may lead to the departure of one or more clusters. The communities which are produced by the interaction of these centrifugal and centripetal forces are generally small, with an average population of thirty-five members including approximately eight adult (ever-married) men (tables 12 and 13).

Change of residence occurs relatively frequently. Ten of the eighty-seven ever-married men (11.5 percent) moved from one longhouse to another during the fifteen-month period of fieldwork. Four

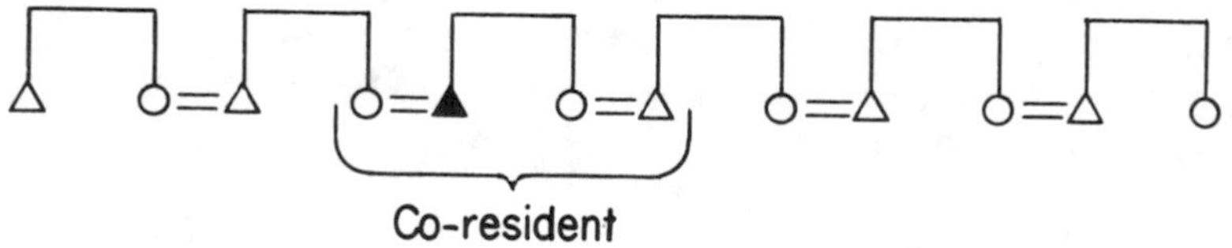

Co-resident

FIG. 19.   Co-residence and Separation in Chains of Marriage-Linked Sibling Sets

of these changes were occasioned by the dissolution of one longhouse community (Haifi) which was depleted by the deaths of five adults and fragmented by the aftermath of witchcraft accusations and lingering suspicions. However, the rate of internal migration for this particular period does not appear to be unusually high inasmuch as nearly everyone has changed his residence during the past ten years.

The Etoro invariably ascribe one of four motives to every change of residence, i.e., witchcraft accusation, desire to live with a particular kinsman, dissolution of the community, or construction of a new longhouse at an inconvenient location with respect to ego's customary hunting areas and currently mature sago. These characterizations appear to be relatively accurate. Public arguments are extremely rare outside of the context of witchcraft accusations and brawls apparently do not occur within the confines of the community. Ill feelings toward a co-resident are never brought out into the open (although they may be expressed privately to third parties) and usually are forgotten in time. An uncongenial relationship with one or two co-residents may have some bearing on changes of residence but does not appear to be sufficient in itself to precipitate relocation.

CHOICE OF RESIDENCE AND ACCESS TO RESOURCES

Consideration of Etoro residence patterns has been prefaced by the observation that the kinship structure is capable of providing an organizational framework for whatever happens "on the ground," but that any random aggregation of individuals does not constitute a potential local group because other factors—such as access to resources—impose some limits on an individual's choice of residence. The nature of these limitations may be simply specified as follows: an individual will normally own sago and may acquire access to garden land at every longhouse where he has a close consanguineal kinsman or affine. Usufructary privileges and gifts of additional sago palms are quite easily obtained through any close relative who is a member of the owning lineage, including female agnates. An individual may thus reside in any of these communities.

Suitable garden land and mature sago are currently abundant as a consequence of depopulation. This is particularly evident in the case of long-maturing crops such as sago, Tahitian chestnut, and *Marita pandanus*. Present supplies represent a resource base that was planted and maintained twenty-five years ago when the Etoro population was twice as large as it is today. It is difficult (if not impossible) to ascertain whether any of these resources were

TABLE 12

Demographic Composition of Longhouse Communities
(May, 1968)

Longhouse Community (Listed by Lineage Territory)	Adult (Ever-Married) Males	Wives	Young Men Age 16–35	Young Women Age 12–20	Children M	Children F	Widows	Total
Turusato	9	11	3	1	6	4	1	35
Gemisato	8	7	4	3	3	1	3	29
Sarado	6	6	4	1	2	3	0	22
Poboleifi	12	17	8	6	16	2	6	67
Kaburusato	6☆	7	6	3	6	3	4	35
Ingiribisato	14	15	6	1	13	5	4	58
Haifi	6☆☆	7	2	2	10	2	0	29
Katiefi	8	7	5	0	5	4	6	35
Hilisato	9	9	7	0	9	5	3	42
Kasayasato	4	4	0	0	4	2	1	15
Nemisato	5	5	5	0	3	1	0	19
Total	87	95	50	17	77	32	28	386
Average	7.9	8.6	4.5	1.5	7.0	2.9	2.5	35.1
Etoro living outside tribal territory	6	3	6	2	5	4	5	31
Grand Total	93	98	56	19	82	36	33	417

Note: Each ☆ indicates one man of the Petamini tribe.

TABLE 13

Demographic Composition of Longhouse Communities
(July, 1969)

Longhouse Community (Listed by Lineage Territory)	Adult (Ever-Married) Males	Wives	Young Men Age 16–35	Young Women Age 12–20	Children M	Children F	Widows	Total
Turusato	9	10	3	2	7	5	1	37
Gemisato	8	7	4	3	3	1	3	29
Sarado	5	5	5	1	4	3	2	25
Poboleifi	10	16	6	6	16	4	6	64
Kaburusato	6	6	4	2	8	5	6	37
Ingiribisato	14	15	5	0	13	5	4	56
Haifi			Disbanded					0
Katiefi	9☆☆	7	5	1	10	3	3	38
Hilisato	7	5	7	0	9	4	5	37
Kasayasato	4	4	1	0	4	2	1	16
Nemisato	5	5	5	0	3	1	0	19
Total	77	80	45	15	77	34	31	359
Average	7.7	8.0	4.5	1.5	7.7	3.4	3.1	35.9
Etoro living outside tribal territory	6	3	9	2	5	4	3	32
Grand Total	83	83	54	17	82	38	34	391

Note: Each ☆ indicates one man of the Petamini tribe.

once scarce relative to the size of the population, but it is clear that they were not as abundant as they are at present. One story of events thirty years ago recounts a feud which was initiated when a man shot a woman on sight for having cut down one of his sago palms (which she had mistaken for a neighboring palm given to her by her mother's brother).

Are current residence patterns then a product of depopulation and an easing of access to the resultant surfeit of resources? The available evidence suggests that the answer to this question is no; traditional residence patterns have been largely maintained. However, it will be necessary to return to this question at several points throughout the chapter where population changes come readily to mind as a plausible explanation.

Sago exploitation differs from swidden agriculture in one very important respect: sago which is not cut at maturity goes to seed and is worthless while garden land becomes more fertile the longer it lies fallow. A mature sago palm which is not currently needed by the owner is thus an ideal gift. The donor can expect that a reciprocal request will be granted in the indefinite future should he sometime lack a proximate palm suitable for processing. There are presently many more mature sago palms than there are people to give them to and I was frequently offered specimens in which I expressed an interest regarding ownership. The acceptance of such an offer on one occasion yielded the insight that he who gives away a sago palm to a co-resident invariably partakes of the product while avoiding many days of arduous labor.[2] Sago palms, then, are not hard to come by and an individual's choice of residence is unlikely to be restricted for the want of such resources.

Residence choices, however, are not dependent upon acquiring gifts of sago palms. Patterns of inheritance ensure that every individual will own sago palms in a number of different lineage territories. An elderly man divides his sago holdings among both his sons and daughters, although favoring the former. A woman who inherits sago may transmit it to her sons and, to a lesser extent, her daughters (or may give it to her brother). Although the majority of a man's sago holdings are within his own lineage territory, he will also own substantial quantities of sago in the territory of his mother's and father's mother's lineage respectively. His wife also has sizable holdings on the lands of her natal lineage (which may well be his FZHusband's or FFZHusband's line). In general, members of lin-

---

2. Only the particular palm is given. The regrowth is retained by the owner.

eages which are major wife-suppliers to each other own substantial amounts of sago in each other's territories. It follows that an individual will usually have significant sago holdings on the territories of all his close kinsmen (except MZS). The Etoro preference for residing with affines and close kinsmen of every type is not in the least constrained by access to sago resources inasmuch as the distribution of sago and relatives is nearly isomorphic (the exception being MZSons). Indeed patterns of sago inheritance definitely encourage residence outside the lineage territory even though the bulk of an individual's sago stands are located therein. The reasons for this are elaborated in subsequent discussion.

In the foregoing discussion I have been concerned only with substantial sago holdings that would sustain a family through several gardening cycles. Individuals own lesser quantities of sago in many different lineage territories. One of the more important factors in this pattern of widely dispersed holdings is the custom that a nonagnatic resident of the longhouse can plant sago on his host's territory and subsequently transmit these palms to his children. The distribution of sago palms which men have acquired from their fathers' plantings bears witness to the fact that residence patterns have not been significantly altered by depopulation.

It should be noted that nonagnatic residents are the owners of some of the resources on which the local group subsists and thus do not suffer the disability of being continually indebted to their hosts for their daily bread. The reciprocity inherent in the Etoro situation promotes an equality of status among co-residents irrespective of agnation.

Patterns of sago ownership are of primary importance because effective access to garden land is governed by access to sago. When a garden is made on a particular site the sago adjacent to the garden is cut and processed to supply food while the garden is being prepared. Selection of a garden site thus depends on the availability of proximate sago which is ready to cut. It follows that garden fallows are largely regulated by the twenty-five-year maturation period of sago. The palms cannot be cut too long before maturity without a significant sacrifice in yield. On the other hand a large sago stand that was cut twenty-five years ago must be cut again or it will go to seed. The effective utilization of garden land thus requires proximate sago resources. Conversely, sizable sago stands can be most conveniently utilized only when they are near current gardens (or the longhouse). The problem here is primarily one of timing. Distant sago would have to be worked when gardening labor was not required elsewhere. But this is primarily when the garden is producing and then substantial quantities of sago are not really needed (see chapter 2).

This interrelationship between the exploitation of sago and garden resources creates a dialectical relationship between the patrilineal corporate group's ownership of land and the cognatic, individual ownership of sago palms. The contradiction could conceivably be resolved in two quite different ways. On one hand, the lineage might deny usufructary privileges to nonagnates and thereby curtail convenient access to the sago stands they own. These would then ultimately revert to the lineage as a consequence of the failure to manifest ownership through use. On the other hand, men who own sago on the territories of other lineages must utilize these palms or allow them to go to seed and thereby forfeit claims to ownership. Effective utilization requires residence on the lineage territory where the palms are located. In other words, individuals are disposed to take up residence where they (or their spouses) own mature sago. When faced with a surfeit of mature sago both at home and abroad, it is advantageous to process the palms on another lineage's lands in order to maintain ownership. The sago palms in one's own territory may be given away or even allowed to go to seed since ownership of the regrowth is not at stake.

At present the second of these two possibilities clearly prevails and available evidence suggests that this has always been the case. The structural balance weighs heavily in favor of welcoming nonagnates who own sago within the lineage's territory rather than denying them usufructary privileges. All of these individuals are the descendants of female agnates (through whom they inherited the sago) and are therefore potential or actual wife-givers to the lineage which owns the land. Moreover, exclusion would require an abrogation of the obligation to assist close kin, or specifically, that a MB (or MBS) refuse the request of his sister's child (or FZ child). This is extremely unlikely irrespective of the relative scarcity or abundance of resources. Indeed, the story of the shooting incident cited earlier in this chapter as an indication of the possibility of past scarcity also relates a MBrother's gift of a sago palm to his ZD.[3]

---

3. This suggests that any demographic pressure on resources which may have existed in the past was alleviated by the lineage membership's exercise of external residential choices rather than by foreclosing the options of nonagnates. I have argued elsewhere (Kelly, 1968*b*) that demographic pressure is mediated by the existing structure and that the social structure itself is not a dependent variable with respect to the scarcity or abundance of land. The point is equally applicable to the demographic decompression of the present context.

The denial of gardening rights to the descendants of female agnates who own sago within the lineage territory would not in any event be sufficient to reserve land resources exclusively to lineage members. Access to these resources by nonagnates is ensured by female agnates' equivalent rights in the lands of the corporate descent group. A woman may garden anywhere within her natal territory at her own discretion, being joined by her husband and also by his true siblings and their spouses. Any agnate, male or female, can grant usufructary privileges. The decision is not subject to lineage approval (although an individual would not disregard the wishes of his or her close agnatic kinsmen). In short, the descent group's corporate ownership of land is not accompanied by group control over access to it.

The contradiction between corporate lineage ownership of land and cognatic, individual ownership of sago (which is posed by the integration of these two aspects of the Etoro economy) has thus been partially resolved—but at the expense of the descent group's corporate control over access to land. This raises more general questions concerning the relation of the lineage to its corporate possessions to which we shall momentarily return.

Of all resources to which the lineage lays claim, rights over game animals are the most jealously guarded. The corporate descent group maintains hunting and trapping rights over all the animal products of its territory. Wild pigs, cassowaries, marsupials, rodents, lizards, snakes, frogs, fish, eels, birds, bird eggs, and woodgrubs may not be taken on lineage lands without first obtaining the permission of a lineage member. As game is the property of men, the husband of a female agnate must also request permission.

These restrictions apply most stringently to neighbors and passersby. Nonagnatic residents of the community are granted customary rights to take rodents, snakes, lizards, frogs, birds, and bird eggs during the period of time they reside at the longhouse. However, specific permission is still required in every instance for the hunting or trapping of wild pigs, cassowaries, marsupials, fish and eels, and the collection of woodgrubs.

The Etoro concept of ownership does not entail a principle of exclusive utilization. Property cannot be withheld from others simply by virtue of ownership. This attitude is particularly apparent with respect to mother-of-pearl shells, the most valuable wealth item. The owner of a shell crescent is usually not in possession of it; such ornaments are given to other kinsmen to wear. Everyone is adorned with a shell ornament, but it is generally someone else's. This concept of the relationship between ownership and use is also applicable to the corporate property of the descent group. Corporate ownership does not convey exclusive access. Lineage membership confers rights in lineage property and these include the right to grant usufructary privileges. These privileges are not denied to kinsmen and affines. An individual would not cede the use of garden land that he required for his own subsistence, but otherwise a request will be granted. It does not matter whether the petitioner himself needs the land; that he desires the use of it is sufficient.

KINSHIP AND CO-RESIDENCE

Every Etoro has a wide range of residential options; he may choose among a number of different longhouse communities which each contain a different array of kinsmen and affines. Other things being equal, the process of selection will be governed by the social significance of the kin relationships themselves. In other words, the frequency with which men reside with their true sisters and sister's husbands may be taken as an indication of the social importance of those relationships (B/Z and ZH/WB). In more general terms, frequencies of co-residence reveal the relative drawing power of siblingship, affinity, and agnation.

Other things, of course, are never equal in any social equation; that they are not primary determinants of the outcome is sufficient for our purposes and this condition is satisfied. Residence is not narrowly determined by access to resources inasmuch as a man generally owns sago and can obtain usufructary privileges in those communities where he has kin. However, a man and his wife are inclined to reside where one or the other owns currently mature sago palms and more than half of an individual's holdings are within his or her lineage territory. Although ego may reside with his MB for a gardening cycle or two he spends many more years on his or his wife's lineage territory and the frequencies of agnatic and affinal co-residence reflect this. The choices between these two types of kinsmen are of particular interest.

The following discussion is concerned with the co-residence of true kinsmen and affines irrespective of the lineage territory where this takes place. A pair of men related as WB and ZH may live together on either's lineage territory or at some third location where another kinsman of one of the two resides. The important fact, for present purposes, is that the two men have chosen to live together in the same longhouse community. This focus is commensurate with the Etoro's expression of residential preferences in terms of living with close kinsmen and affines rather than with the agnatic group of these relatives or within their respective lineage territories. (The distribution of lineage members among local groups will be con-

sidered in another context.) More importantly, however, the observed statistical frequencies of co-residence across all the various
dyads individually considered are predictable in terms of two related
models of cross-sex sibling co-residence which will be presented in
due course. The attraction of living with each of a number of close
kin and affines simultaneously is resolved by residential arrangements which are conducive to this larger pattern.

The figures presented in the following tables are drawn from a
total sample which consists of the entire tribe with the exception of
three men currently serving jail terms for homicide. Etoro residing
outside the tribal territory of their own volition are not excluded.
The figures refer to residential arrangements at the inception of my
fieldwork in May, 1968. Each particular computation includes only
those adults who have a true, living, adult (i.e., ever-married) kinsman or affine of the type under consideration. The co-residence of
unmarried young men and their married kin is figured separately
when of special interest as they have a different range of residence
choices. Every person is included in all applicable categories so
that a given ego will figure in as many pairings as he has true, living
relatives. The frequencies for different types of relationships thus
indicate kinship priorities in Etoro choice of residence.

The Co-residence of Siblings

True full and half-brothers[4] reside together more frequently than
any other category of kinsman, 92.6 percent being co-resident
(table 14). Brothers may live at different longhouses for one or two

TABLE 14

Co-residence of Brothers
(True, Living, Ever-Married Full or Half-Siblings)

	Size of Brother Group			
	4	3	2	*Total*
Number of cases	1	1	10	12
Number of individuals	4	3	20	27
Number co-resident	4	3	18	25
Percentage co-resident	100	100	90	92.6

Note: Sixty of the 87 (69 percent) ever-married, living men have no brothers (ever-
married and living).

---

4. The sample includes all patrilateral half-brothers and those matrilateral half-brothers who are also agnates—i.e., the sons of women involved in
the levirate. Matrilateral half-brothers of different lineages (as a result of
widow transfers) are excluded. This applies to the samples included in
subsequent tables as well.

gardening seasons but are never permanently separated. The two
married brothers who initially resided in different communities
(each with WF) were planning a joint garden when I left the field.
Although the co-residence of brothers is compatible with the localization of the lineage, the former does not necessarily imply the
latter. Only 55.6 percent (15/27) of the brother groups lived on their
lineage territory. The high frequency of co-residence reflects the
strong tendency for brothers to move as a unit and this is related to
the fact that they share the same kin and affines—with the exception of WB and WF.

The Etoro preference for living with true siblings includes sisters (Z/Z) as well as brothers. Although the 43.2 percent frequency
of co-residence among ever-married sisters (table 15) is much less
than that for brothers, it is nevertheless quite high for a society
containing exogamous, patrilineal descent groups. The co-residence
of sisters necessarily entails the separation of at least some husbands from their agnates—except in the event of agnatic parallel
marriage. Thirty-six percent (16/44) of the sisters in the sample are
married to men of the same lineage and 62.5 percent (10/16) of these
live together (or 57.1 percent [8/14] excluding one pair of sisters
married to the same man). Comparatively, 32.1 percent (9/28) of the
siblings married to men of different lineages co-reside (table 16).

TABLE 15

Co-residence of Sisters
(True, Living, Ever-Married Full or Half-Siblings)

| | Size of Sister Group | | | |
	4	3	2	Total
Number of cases	2	4	12	18
Number of individuals	8	12	24	44
Number co-resident	4	5	10	19
Percentage co-resident	50	41.7	41.7	43.2

Note: Sixty-eight of the 112 (60.7 percent) ever-married, living women have no true,
ever-married sisters.

TABLE 16

Co-residence of True Sisters in Relation to Agnatic Parallel Marriage

	Sisters Co-resident	Sisters Not Co-resident
True sisters married to men of the same lineage	10*	6
True sisters married to men of different lineages	9	19

*Includes one pair of sisters married to the same man.

Agnatic parallel marriage thus contributes to the observed frequency of sister co-residence—and also to the co-residence of agnates. Sisters do not live together only when they are married to agnates; nearly one-third (32.1 percent) of those married to men of different lineages also co-reside.[5] It follows that fewer male agnates would live together in the absence of agnatic parallel marriage.

The preceding discussion illustrates a more general principle, namely, that agnatic parallel marriage mediates the relationship between siblingship and descent. The principle of siblingship, when applied to brothers, introduces invidious distinctions of consanguinity into the lineage which leave the basic structure weakened but intact. Similarly, the co-residence of brothers is clearly compatible with localization of the lineage. However, application of the principle of siblingship to sisters introduces distinctions which are not confined within a framework of patrilineality. The solidarity of male agnates is diluted by the competing solidarity of MZSons. Moreover, the extensive co-residence of sisters would entail the dispersion of male lineage members. In more general terms, siblingship engenders a consanguineal solidarity which is not constrained by lineality and this is the nexus of a fundamental contradiction between siblingship and descent. In Etoro society, this contradiction is resolved by agnatic parallel marriage (and the levirate). The invidious distinctions of patrilateral consanguinity which follow from the siblingship of brothers are overlaid with matrilateral consanguinity when FFBSSons marry true sisters (or when a woman passes between them in the levirate). Agnatic parallel marriage thus aligns consanguinity with lineality. This is readily illustrated by consideration of generalized exchange which is the limiting case of agnatic parallel marriage and the logical culmination of this mode of resolution of the siblingship-descent contradiction. Under a regime of generalized exchange all agnates have mothers of the same lineage and are both matrilateral and patrilateral consanguines. Sisters always co-reside without this necessitating the dispersion of male agnates. Finally, the external relationships of lineage members are perfectly congruent.

---

5. There is a general tendency toward the co-residence of female agnates; 26.5 percent (9/34) of the women related as true FZ/BD co-reside, as do 21.6 percent (11/51) of the women related as true FBD. In all, 45.7 percent (43/94) of the ever-married women live with one or more female agnates (including those listed above). The significance of close consanguinity is evident from the fact that these frequencies are inversely related to genealogical distance. This is equally true for male agnates and the point will be raised again in that context.

Cross-Sex Siblings

True sister exchange facilitates the co-residence of cross-sex siblings (and affines) in the same way that agnatic parallel marriage
facilitates the co-residence of same-sex siblings (true sisters and
lineage "brothers"). In both cases the spouses of siblings will themselves be siblings (or lineage brothers) so that co-residence of two
sibling sets is consistent with the co-habitation of husband and wife.

This interrelationship is also significant for the statistical questions at hand: the potential frequency of brother-sister co-residence
is limited by the frequency of the enabling condition—true sister
exchange. In the absence of true sister exchange (and it is usually
absent) the co-residence of true brothers and sisters entails the
separation of ego's wife and his ZH from their respective brother
and sister. Under these circumstances, the co-residence of true,
married, cross-sex siblings could not exceed a frequency of 50
percent. This is illustrated in figures 20 and 21.

These diagrams reveal another dimension of the dialectical relation between siblingship and descent which is played out at the
residential level in terms of sibling co-residence vs. localization of
the lineage. Maximum co-residence of brothers and sisters provides that each local group will be only 50 percent agnatic in (adult
male) composition. However, this result can be realized in two
quite different ways, that is, there are two possible models of
cross-sex sibling co-residence (without true sister exchange) and
each has different effects on localization of the lineage. In the first
model (fig. 20) there are only half as many longhouse communities
as there are exogamous lineages. Half of the patrilines are localized
on their respective territories while the other half are dispersed
among affinally related descent groups. This model squares rather
nicely with the Etoro statistics. There are twenty-two lineages but
only eleven local groups; the average agnatic composition of these
communities is 48.3 percent.[6]

In the second model (fig. 21) there are an equal number of
lineages and local groups. Half the sibling sets of each patriline
remain on their agnatic territory and half reside with affinally related lines. In this case each lineage is 50 percent localized (rather
than half the lineages being 100 percent localized and half dispersed). This model is also applicable to Etoro residential arrangements and we shall return to it later in the chapter.

----

6. The figure for lineages includes only those which contain males.
The nearly extinct Tifanafi line, represented by only two women, is thus
omitted. The figures for local groups and agnatic composition refer to the
initial census.

Lineages

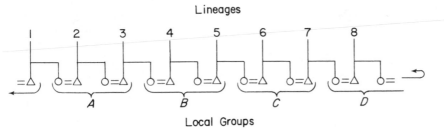

Local Groups

FIG. 20. Model of Cross-Sex Sibling Co-residence for Eight Lineages and Four Local Groups

Under the prevailing conditions of Etoro society, cross-sex sibling co-residence can be achieved only at the expense of localization of the lineage (or at least half of the lineages). If brothers and sisters are to live together then some male agnates will necessarily be separated. This dimension of the siblingship-descent contradiction hinges on the co-habitation of husband and wife and therefore cannot be resolved by any ingenious form of marriage save one—endogamy.[7] This solution is entertained by certain desert tribesmen,[8] but not by the Etoro. The contradiction is thus

Lineages

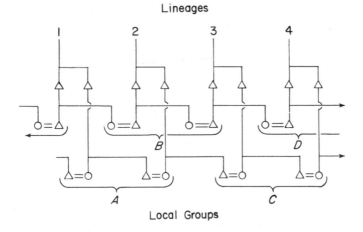

Local Groups

FIG. 21. Model of Cross-Sex Sibling Co-residence for Four Lineages and Four Local Groups

---

7. True sister exchange increases the frequency of brother-sister co-residence but not the degree of localization or agnation. It accommodates cross-sex siblingship with no benefit to descent.

8. Interestingly, endogamy and generalized exchange are equally effective in resolving the contradiction between siblingship and descent.

given full effect in residential arrangements: either the lineage will be localized and cross-sex siblings separated or else 50 percent of the latter will be united and the lineage must settle for half a loaf in terms of localization. The third and more likely possibility is that the result will be the vectorial product of these opposed tendencies, viz., less than the maximum 50 percent co-residence of true brothers and sisters will be achieved and the lineage may then attain more than 50 percent agnatic composition (or will arrive at this figure for different reasons).

Several factors besides sister exchange enter into a determination of the maximum attainable frequency of co-residence among cross-sex siblings. One of these, anticipated in the preceding discussion, is that the incidence of co-residence can be increased by decreasing the ratio of local groups to lineages. For example, the residential units *A* and *B* and *C* and *D*(fig. 20) could be combined and only two of the eight sibling bonds would then be broken by the co-habitation of husband and wife.[9] The effect of such a reduction in the number of local groups (with the number of lineages remaining constant) does not enter into present computations but will be pertinent to a later discussion of a decrease in the number of Etoro longhouses from eleven to ten which occurred during the course of fieldwork.

The final factor is demographic: many individuals do not have a living, married, cross-sex sibling. This increases the potential frequency of co-residence among those who do since the residential union of one sibling pair does not necessarily entail the separation of one or two others. If a male ego's wife has no brother and ego's ZH also has no sister, then ego and his sister can live together without precipitating the residential separation of other sibling sets. Reality also deviates from the model presented above in that some sibling sets include three, four, or five brothers and sisters. In view of these demographic complications, the maximum attainable frequency of cross-sex sibling co-residence can be com-

---

In both cases all agnates have mothers of the same lineage and matrilateral consanguinity is introduced into the descent group; in both cases siblings co-reside. However, with generalized exchange only same-sex siblings live together (B/B, Z/Z) while endogamy accommodates cross-sex siblings as well. These consanguineal benefits of endogamy are recognized by the Iatmul (Bateson, 1958:91).

9. The limiting case—the single-village tribe—is an ethnograhic reality among some Purari tribes. This is still another possible accommodation of siblingship within a framework of descent.

puted only by an examination of all extant chains of marriage-linked sibling sets in order to determine where residential unions at some points have necessarily induced disjunctions elsewhere.

TABLE 17

Co-residence of Brothers and Sisters
(True, Living, Ever-Married Full or Half-Siblings)

	Type and Size of Sibling Group						Totals
	4B / 1Z	2B / 2Z	1B / 3Z	2B / 1Z	1B / 2Z	1B / 1Z	
Number of cases	1	1	1	5	4	18	30
Number of individuals	5	4	4	15	12	36	76
Number of co-resident brothers and sisters	5	0	0	6	3	12	26
Percentage co-resident	100	0	0	40	25	33.3	34.2

Note: Forty-nine of the 87 (56.3 percent) living, ever-married men have no true sisters, and 74 of the 112 (66.1 percent) living, ever-married women have no true living, ever-married brothers.

As shown in table 17, the observed frequency of brother-sister co-residence is 34.2 percent (26/76). The maximum attainable frequency is 72.4 percent (55/76). The actual extent of cross-sex sibling co-residence thus represents 47.3 percent (26/55) of what is attainable.[10] (The latter figure is comparable to those for B/B and Z/Z co-residence.)

Many of the cases in which ever-married brothers and sisters do not live together are distinguished by the absence of ZH due to the fact that the sister is an unremarried widow. Only two of eleven men live with a widowed sister. These nine negative cases account for thirteen of the twenty-nine non-co-resident cross-sex siblings. In three other cases (involving six siblings) the sister is married to a man of another tribe so that co-residence would entail the separation of the brother (or ZH) from all other kinsmen. In sum, 65.5 percent (19/29) of the negative cases involve deceased or non-Etoro affines. If all cases of these two types are excluded, the frequency of brother-sister co-residence is 68.8 percent (22/32) of the maxi-

---

10. The co-residence of unmarried young men (fifteen or older) and their married sisters is not limited by the factors previously discussed and a frequency of 100 percent is possible. Fifty-six percent (43/77) of these unmarried brothers and married sisters live together.

mum attainable.[11] The point here is simply that brothers and sisters usually live together (insofar as this is possible) when ZH is alive and also a fellow tribesman.

The interrelationship between cross-sex siblingship and affinity is particularly apparent in a consideration of residential arrangements. A man who resides with his married sister necessarily lives with ZH as well. This raises the question of which relationship draws a man to the local group where both his Z and ZH reside. Is the co-residence of ZH and WB merely an artifact of the co-residence of cross-sex siblings or, conversely, is the co-residence of brothers and sisters simply the by-product of a preference for living with affines? In point of fact neither relationship takes precedence. If either the sibling or affinal relationship is absent, co-residence is unlikely. This is evident from the cases where either Z or ZH is deceased (tables 18 and 19). Although thirteen of thirty men (43.3 percent) live with currently married sisters, only two of eleven (18.2 percent) reside with a widowed sister. While the same thirteen of thirty men live with the husband of a living, currently married sister, only one of twelve (8.3 percent) resides with the husband of a deceased sister.[12]

The question posed above concerning the precedence of sibling or affinal relations is thus an either-or fallacy; it is the intersection of the two relations that is important. The Etoro aspire to live with as many close kinsmen and affines as possible. When death depletes the cluster of relatives at one location, other possibilities become more attractive. If ZH dies, ego is likely to go elsewhere. Ego's widowed sister generally remains with her deceased husband's brothers throughout the mourning period and until the question of her remarriage is decided (as discussed in chapter 8). Simi-

---

11. The two cases in which men live with their widowed sister are, of course, also excluded. The number co-resident is thus reduced from twenty-six to twenty-two. The number who could live together is decreased by twenty-three (nineteen who don't and four who do), from fifty-five to thirty-two. The co-residence of a man and his widowed sister does not induce any separations elsewhere since the deceased ZH represents a break in the marriage-linked sibling chains. The attainable frequency of co-residence is therefore not increased by the exclusion of these cases. The same applies to cases of non-Etoro sister's husbands since their sibling sets fall outside the sample and therefore were not considered in the initial computation.

12. These figures also indicate that change of residence follows dissolution of a union by death.

TABLE 18

Cross-Sex Sibling Co-residence in Relation to
Presence or Absence of a Living ZH

	B/Z *Co-resident*	B/Z *Not Co-resident*	*Total*
ZH living	15	12	27
ZH deceased	2	8*	10
Total	17	20	37

Note: Men whose only ZH is non-Etoro are excluded.

*One man in this category is also in the category ZH living, B/Z not co-resident due to the fact that he has two sisters, one of whom is widowed and one of whom is not.

TABLE 19

Wife's Brother–Sister's Husband Co-residence in Relation to
Linking Sister (Wife) Living or Deceased

	WB/ZH *Co-resident*	WB/ZH *Not Co-resident*	*Total*
Z (wife) living	15	12	27
Z (wife) deceased	1	7*	8
Total	16	19	35

Note: Men whose only ZH is non-Etoro are excluded.

*Two men in this category also appear in the category WB/ZH not co-resident, Z living due to the fact that these men have two sisters, one living and one deceased.

larly, when a man's sister dies, he or his ZH is likely to be drawn to a different longhouse community.

The Co-residence of Affines and Parties to an Exchange of Women

The ideal residential group composed of the parties to a true sister exchange and their true brothers is infrequently realized as there are very few true sister exchanges. Arigadabo (fig. 18) is the only longhouse (of eleven) which presently conforms to this ideal. The exchange group which forms the organizational core of this community also represents the only extant true sister exchange in which all four participants are living. The reasons for this paucity are primarily demographic. There are only thirty sibling sets containing married cross-sex siblings (see table 17). Any given lineage will thus find only three to six true brother-sister pairs among its major exchange groups. This field is further narrowed by the fact that men age twenty-five to thirty-five marry women fifteen to twenty. A true sister exchange thus requires two sibling sets in which the brother is ten to fifteen years older than his sister. However, in half of the thirty sibling groups the sister is elder, and in most of the remaining fifteen the age differential is more than fifteen years or less than ten. Finally, both brother-sister pairs would have to come of age at the same time. True sister exchange, then, is rarely possible.

The Etoro consider a longhouse community composed of the parties to a true sister exchange and their true siblings to be ideal because it provides for maximum co-residence among true siblings and affines while the children of the community grow up with nearly all of their close consanguineal kin. In other words, such a community achieves the localization of the valued relationships of siblingship, close consanguinity, affinity, and exchange. This is not only an ideal, but also an Etoro ideal type representing the conjunction of these four important relationships. The ideal is encompassing rather than limiting; the closest approximation for any particular ego is simply the longhouse community which contains the greatest number of true siblings, affines, and close consanguineal kinsmen. The structure of the kinship system then imposes classificatory relationships wherever true relationships are lacking and thus molds reality to ideology. The organizational ideal does not yield to demographic defects.

Etoro residential preferences extend to all affines and to the participants in classificatory exchanges, including those involving cross-generational marriage (i.e., "B"/"Z," "F"/"D"). There are eight cases in which all four of the parties to an exchange of women are living[13] and six of these are co-resident (table 20). These co-residential clusters also include the true brothers of the exchange group (and their wives) so that, in all, the six groups encompass forty-four individuals or 22 percent of the adult (ever-married) population. These exchange groups often form the organizational cores of longhouse communities to which still other individuals attach themselves (e.g., the WB of the true B of the parties to the exchange).

Affinal Co-residence

The models of maximum cross-sex sibling co-residence presented in figures 20 and 21 provide that every man will live with either his

---

13. The sixteen marriages represent 23.2 percent of current intratribal unions (excluding women's second marriages). An additional 11.6 percent of these extant unions are parts of exchanges dissolved by death. Another 5.8 percent represent incomplete exchanges which will be completed in the next few years.

TABLE 20

Co-residence of Parties to an Exchange of Women

Type of Exchange	Number of Cases	Number Co-resident
B/Z = B/Z	1	1
B/Z = "B"/"Z"	3	3
B/Z = "F"/"D"	1	*
"B"/"Z" = "F"/"D"	2	1
"F"/"D" = "F"/"D"	1	1
Total	8	6

*The "F" in this exchange group is the true father of the "Z" in one of the B/Z="B"/"Z" exchange groups and resides with them, i.e., with DH rather than with his WB (and "D"H).

WB or ZH but not both. In the absence of true sister exchange ego must choose between the two. Similarly, a man must choose between residing with his WF or his own F and, reciprocally, between living with D and DH or with S and SW. The desired co-residence of B and Z dictates a fifty-fifty compromise here as all men can live with WF (or own F) only if brothers and sisters always live apart. In terms of the models, then, the maximum frequency of co-residence with each of the four types of affines, respectively, is 50 percent. However, everyone (100 percent) can live with at least one of the four. In practice, 70.7 percent (41/58) of the adult men who have a DH, WF, ZH, or (ever-married) WB reside with one or more of these affines.[14]

The choices required by the models of cross-sex sibling co-residence are considerably eased by the demographic disparities between model and reality. Thirty-five of the fifty-eight men have only one type of affine, twenty-two have two, one has three, and none of them have four. In six cases pairs of affines are themselves co-resident so that only seventeen men must choose between several affines at different longhouses. Similarly, a choice between F and WF is rarely required. Few married men have a living father due to the late age of marriage for males (twenty-five to thirty-five).

---

14. This figure includes only those affines who are related to ego or ego's spouse through a true sibling or parent, i.e., the husband of a true sister, wife's true father, etc. Cases in which the linking female is deceased, or the only affine is of another tribe, are also excluded. Only two of ten men live with a non-Etoro affine; only one of twelve men resides with the brother of a deceased wife. Two-thirds (58/87) of the ever-married men have one or more Etoro affines related through living women. The figure of 70.7 percent (and subsequent figures) refers to this sample.

The eighty-seven currently married men include only five fathers and six sons. In four of the five cases father and son(s) are co-resident while in the remaining case the son lives with his WF (and the father with WB). Only one of the five men who lives with his father also has a living WF and in this instance they also live together. In other words the son lives with both F and WF (and also with Z and ZH). This cluster illustrates the manner in which theoretically incompatible residential preferences can be resolved in practice.[15]

The Etoro preference for living with a true brother poses still another potential choice since each brother will have a different WB and WF. Under these circumstances, brother co-residence would deplete the frequency of co-residence with WF and WB. If a man resided with his WF and was joined by his true brother, the latter would not live with any of his own affines.

There is a marital solution to this problem—the union of two true brothers and two true sisters. There is one agnatic parallel union of this type (among current marriages). Gaps in individual affinal networks resolve the difficulty for all but two of the remaining brother groups.[16] In most cases, only one of the brothers has a WF and/or WB while the second brother's wife has no living father or ever-married brother. Affinal and true brother co-residence are thus compatible and no choice between B and WF is necessary.[17]

Etoro residential preferences theoretically pose a wide range of choices between various true kinsmen and affines such as the WF vs. F and B vs. WF (WB) choices considered above. It is important to note that these decisions are very rarely required in practice due to gaps in individual kin and affinal networks, i.e., no one has a full complement of relatives. These demographic disparities do not militate against the fulfillment of the many Etoro residential preferences but instead make their concurrent attainment possible. Everyone lives with whatever relatives he has. The seemingly awkward models based on the rule of cross-sex sibling co-

---

15. The number of fathers whose daughters have married exceeds the number who have married sons because women marry at an earlier age than men. Nine fathers live with their (ten) daughters (and DH) while five father-daughter pairs reside at different longhouses. Three of the nine fathers have moved to their daughter's husband's place of residence with their daughter. These three include the WF mentioned above.

16. In the single case in which both brothers have a WF the brothers themselves live apart, each with his respective WF. In the second case a man resides with his B and BDH and is consequently separated from his ZH (so that he does not reside with any of his own affines).

17. There may still be a choice between WB and ZH if the sibling set also includes a Z. In the event, all siblings usually co-reside.

residence are thus quite simple in practice since they merely capitalize on inevitable, expectable, demographic circumstances.

Affinal co-residence is described and measured in the series of tables which follow. The fifty-eight men who have Etoro affines are divided among tables 21, 22, and 23 according to (1) the number of different types of affinal relatives, and (2) whether the two types of affines are themselves co-resident or live at different longhouses. This format separates those instances where the only choice is between co-residence or non-co-residence from cases where there is a choice of residing with either one of two affines or with neither. (Each ego appears on only one of these tables and pairs of reciprocally related individuals may be separated if, for example, the DH of a WF/DH pair has a ZH as well.) Table 24 gives the observed frequency of co-residence for each type of affinal relationship and also the percent of maximum attainable co-residence, giving effect to instances where living with one affine entails separation from another.

TABLE 21

Frequency of Co-residence for Men with Only One Type of Affine

| | Type of Affine | | | | |
	ZH	WB	DH	WF	Total
Number of egos with affine of each type	10	10	8	7	35
Number of egos co-resident	5	5	5	4	19
Percentage co-resident	50	50	62.5	57.1	54.3

TABLE 22

Choices Made by Men with Two Types of Affines
Who Reside at Different Longhouses

Choice between (Types of Affines)	Ego Co-resident with	Number of Cases	Total Cases
ZH vs. WF	ZH	2	
	WF	3	
	Neither	0	
			5
DH vs. WB	DH	2	
	WB	2	
	Neither	0	
			4
ZH vs. WB	ZH	4	
	WB	2	
	Neither	1	
			7

Note: The only man with three types of affines—WB, ZH, and DH—lives with his DH.

TABLE 23

Residence of Men with Two Types of Affines Who Are Themselves Co-resident

Ego Co-resident with	Number of Cases
WF and WB	2
WB and ZH	2
ZH and DH	1
WF and ZH	1
None	0
Total	6

TABLE 24

Frequency of Co-residence for All Affinal Relationships

	Type of Affine			
	ZH	WB	DH	WF
Number of cases (men who have an affine of type)	27	26	14	15
Number of co-resident cases (men who live with the affine)	15	13	9	10
Percentage co-resident	55.6	50.0	63.4	66.7
Number of separations entailed by co-residence with another affine	6	7	2	2
Maximum possible number co-resident	21	19	12	13
Percentage co-resident out of maximum possible number co-resident	71.4	68.4	75.0	77.0

Note: Men with two types of affines are counted in two columns, while men with two or more of the same type affine are counted only once in the appropriate column. The lack of equivalence in the number of cases of ZH and WB co-residence is due to the fact that pairs of brothers living with a single ZH produce two cases of ZH co-residence (two men who live with a ZH) but only one case of WB co-residence. Similarly, one man lives with the husbands of two daughters.

158

This series of tables indicates that residing with WF and DH is slightly favored over residence with WB and ZH. The frequency of co-residence with ZH is also slightly higher than with WB because pairs of true brothers tend to live with the Z and ZH they have in common rather than with the WB of one. However, the number of different types of affines has the most marked effect on the frequency of co-residence. Nearly all the men (22/23 or 95.7 percent) who have two types of affines live with one or both while 54.3 percent (19/35) of the individuals with only one affine co-reside. The residence of men with two types of affines thus corresponds exactly to the models of cross-sex sibling co-residence. In other words, the statistics are intelligible in terms of these models.

The Co-residence of Agnatic Kinsmen

There are a number of factors other than preference which are conducive to the co-residence of agnatic kinsmen. Married sons usually reside with their fathers and true brothers are rarely separated. This creates a predisposition to the co-residence of FB/BS and of FBSons. These kinsmen will live together (as a consequence of ego's living with his father and the latter's co-residence with his brother) unless, or until, one or more changes his place of residence. This residual residence with FB and FBS is further perpetuated by the fact that affinal co-residence only requires that one man leave his current dwelling place; for each WB who moves there is a ZH who remains. Finally, several agnates may live together as a result of the concentration of marriages, i.e., both may have affines at the same longhouse community. All of these factors contribute to the co-residence of pairs and clusters of agnatic kinsmen both on the lineage territory and elsewhere. Thus, while local groups average less than 50 percent agnatic in composition, 73.8 percent (59/80) of the ever-married men who have patrilateral kinsmen outside their nuclear family reside with one or more of these agnates (i.e., FB, FBS, FFBS, etc.). This figure is comparable to the 70.7 percent co-residence with one or more affines.

Living with close agnatic kin (FB and FBS) is considered to be desirable in itself and is not merely the by-product of other factors. However, these factors do augment the frequency of co-residence and this is relevant in a comparative context (vis-à-vis the incidence of co-residence with other kin and affines). The following figures elucidate the extent to which FB/BS co-residence is a residuum of other preferences. The frequency of co-residence among FBrothers and their married and unmarried BSons (over the age of fifteen) is 68.4 percent (26/38). Excluding those cases which are a

direct product of the current co-residence of ego's father and FB
reduces this to 56.5 percent (13/23). In nine of the thirteen cases in
which FB and BS live together this is due to the fact that neither
has changed his residence after the death of the linking father
(brother). Only two pairs of FB/BS co-reside as a result of having
moved to the same longhouse (and in one of these cases BS resides
with his Z as well as his FB and the latter lives with his D as well
as his BS). In ten of fourteen instances BS and FB were separated
by change of residence. When one of the two moved, the other did
not accompany him.

The significance of close consanguineal ties within the lineage
is clearly evident in residential arrangements; the frequency of co-
residence with agnatic kinsmen is inversely related to genealogical
distance. The figures, presented below, include only ever-married
individuals and do not discount cases where ego lives with FB or
FBS as a consequence of living with F.[18]

B/B	25/27	92.6 percent
F/S	9/11	81.8 percent
FB/BS	15/18	83.3 percent
FBS/FBS	22/43	51.2 percent

The incidence of FBS co-residence is remarkably low in view
of the fact that it is augmented by the residual effects of B/B, F/S,
and FB/BS co-residence. Fewer men reside with their patrilateral
parallel cousins than with three of the four types of affines respectively even though affinal co-residence requires a change of residence on the part of some individuals while FBSons can live together simply by remaining where they are. This indicates that men
are inclined to leave their FBSons in order to join their affines.

The relative importance of relationships with cross-sex siblings
and affines as opposed to those with agnatic kin is evident from the
residential choices made by men after their father's death. These
choices are illustrated by consideration of the same group of

---

18. The frequency of FB/BS co-residence is higher when only ever-
married men are considered than when both married and unmarried BSons
(over fifteen) are included. This is partially due to the fact that the former
group is smaller and includes one man who lives with his father and his
father's three brothers. Even so, more married men live with FB than
unmarried men. A larger proportion of the young men move to their Z and
ZHusband's place of residence. This is probably due to the cultural preference for ZH as a homosexual partner (discussd in chapter 7).

FBrothers and their married and unmarried BSons discussed above. Ten of the fifteen men whose F is deceased have a married sister as well as a FB. Three of the ten reside with both, five with Z and ZH (but not FB), and two with FB alone. Of the five men without a married Z, three stayed with their FB and a pair of brothers joined the WB of one. All told, eight men remained with their FB after their father's death and seven moved elsewhere. But three of the eight who remained lived with Z and ZH as well and three had no sister. Of the seven who moved away, five resided with Z and ZH and two with WB (and BWB). When a choice is required men favor Z and ZH over FB by a margin of five to two —but at the same time more than 50 percent of the men reside with FB. This reflects the general strategy of Etoro residential arrangements which is to bring together as many close kinsmen and affines as possible by exploiting the gaps in individual kin and affinal networks.

The substantial frequencies of co-residence recorded for siblings, affines, and agnatic kin respectively indicate that Etoro residential arrangements are in conformity with the models of cross-sex sibling co-residence presented in figures 20 and 21. Although Etoro residential preferences encompass all close kinsmen, the frequencies of co-residence for those not accommodated by the cross-sex sibling models are generally lower. (These figures are listed below.) The Etoro aspire to live with as many of the preferred affines and close kinsmen as possible. Residing with MB or MZS is desirable but difficult to combine with other preferences and therefore occurs less frequently in practice.

MB/ZS	5/45	11.1 percent
MBS/FZS	6/38	15.8 percent
MZS	5/27	18.5 percent
MBDS/MFZS	2/17	11.8 percent

The kinship priorities evident in Etoro residential choices and in the frequencies of co-residence presented in this section clearly document the extent to which solidarity is vested in siblingship and the emphasis on close consanguinity and affinity which follow from this. Although closely related agnatic kin such as FB and FBS are clearly favored over equally closely related nonagnates (MB, MBS, and FZS), the relative attractiveness of living with agnates definitely declines as genealogical distance increases. Residence choices provide a further illustration of the structural weakness of descent relationships that are not underwritten by close consanguinity.

LINEAGE LOCALIZATION AND THE AGNATIC
COMPOSITION OF LOCAL GROUPS

Both of the models of cross-sex sibling co-residence provide that local groups will be 50 percent agnatic in adult male composition, but each involves a somewhat different pattern with respect to localization of the lineage.[19] In the first model (fig. 20) there are only half as many local groups as there are lineages. Half of the lineages are 100 percent localized and half are dispersed among the longhouses of affinally related descent groups. In the second model (fig. 21) the number of local groups is equivalent to the number of lineages. Half of the men of each lineage remain on their agnatic territory and half reside with affinally related lines so that each descent group is 50 percent localized. This model is applicable to a general condition of classificatory sister exchange between lineages.

Etoro residence patterns conform to the first of these models in that there are twenty-two lineages but only eleven longhouse communities. However, the eleven patrilines which have a longhouse on their territory are not all 100 percent localized and in some cases the degree of localization more nearly corresponds to the second model. This is exemplified by Turusato and Kaburusato, the two patrilines which are parties to the true sister exchange which forms the basis of the Arigadabo community (at Turusato). Fifty-five percent of the members of Turusato lineage reside at their longhouse and the comparable figure for Kaburusato is 22 percent. There are more members of Kaburusato at Arigadabo than at the Kaburusato longhouse.

The distribution of lineage members among local groups, the agnatic composition of longhouse communities, and the percent of localization among the eleven localized descent groups are given in tables 25 through 30, respectively. These data are intelligible in terms of the two models previously discussed and do not require extensive explication. Several points may be noted. The eleven localized lineages are generally larger than the eleven dispersed patrilines and the former account for 71.3 percent (62/87) of the adult male population. However, there are some exceptions to this pattern. Waysato is larger than all but three lineages and does not

---

19. Localization is measured by the percentage of adult male lineage members assembled on the lineage territory; agnatic composition by the percentage of agnates in the adult male population of the lineage territory. A lineage which is aggregated outside its territory is not considered to be localized.

TABLE 25

Distribution of Adult Male Lineage Members among Longhouse Communities, May, 1968

| | Longhouse Communities (Listed by Lineage Territory) | | | | | | | | | | | | |
	Turusato	Gemisato	Sarado	Poboleifi	Kaburusato	Ingiribisato	Haifi	Katiefi	Hilisato	Kasayasato	Nemisato	Extratribal*	Total Lineage Members
Lineage:													
Nagefi								1					1
Turusato	5					2				1		1(p)†	9
Alamafi												1(p)	1
Salubisato					1							1(p)	2
Kobifi		3											3
Gemisato		3									1		4
Haũasato									1				1
Sarado			5						2			1(h)‡	7(8)
Poboleifi				3		1						1(h)	4(5)
Masianifi				2									2
Somosato		1											1
Kaburusato	5				2		1	1					9
Ingiribisato						10							10
Haifi			1		1		2		1				5
Owaibifi								2					2
Katiefi							1	4	1				6
Hilisato									1				1
Somadabe									3				3
Kasayasato										3			3
Waysato				7	1							1(h)	8(9)
Kudulubisato		1											1
Nemisato											4		4
Petamini tribe§				1	2								3
Total	10	8	6	12	5	14	6	8	9	4	5	3(p)3(h)	90(93)
Number of lineages represented at each community	2	4	2	3	4	4	4	4	6	2	2		37

*Three of the Etoro men who reside outside the tribal territory are in jail in Mt. Hagen for homicide. The other three reside in the Petamini tribal territory. One lives with a WF and another with a MZS of that tribe. The third resides with his WBrothers of the Etoro Mamunasato lineage which has migrated to the Petamini territory.

†p = Residing in Petamini territory.

‡h = Residing at Mt. Hagen.

§Three members of the Petamini tribe reside at Etoro longhouses where they are related to the host lineage as ZS, WB, and BWB, respectively.

have a longhouse on its territory, while Hilisato does although it is represented by only a single lineage member. There are four cases in which all agnates live together at a longhouse on another lineage's territory (this figure excluding the six patrilines with only a single adult male member). Nearly all of the descent groups which are aggregated (irrespective of location) are genealogically shallow and in several cases include only brothers. In about half of the communities agnates are outnumbered by nonagnates although there are usually more members of the owning line than of any of the several guest lineages. Two to six patrilines are represented at each longhouse, the median being four. This reflects the tendency of communities to incorporate a number of marriage-linked sibling sets.

The distribution of lineage members among local groups at the end of the fieldwork period shown in table 28 reflects substantial changes due to deaths and change of residence.[20] During this period the Haifi community disbanded as a consequence of death and witchcraft accusations, reducing the number of longhouses to ten, and the Hilisato community achieved the distinction of becoming zero percent agnatic. The average agnatic composition of local groups decreased to 42.9 percent (from 48.3 percent) due partly to the smaller number of localized lineages but primarily to the fact that nine (of forty-three) agnates died as opposed to only three (of forty-four) nonagnates.[21] The idea that the Etoro were once organized in terms of exclusively agnatic lineage communities and have been reduced to their present state by depopulation is beguilingly simple, but there is no evidence whatsoever which would support this. Several important indications to the contrary have already been noted. What appears to have happened during the course of population decline is that the Etoro have favored the first model of cross-sex sibling co-residence over the second. Smaller lineages which were once 50 percent localized have moved in with larger affinally related lines. In other words, an earlier condition where each descent group was 50 percent localized has shifted toward the present arrangement where the larger lineages are 68 percent localized and the smaller patrilines dispersed among them. This change

---

20. Table 28 also differs from table 25 in that it includes three men who joined the ranks of "adults" through marriage. Men often change their residence at marriage but these changes do not follow any regular pattern. One of the three newly married men left his MB and returned to his own lineage longhouse, another continued to reside at his ZHusband's group, and the third moved to his wife's natal community.

21. The dissolution of Haifi added only one nonagnate to the population.

facilitates co-residence with a greater number of siblings, close kinsmen, and affines in accordance with Etoro preferences. The reduced number of localized lineages represents the maintenance of siblingship rather than the decline of agnation.

TABLE 26

Agnatic Composition of Longhouse Communities, May, 1968

*(Agnates as a Percentage of Total Adult Male
Population of the Community)*

Longhouse Community (Listed by Owning Lineage)	Total Adult Male Population	Number of Agnates	Agnates as a Percentage of Total
Turusato	10	5	50.0
Gemisato	8	3	37.5
Sarado	6	5	83.3
Poboleifi	12	3	25.0
Kaburusato	5	2	40.0
Ingiribisato	14	10	71.4
Haifi	6	2	33.3
Katiefi	8	4	50.0
Hilisato	9	1	11.1
Kasayasato	4	3	75.0
Nemisato	5	4	80.0
Total	87	42	48.3

TABLE 27

Degree of Localization among the Eleven Lineages Which Have a
Longhouse on Their Territory, May, 1968

*(Percentage of Total Lineage Membership
Residing at the Lineage Longhouse)*

Lineage	Total Adult Male Members*	Number Residing at Lineage Longhouse	Percentage of Total Lineage Membership Residing at the Lineage Longhouse
Turusato	9	5	55.6
Gemisato	4	3	75.0
Sarado	7	5	71.4
Poboleifi	4	3	75.0
Kaburusato	9	2	22.2
Ingiribisato	10	10	100
Haifi	5	2	40.0
Katiefi	6	4	66.7
Hilisato	1	1	100
Kasayasato	3	3	100
Nemisato	4	4	100
Total	62	42	67.7

*Excluding three men serving jail terms.

TABLE 28

Distribution of Adult Male Lineage Members among Longhouse Communities, July, 1969

	Longhouse Communities (Listed by Lineage Territory)												
	Turusato	Gemisato	Sarado	Poboleifi	Kaburusato	Ingiribisato	Haifi	Katiefi	Hilisato	Kasayasato	Nemisato	Extratribal*	Total Lineage Members
Lineage:													
Nagefi					2								2
Turusato	5					2			1			1(p)†	9
Alamafi												1(p)	1
Salubisato						1						1(p)	2
Kobifi		3											3
Gemisato		3									1		4
Haũasato									1				1
Sarado			1						2			1(h)‡	3(4)
Poboleifi				2	1							1(h)	3(4)
Masianifi				2									2
Somosato		1											1
Kaburusato	4	1			3			2					10
Ingiribisato		1				10							11
Haifi			2				---	1	1				4
Owaibifi								2					2
Katiefi								2	1				3
Hilisato									---				0
Somadabe									2				2
Kasayasato										3			3
Waysato			6		1							2(h)	7(9)
Kudulubisato	1												1
Nemisato											4		4
Petamini Tribe§								2					2
Total	9	8	5	10	6	14	---	9	7	4	5	3(p)4(h)	80(84)
Number of lineages represented at each community	2	4	4	3	3	4	---	5	5	2	2		34

*Four of the Etoro men who reside outside the tribal territory are in Mt. Hagen—three in jail for homicide and one working on a plantation. The other three reside in the Petamini tribal territory. One lives with a WF and another with a MZS of that tribe. The third resides with his WBrothers of the Etoro Mamunasato lineage which has migrated to the Petamini territory.

†p = Residing in Petamini territory.

‡h = Residing at Mt. Hagen.

§Two members of the Petamini tribe reside at Etoro longhouses where they are related to the host lineage as WB and BWB, respectively.

TABLE 29

Agnatic Composition of Longhouse Communities, July, 1969

(Agnates as a Percentage of Total Adult Male
Population of the Community)

Longhouse Community (Listed by Owning Lineage)	Total Adult Male Population	Number of Agnates	Agnates as a Percentage of Total
Turusato	9	5	55.6
Gemisato	8	3	37.5
Sarado	5	1	20.0
Poboleifi	10	2	20.0
Kaburusato	6	3	50.0
Ingiribisato	14	10	71.4
Haifi	———Disbanded———		
Katiefi	9	2	22.2
Hilisato	7	0	0.0
Kasayasato	4	3	75.0
Nemisato	5	4	80.0
Total	77	33	42.9

TABLE 30

Degree of Localization among the Eleven Lineages Which Have a Longhouse on Their Territory, July, 1969

(Percentage of Total Lineage Membership Residing
at the Lineage Longhouse)

Lineage	Total Adult Male Members*	Number Residing at Lineage Longhouse	Percentage of Total Lineage Membership Residing at the Lineage Longhouse
Turusato	9	5	55.6
Gemisato	4	3	75.0
Sarado	3	1	33.3
Poboleifi	3	2	66.7
Kaburusato	10	3	30.0
Ingiribisato	11	10	90.9
Haifi	4	Disbanded	——
Katiefi	3	2	66.7
Hilisato	0	0	0.0
Kasayasato	3	3	100.0
Nemisato	4	4	100.0
Total	54	33	61.1

*Excluding three men serving jail terms.

CHAPTER 7

Marriage and
Affinal Relationships

The general characteristics of exchange relationships between lineages (as units) have been discussed in chapter 5. In contrast, the foci of the present chapter are the event of marriage, the process of obtaining a wife, marriage preferences and prohibitions, the frequency of preferred matches, the distribution of recorded unions by lineage and moiety, and the relation of rule and practice to the larger structure. In evaluating marriage rates, both demographic and structural factors are considered. In the latter connection I will be particularly concerned to examine the respective roles of lineage and kin relationships in the regulation of marriage and the manner in which these are intertwined. At one level, classificatory kin designations and lineage exchange relationships constitute separate social categorizations which mutually govern the availability of women to any particular ego; at another level they are interdependent. Kinship designations are themselves responsive to lineage relationships of siblingship and exchange—and to the state of reciprocity between exchange groups—such that individuals tend to be ascribed to kinship categories on these bases. Thus it is not genealogical kinship per se which regulates marriage but rather kinship categories which encode elements of reciprocity and interlineage relationship as well as genealogical connection.

These conclusions guide the subsequent evaluation of marriage rates, which are considered in terms of both recorded genealogical relationships and their Etoro classification. The examination of marriage rules and rates also provides a basis for consideration of the question of moiety recognition (raised in chapter 4) and the relation of marriage rules to the larger structure. In the final section of the chapter, marital payments and affinal exchange are analyzed and related to the pervasive dualism of the structure as expressed in the dual organization of local groups.

The Effects of Depopulation on the
Age Differential between Spouses

At present, Etoro men are generally between the ages of twenty-six and thirty-five when they take their first wife. Women are married for the first time at sixteen to eighteen (see tables 53 and 54, Appendix). However, both the age at first marriage and the age differential between spouses have been altered by the direct and indirect effects of contact. Girls were traditionally wed at age ten to twelve (by men about ten years their senior). In 1966, the government dissolved several of these "child marriages" and stipulated that future marriages be postponed until the prospective bride's breasts are fully developed. (As a result of this injunction relatively few marriages took place between 1966 and 1969.)

The age difference between husband and wife at first marriage has increased in the last fifteen years due to the effects of epidemics of introduced diseases on the age structure of the population. The most severe of these epidemics took place in 1948 to 1949 and produced very substantially increased rates of mortality among children five years and under.[1] Men of twenty-six to thirty-five (in 1968) were already over five during this period of heavy infant mortality and their rate of survival was substantially higher than that of the younger women (sixteen to twenty-five) who would traditionally have been their wives. Men in these cohorts (twenty-six to thirty-five years of age) outnumber women age sixteen to twenty-five by a ratio of 1.85 to one. The difficulties inherent in this situation have been partially alleviated by the fact that epidemic mortality has also increased the supply of widows, many of whom have been wed by bachelors (see table 62, Appendix). However, other unmarried men in this age group have arranged betrothals to still younger girls and this has increased the age differential between spouses.

The present age differential is a product of the cumulative effects, over the past fifteen years, of balancing the sex ratio by arranging marriages with successively younger girls. Each male cohort has taken some wives from the age groups that traditionally would have been reserved for their junior brothers, and the latter have thus been forced to look to still younger girls. This process is

---

1. The "pinch" in the age structure of the Etoro population (presented in fig. 3) in the twenty-one to twenty-five cohort clearly reveals the date of these severe epidemics and their effects on infant mortality.

clearly evident in table 31 which gives the age differential between spouses by female cohort. The median age difference between husband and wife has increased from ten years, for marriages which took place sixteen to twenty years ago, to sixteen years for current betrothals.

It seems very likely that this cumulative process will begin to stabilize over the next ten years and then reverse itself. The reversal will be brought about by three factors that are already apparent, viz., (1) that an expanded age differential between spouses aug-

TABLE 31

Age Differential between Husband and Wife in First Marriages

(Distribution of Cases for Current Betrothals and Recent Marriages,
by Woman's Cohort)

Age Difference between Husband and Wife in Years	Current Betrothals	Recent Marriages		
	Females Age 6–15	Females Age 16–20	Females Age 21–25	Females Age 26–30
21	xx			
20	x			
19	xx			
18				
17	xxx	x		
16	xx		x	x
15	x	x	x	xx
14		xx		
13		x	x	
12	x	x	xxx	
11	xx		xx	
10	xx	x	x	x
9				x
8			xx	x
7	x			
6				x
5				
4				
3			x	
Total cases	17	7	12	7
Average age difference (in years)	15.2	13.8	10.9	11.3
Median age difference (in years)	16	14	11–12	10

Note: Each x represents one case.

ments the incidence of widowhood, (2) that bachelors are increasingly taking widows as first wives, and (3) that unmarried men are favored over married men in arranging future unions. The most recent betrothals involve men eighteen to twenty years older than their prospective wives of five or six. When these girls reach government-stipulated maturity at about fifteen and marry, their husbands will be thirty-three to thirty-five. These men will, at that point, be entering the age groups where mortality becomes increasingly heavy (largely due to pneumonial complications following introduced influenza). A substantial proportion of these men will leave widows of twenty to thirty who will be married by bachelors of the same age or a few years older—this being an emergent pattern. The men of twenty-five to thirty years of age who acquire widows at this time will not yet have arranged betrothals as all girls over five will be promised to others, while girls below this age are not customarily betrothed (for reasons which will be discussed). The next cohort of females (one to five years of age) will then become available to younger men and the age differential between spouses will begin to contract.

One of the most important factors in the predicted reversal of the present trend comes into play at this point, i.e., that unmarried men are clearly favored over married men in the arrangement of prospective unions. A bachelor who weds a young widow cannot thereafter argue that he *needs* a wife and this markedly decreases his chances of negotiating a betrothal to a young girl. The cumulative expansion of the age differential between husband and wife thus ceases when the difference becomes twenty years as unbetrothed men of twenty-five will then marry young widows—who become increasingly available—in lieu of attempting to arrange a betrothal over the next few years. This is already beginning to occur on a limited scale. In addition, a few bachelors who recently wed widows have had their prior betrothals broken off on the grounds that they now had a wife and were not in need of one. (These stated grounds probably do not adequately reflect the girl's father's motivation in revoking the betrothal. One of the fathers also expressed concern that his daughter would be the junior cowife of a woman twenty years older.)

Eventually the increased number of young widows engendered by an expanded age differential will offset the present imbalance in the ratio of eligible bachelors to prospective wives. Once the cumulative effect of arranging marriages with successively younger girls is broken in the manner described above, the age differential between spouses will come to reflect the frequency of polygyny and the sex ratio of the unmarried segment of the population—then no longer under the influence of the present disjunctions in the age structure. The observed increase in the age difference between husband and wife over the past fifteen years therefore does not represent a permanent change but the initial phase of a temporary oscillation.

Disjunctions in the age structure of a population (of the type just discussed) set in motion processes which create the preconditions for the development of gerontocracy. However, gerontocracy cannot be permanently established unless prospective wife-givers favor older, married men over younger, unmarried men—in which case the essential feature of the institution would already be present. This suggests that the instrumentalities of social change are sociocultural rather than demographic. Demographic factors may create the preconditions for social transformation but they do not constitute sufficient causes in the process of social change because they do not impinge on the system of rules which governs social events and their cultural interpretation. Changes in demographic parameters also tend to be transitory because the variables are characteristically embedded in homeostatic systems.

The sex ratio of the Etoro population is 79.1 (121/153) females per hundred males.[2] This ratio appears to be relatively constant inasmuch as both the pre- and post-1943 segments of the population—above and below age five in the severe 1948–49 epidemics—do not deviate significantly from the figure for the whole. The sex ratio for the population twenty-six and over is 81.8 (63/71) females per hundred males, and for the population twenty-five and under 76.3 (58/76) females per hundred males. This unbalanced ratio requires some difference in age between husband and wife, as does the extant frequency of polygyny which entails a ratio of 120 married females per 100 married males. Both of these factors could be accommodated by an age differential of about seven to ten years. There are, for example, sixty-seven women over the age of twenty-three and fifty-six men over thirty, producing the desired ratio of 1.2 to one. To achieve this ratio at a marriage age of twenty

---

2. This sex ratio and other figures presented here are drawn from the age structure which includes 71.0 percent (274/386) of the initial population of the tribal territory (eight of eleven communities). However, the sex ratio for the total initial population is almost the same—80.4 (172/214) females per 100 males. If the three men serving jail terms were included, the ratio would be 79.3 (172/217) for the entire population—virtually identical to that of the sample, i.e., 79.1.

to twenty-two for men would require an estimated ten-year difference between spouses using a reconstructed pre-epidemic age structure.

Polygynous unions represent 18.3 percent of current marriages and 15.3 percent of completed unions with one spouse still surviving (table 32). The latter category includes marriages contracted, on the average, about ten to fifteen years earlier than current marriages. The frequency of polygynous unions has thus increased by 3 percent in the last ten to fifteen years, although the average number of wives per man has only changed by 0.02 (from 1.19 to 1.21). This slight rise in polygynous unions is probably a product of the increased incidence of widowhood following from the expanded age differential between spouses discussed above. The increase is modest because 70.6 percent (24/34) of the widows are remarried by men without wives—bachelors, widowers, and divorcees. Forty-seven percent are wed by bachelors alone (see table 62, Appendix).

TABLE 32

Frequency of Polygynous Unions and Number of
Wives Per Husband for Current and Completed Unions with
One Spouse Still Surviving

	Current Unions		Completed Unions with One Spouse Still Surviving	
	Number of Men	Percentage of Total Men	Number of Men	Percentage of Total Men
Men with				
One wife	67	81.7	50	84.7
Two wives	13	15.9	7	11.9
Three wives	2	2.4	2	3.4
Total men	82	100	59	100
Total wives	99		70	
Average number of wives per man	1.21		1.19	
Additional wives of these men lost through				
Death	9		5	
Divorce	2		3	
Total number of simultaneous and successive wives	110		78	
Average per man	1.34		1.32	

THE ROLE OF LINEAGE AND KIN RELATIONSHIPS IN THE REGULATION OF MARRIAGE

Girls are (and traditionally were) betrothed at about the age of five. Both sororate and levirate rights are applicable during the betrothal. If the prospective bride dies, her agnates should provide a replacement; if the prospective groom dies, his intended spouse should be promised to one of his agnates. The obligation to give and the right to receive women are held in common by all lineage members, and the extension of sororate and levirate rights to the betrothal period is consistent with this. This extension also illustrates the Etoro conception of marriage as a transaction between patrilines. The obligation to provide wives for major exchange groups and to fulfill the requirement of balanced reciprocity in the exchange of women is not altered by the death of one of the parties to a prospective union.

Sororate claims may be invoked when a young woman recently given in marriage dies without having borne a child and following a divorce (the latter circumstance will be discussed more fully in chapter 8). The requirement of sororal replacement is therefore applicable only to females between the ages of five and twenty and the mortality rate for this age group is lower than that for any other segment of the female population.[3] The occasions on which sororate rights may be exercised are consequently few in number. Whether or not this custom is honored in particular cases depends on the nature of the relationship between the lineages linked by the betrothal and the balance of exchange between them. If the two patrilines are major wife-suppliers to each other and the wife-giving group has received more women than it has given, then a replacement is likely to be arranged.

Decisions which pertain to the lineage's obligation to provide wives for major exchange groups are generally made by individuals following consultation and discussion with their close agnates. In most instances, the latter group is co-extensive with the lineage membership (or very nearly so). Although all agnates do not assemble as a body for the purpose of considering the betrothal of a daughter of the line or a sororate claim, intentions and responses to them are communicated during the course of daily activities. No one will question a father's decision when the proposed union conforms to established exchange relationships, but objections may be

---

3. Girls are not betrothed until they attain the age of five and are well past the period of heaviest infant and childhood mortality in order to minimize the chances that a sororal replacement will be necessary.

raised to other matches by close and/or distant agnates. However, persuasion and social pressure are the only means available for dissuading a man from proceeding with an undesirable union and distant agnates who are normally outside an individual's personal network of supporters are unable to exert such pressure effectively. (Thus, segmentation occurs when two groups of distantly related agnates disagree concerning the deployment of women in exchange.) In spite of the absence of any strong mechanisms for ensuring lineage control, marital decisions are generally made with a view to the established obligations and enduring corporate interests of the descent group in maintaining dependable exchange relationships. This is largely guaranteed by the constitution of the descent group itself, a constitution which is predicated on a congruence in external relationships which follows from agnatic parallel marriage and the concentration of marriages in general. The majority of lineage members will be related through past or present marriages (as WB, ZH, WF, DH, MB, ZS, MBS, FZS, etc.) to at least one of the three major exchange groups with which 50 percent of the patriline's unions are contracted. Any agnates who are not personally related in one of these ways will usually be close patrilineal kin of those who are. The descent group's corporate obligations in the domain of exchange relationships are thus largely congruent with the kin and affinal obligations of individual lineage members. Lineage interests and individual interests coincide. The fulfillment of obligations which are defined with respect to the corporate descent group therefore does not depend upon lineage solidarity. A lineage consensus in all social transactions with major exchange groups is ensured by the structural constitution of the lineage.

The Etoro lineage is not dissimilar from African or other modeled varieties of corporate descent groups with respect to the delineation of rights and duties but differs with regard to the mechanisms by which rights are exercised and duties discharged. The corporate "estate" of the lineage encompasses rights to wives and rights of disposal over sisters, daughters, and widows. The obligation to give and the right to receive women are vested in enduring exchange relationships which are defined at the lineage level (and may be validated by totemic myth). However, performance is based upon a mechanical congruence in individual external relationships rather than an internal agnatic solidarity and appeals to agnatic sentiments. The mobilization of the Etoro lineage in corporate affairs does not proceed from the ideological notion that "we are all brothers" but from the conception that "we are all related to the same people." (This condition is structurally ordained since the lineage fissions when congruence is diluted.) This mode of operation is remarkably dependable. The extent to which particular decisions concerning widow remarriage reflect the interests of the descent group will be considered in detail in chapter 8.

The Etoro are well aware of the significance of congruence within major exchange groups and the creation of this condition is an important element in the strategy of exchange. Giving a number of "sisters" (and "daughters") to a major exchange line simultaneously is considered to be highly desirable; such generosity is an ideological virtue. But at the same time, the interests of the wife-giver are well served; generosity establishes congruence in the receiving lineage and this ensures an ample supply of wives (FZSDaughters) for the sons of the donor patriline. A true FZSon cannot legitimately refuse to give his daughter to ego in marriage. However, when FZS does not have a daughter of his own, ego's success in obtaining a wife from FZSon's lineage is partly contingent upon the degree of congruence within that descent group. If FZSon's agnates have mothers, wives, and cross-cousins of other lineages than FZS, they will be bound by other obligations and objectives. Reciprocity is comparatively tenuous when marriages are dispersed rather than concentrated and dispersion is an inferior strategy with respect to both exchange and alliance. Concentrating marriages confers the advantage of unqualified support from major exchange groups in internal disputes and in carrying out retributive counter-raids against external enemies. An exchange line which will readily provide its daughters in marriage will, for the same reasons of congruence, readily lend its support in other affairs.

A young bachelor's betrothal is generally arranged by his father (or elder brother) and his mother's brother. Although the MBrother's role in these proceedings is enjoined by kinship obligations, it is also the case that his (MBrother's) son will ideally marry ego's daughter (as a FZSD) and a MB therefore has a special interest in securing a bride for his ZS. The MB is in a position to act as matchmaker as a consequence of the general structure of sibling and exchange relationships between lineages. Mother's brother will generally be a matrilateral sibling of the bachelor's (ego's) potential wife-givers[4]

---

4. Major exchange groups of the same lineage (the bachelor's in this case) are "brother" lines as a consequence of parallel marriage. Ego's MBrother's patriline will generally have received women from ego's line in the past and will therefore be linked by ties of matrilateral siblingship to ego's "FZSon's" lineages who have also received women (father's sisters) from ego's line.

and can draw on this relationship in attempting to persuade them to provide a wife for his ZS.

Personal preferences do not normally enter into the selection of a spouse (unless the prospective bride is a widow or divorcée). Although an ideal wife should be attractive, hardworking, and compliant, it is difficult to determine which five-year-old girls will eventually possess these desired qualities. The selection is made by the bachelor's father or elder brother and the primary considerations are those of kinship, reciprocity, and availability rather than personal characteristics. A girl's father is guided by these same considerations in selecting among a number of suitors. The kin relationship between the bachelor's and girl's respective fathers is often an important factor. Ideally (i.e., in the context of FZSD marriage), the bachelor's father will be the prospective wife-giver's MB—the kinsman who helped arrange his own marriage, contributed to his brideprice, presided over his final initiation into manhood, and who has given small gifts to his ZS throughout the latter's lifetime. In short, the MB requests a wife for his son after some thirty years of continuous prestations. The request cannot be refused.

The process of seeking a prospective wife and successfully negotiating a betrothal is governed both by the existing exchange relationships between lineages and by preferences and prohibitions which are defined in terms of egocentric kin relationships. The total group of girls of betrothable age available to any particular male ego is thus culturally categorized by two sets of criteria which are not necessarily consistent. In the event of conflicting determinations, lineage relationships generally take precedence over individual kin relationships. The strategy of exchange is keyed to the larger system and the decisions of wife-givers are responsive to this strategy. Although an individual's claim to a true FZSD is compelling, classificatory relationships admit of considerable manipulation. If there are five prior marriages between a pair of patrilines, then classificatory relationships between the members of these respective descent groups can be traced in five ways (for those lacking a true relation). Under these circumstances, a "correct" relationship can always be selected in order to justify a desired union, while an alternate classification that would preclude the match is simply overlooked. The concentration of marriages between major exchange groups is considered desirable in itself and the Etoro are not deterred from the attainment of this goal by an inflexible adherence to kin category prohibitions.

The strength of a classificatory kinship claim or prohibition thus varies according to the sphere of lineage relationships. Claims weaken and prohibitions are more rigidly interpreted as ego moves from major wife-suppliers to minor exchange groups to partial brother lines and finally to putatively exogamous major brother lines. The influence of lineality may be readily illustrated by a hypothetical case of incest. If ego's father married a lineage sister, ego's true FZSD would be an agnate. However, ego's claim to this girl would not be universally acknowledged by his fellows. The same principle applies to relationships stemming from a previous irregular marriage to a partial brother line. The Etoro do not feel compelled to honor a "FZSD" claim, or the reciprocity upon which it is based, when this entails a repetition of past errors. This is evident from the data presented in chapter 5. Most marriages within the moiety (57 percent) are single, nonreciprocal unions.

Individual kin relationships are of particular importance when lineage relationships are equivalent or near-equivalent (i.e., other things being equal). Every available girl is sought by suitors from a number of different lineages with which the girl's line customarily intermarries and kinship is generally the decisive factor in a wife-giver's selection among them. The preeminent claim to a true FZSD is rarely denied and a classificatory FZSD, FFZD, or FFZSD relationship based on unfulfilled reciprocity also confers a high degree of success. In addition, a man may be disqualified, vis-à-vis other suitors, by a secondary "sister" or "daughter" relationship as has been discussed in chapter 4. In this context, kinship serves as a basis for avoiding and adjudicating disputes over women; it provides justification for a wife-giver's allocation of women among exchange groups so that these important relationships are not debilitated by the rancor of unsuccessful suitors. This also promotes harmony between brother lines which, by definition, seek wives from the same group of lineages.

It is important to distinguish classificatory kin relationships which are consequent upon the exchange of women from those that are traced through brother lines. Almost every woman of ego's moiety in the first ascending generation is a "FZ," i.e., father's classificatory matrilateral sibling. It follows that virtually every potential spouse could be traced as a "FZSD." Such relationships do not confer rights to women as they are not established through women given in the past. The "FZS" in this case is not bound by obligations of reciprocity and a wife cannot be secured on this basis. In other words, it is not classificatory kinship per se which enters into the regulation of marriage, but the elements of reciprocity which kinship encodes. Patrilateral cross-cousin relationships traced through brother lines are therefore not operable in wife

seeking. However, they are frequently activated after the marriage
has taken place so that all unions appear to be in conformity with
the ideal FZSD match. This is achieved by addressing WF as
nesago (FZS) on the basis of a FMZDS or analogous genealogical
connection. (This represents a change from the affinal terminology
employed during betrothal and in the early years of marriage which
will be discussed later in the chapter.)

The preceding discussion illustrates a more general point—that
Etoro kinship terminology engenders multiple possibilities for the
classificatory designation of any particular alter. The possibility of
selective recognition of one of a variety of utilizable connections
provides wide latitude in the ascription of individuals to kinship
categories. In brief, it is possible to call anyone almost anything.
This flexibility enables the Etoro to place a terminological seal of
approval on whatever happens—after the event—and they usually
do. The Etoro operate what may be characterized as an ex post
facto prescriptive system. This is particularly apparent from the
fact that individuals are given to employing the "logic" of conversion and reasoning from the state to the appropriate preconditions.
When asked to explain a marriage that is clearly in violation of
stated rules an informant will invariably say, "if they married, they
must have been *naua*" (the general kin category within which marriage is permissible). By the same logic, WF becomes "FZS" several years after the union is celebrated. However, this ex post facto
imposition of ideology upon reality does not enter into the process
of obtaining a wife. In the latter context, kinship is extended in
accordance with a quite different set of rules and it is these rules
which I am presently concerned to explicate. The basic terminological system is presented in figures 22 and 23.[5]

Category of Permitted Unions

All women with whom marriage is permitted are included in the
single kinship category *aua* (reciprocal *naua*) and the Etoro explain
marital eligibility in these terms. Their statement that "we marry
naua" is somewhat confusing at first, inasmuch as *naua* is the term
men apply to their FF (among others), but it is also instructive. The

---

5. The kinship terms are presented in figures 22 and 23 as they are
used in the terminology of address. The first person form of the terminology of reference employs the same basic terms accompanied by the first
person possessive pronoun (e.g., *niẽ nado,* my father). Since Etoro kinship
terms are inflected for person to agree with the possessive pronoun, the
second and third person forms become *tiẽ tiado* (your father) and *iẽ e:do*
(his father), respectively.

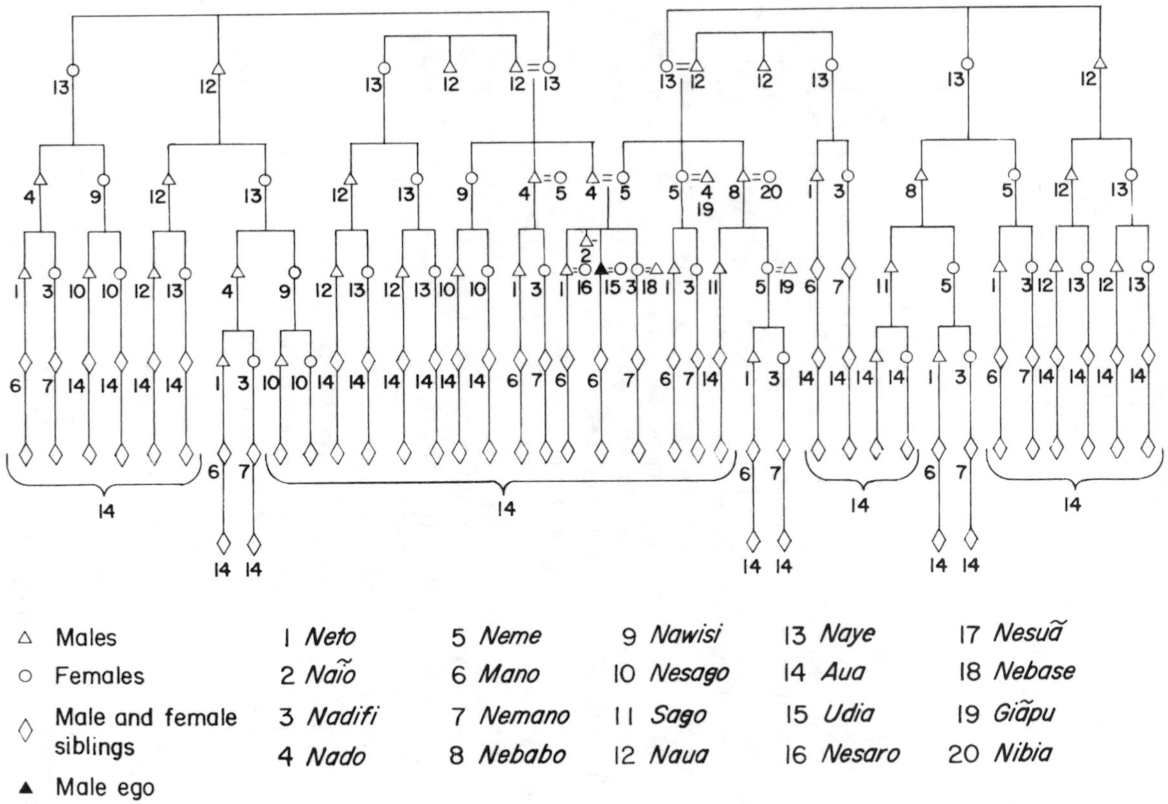

FIG. 22.   Etoro Kinship Terminology (Male Ego)

△	Males	1	Neto	5	Neme	9	Nawisi	13	Naye	17	Nesuã
○	Females	2	Naõ	6	Mano	10	Nesago	14	Aua	18	Nebase
◇	Male and female siblings	3	Nadifi	7	Nemano	11	Sago	15	Udia	19	Giãpu
▲	Male ego	4	Nado	8	Nebabo	12	Naua	16	Nesaro	20	Nibia

180

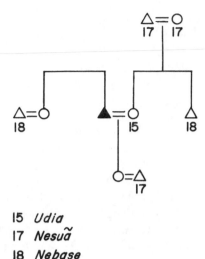

15 *Udia*
17 *Nesuã*
18 *Nebase*

FIG. 23.   Etoro Affinal Terminology (Male Ego)

statement can be elaborated as "we marry women who call us
naua, and whom we call *aua,*" but this provides only partial
clarification since *aua* includes SD, who is definitely not marriageable. The apparent difficulty here is an artifact of extensionist theory rather than Etoro usage. While all marriageable women are
aua, not all *aua* are marriageable. The most prominent exception is
the primary relative SD, who is excluded by the Etoro rule of
lineage exogamy (as are other nonmarriageable *aua*).

It is quite evident that the meaning of the kinship category
naua/aua is not elucidated by the theoretical notion of extension
from a primary relative—unless "meaning" refers to something
other than what this category conveys to the Etoro. However, the
Etoro conception is precisely what we need to know in the present
context, and our understanding is considerably enhanced by regarding *naua* and *aua* as category terms interpretable with respect
to the regulation of sexual relations and hence marital eligibility.

The characteristics of relative age and sex which condition
usage of the *naua/aua* (man speaking) and related *naye/aye*
(woman speaking) terms are described in figure 24. (The genealogical distribution of the former kinsmen is given in figures 22 and 23.)
Naua is applied to elder males by speakers of both sex; *aua* is
applied to hearers of both sex by elder males. The fact that elder
males do not terminologically distinguish the sex of younger individuals within the *aua* category is readily intelligible with reference

to the bisexual orientation of Etoro society. The *aua* term denotes those individuals, both male and female, with whom sexual relations are permitted (excepting lineage members). A brother and sister who are equally appropriate sexual partners for an elder male would both be referred to as *aua,* and both siblings would reciprocally refer to such elder males as *naua.* However, this feature of Etoro terminology also necessitates a somewhat roundabout method of specifying marriageable women (as distinct from permitted homosexual partners). If Etoro men were to say "we marry *aua,*" this would designate males as well as females (while marriage applies only to the latter). The fact that individuals distinguish the sex of *elder* persons spoken to (or of) does not provide a direct solution for male speakers because men always marry younger women. However, this feature does make it possible to clearly designate marriageable women from the standpoint of the women's terminology because female speakers not only distinguish the sex of elders spoken to (or of), but also marry elder men. In short, the Etoro statement that "we marry (women who call us) *naua*" is the only way to describe, unambiguously, the union of an elder male and younger female within the kinship category *naua/aua,* and this accounts for the seemingly unusual phraseology. Etoro kin terminology thus specifies both those individuals who are sexually accessible to a male ego and, by allusion to women's terminology, those whom he may marry.

Sex of Speaker	Sex and Age of Person Spoken to or of			
	Elder		Younger	
	Male	Female	Male	Female
Male	*naua*	*naye*	*aua*	*aua*
Female	*naua*	*naye*	*aye*	*aye*

Reciprocals: *naua / aua*
naye / aye

FIG. 24. Conditioning Factors in *Naua/Aua* and *Naye/Aye* Usage

It is interesting to note that homosexual relationships are regulated by kinship. The ideal homosexual partner is ZH so that a married sister and her younger brother have equivalent relationships of sexual partnership to the same man (ideally a FMBS). This fills a gap in logical possibilities between sororal polygyny and fraternal polyandry. However, the emphasis in the Etoro case is on cross-sex rather than same-sex siblingship.[6] Marriage also involves a direct exchange with respect to sexual access. A man relinquishes such access to his sister, by the incest prohibition, but acquires access to his brother-in-law when she is given (or promised) in marriage. The affective bond between WB and ZH is exceptionally strong.

The Etoro distinguish prohibited and permitted unions by kinship category (and lineage exogamy) as follows:

1. All women with whom marriage is permitted are *aua* and marriage with any other type of kinswoman is prohibited.
2. All *aua* are marriageable excepting those who are members of ego's lineage.

Marriage with *naye* (FM, MM, etc.) is necessarily precluded by the fact that *naye/aua* usage is conditioned by relative age rather than by generation. A classificatory grandmother who is younger than ego is automatically *aua* (not *naye*) and hence a possible spouse. This resolves a potential difficulty with respect to FMBD. Father calls his MBD "mother" (*neme*) and ego would thus normally call her *naye*, while her children would be his "F" and "FZ." However, if FMBD is younger than ego, she is *aua* and consequently marriageable. Sister exchange can thus be combined with the ideal FZSD marriage (FMBS being the reciprocal of FZSD).

The kin category *naua/aua* includes unrelated individuals as well as the genealogical kinsmen designated in figure 22. The terms are applicable when genealogical connection is distant, unknown, or nonexistent. Members of other tribes, including traditional enemies, are referred to as *naua*. To the Etoro, *naua* terminology conveys a sense of social distance and a condition of nonrelationship or elapsed relationship; there are no positive social obligations

---

6. The preference for ZH as a homosexual partner probably accounts for the higher frequency of co-residence among unmarried brothers and their married sisters than among married cross-sex siblings. The sexual relation continues until the young man (the WB) marries and contracts a homosexual relationship with his spouse's sibling.

which are ascribed by this classificatory designation.[7] *Naua* are, in a sociological sense, nonrelatives—people with whom one has no definite ties. They differ from individuals in all other terminological categories in this respect and also with respect to marriageability.

The Etoro conceive of the prototypical *naua* as genealogically unrelated to ego. In semantic terms, then, it might be argued that there is a process of extension which proceeds inward, from a point of unrelatedness, rather than outward from a primary relative. Father's father (and SS) are thereby assimilated to a category which is characterized by social distance.[8] The structural weakness of descent and the genealogical shallowness of the lineage are consistent with this.

Marriage Prohibitions

The Etoro attribute the origin of witchcraft to the mythological union of a true brother and sister. The two copulated secretly in the bush and the girl later gave birth to a son. By this act of incest, the brother and sister were themselves transformed into witches and a witch-child was the fruit of their union.[9] The illicit match was revealed by the discovery of the child; the siblings (parents) were

---

7. There may be an obligation to provide wives between *naua/aua* (as a result of lineage exchange relationships or unbalanced reciprocity in the prior exchange of women) but this obligation is not vested in the kin classification itself.

8. It is very rare for a man to live long enough to see his true grandchildren due to age differential between spouses and the fact that women under twenty do not bear children. (A relatively late age of first birth has also been noted among the Kakoli of the Upper Kaugel Valley [Bowers, 1971].) A man of twenty who marries a girl of ten would be at least thirty when his first child is born and a minimum age of sixty years at the birth of his first son's child. The "distance" which separates true FF and SS is that which separates the world of the living from the spirit world.

9. The witch-child is a product of the act of incest itself not of his parentage by witches. The acquisition of witchcraft is a complex subject which cannot be elaborated here. However, it should be mentioned that the Etoro explicitly deny that the child of a witch and a nonwitch will be a witch. The offspring of two parents who are both witches are likely to be witches but do not necessarily possess the characteristic. Infants that are physically large at birth are thought to be witches and are subject to infanticide. When both parents are witches it is believed that they are unlikely to kill those of their offspring who are large babies (and thus possess witchcraft) and the likelihood that the children of such unions will be witches is related to this.

killed but the witch-child escaped. Incest thus begat witchcraft and introduced sickness and death into the world. Before this time men were immortal.

The marriage of a classificatory sister evokes recollections of this original sin. A man who contracts such a union is definitely suspect since he replicates the behavior of the archetypal witch. If the "sister" is a relatively close kinswoman, it is thought that the offspring of the union will be witches. For these reasons, the Etoro do not marry women whom they acknowledge to be their "sisters." Although marriage with all kinswomen other than *aua* is considered incorrect, the strongest negative injunction is reserved for the terminological category *nadifi* (Z). Marriage with women in the kin categories *nawisi* (FZ), *mano* (child), *neme* (M), and *nemano* (ZD) is also proscribed and these prohibitions are also explained in terms of incest. However, witchcraft is only vaguely associated with incest in these instances; the Etoro do not hold that a witch-child will result from a union with a classificatory member of these categories.

The prohibition of marriage with women in the terminological category *nesago* (FZD) is distinct from all the proscriptions discussed above in that there is no connotation of incest whatsoever. *Nesago* should not be married only because she is not *aua* and thus outside the category of permitted unions. A classificatory FZD marriage is technically incorrect but not actually proscribed. This distinction is significant because a potential *nesago* classification does not constitute an impediment to marriage when an *aua* relationship can also be established through another genealogical connection. In other words, a "FZD" may be married if she is also a "FZSD," "FFZSD," "FMBSD," etc. Such unions are not uncommon between major exchange groups because they facilitate the desired concentration of marriage and the fulfillment of reciprocity.

Although marriage with all women in the *aua* category (other than agnates) is permitted, FZSD unions are definitely preferred.[10] The desirability of this union is directly related to reciprocity. A FZSD match represents the earliest point at which reciprocity can be fulfilled by marriage within the *aua* category (and the first opportunity to recommence an exchange). This emphasis on reciprocity is manifest in the stipulation that a true FZS cannot refuse his daughter to ego as a wife and the fact that this injunction applies to

---

10. Father's sister's son's daughter is terminologically distinguished from other *aua* as *nesago iē mano*, literally "FZS his child."

the wife-giver rather than the wife-seeker. It might be argued that reciprocity is prescribed and FZSD marriage is the preferred vehicle by which this is realized.

The marriage of women within the *aua* category who are genealogically related to ego is considered preferable to the marriage of unrelated *aua* because the latter is inconsistent with the desired concentration of marriages. Moreover, giving a Z or D to an unrelated man generally entails a failure to honor outstanding obligations of reciprocity elsewhere.

There are no genealogically related *aua* other than FZSD which are singled out as ideologically preferred mates. However, unions which are consistent with balanced reciprocity are favored in practice over nonreciprocal unions which occur outside the context of direct or ongoing exchange. Marriages with (true or classificatory) MBSD, FMBD, and FMBSD which involve a unidirectional flow of women in consecutive generations are infrequent although kinswomen of these genealogical types are often married when they are also related through women given in the past (i.e., as FZSD, FFZSD, etc.), or when the union is part of a current exchange. Success in arranging a nonreciprocal union depends upon the significance of the exchange relationship between the suitor's and potential wife-giver's lineages and the extent to which the balance of exchange favors the suitor's line. The greater the number of women that are owed, the more difficult it becomes to obtain additional wives. Generosity in providing wives to major exchange groups generally takes the form of giving two, three, or four women simultaneously, rather than continually over a period of generations. The way in which witchcraft accusations operate as a sanction which enforces reciprocity in the exchange of women over the long term has been discussed in chapter 5. The same principles which actuate witchcraft accusations when reciprocity is significantly unbalanced also militate against FMBSD, FMBD, and MBSD unions under the same conditions.

The way in which kinsmen related through a given type of genealogical connection are allocated to terminological categories also varies according to the prevailing conditions of reciprocity. Cross-cousin terms are applied so as to encode both the state of reciprocity between lineages and the fact that the obligation to give and the right to receive women are held in common by all lineage members. The lineal organization of exchange obligations and prerogatives is evident in the classificatory rule that one marriage engenders cross-cousin terminology between all male members of the wife-giver's and wife-receiver's lineages in the following generation.[11] The state of reciprocity is expressed by the distinction between (male) matrilateral and patrilateral cross-cousins (*sago* and *nesago* respectively). As mentioned previously, ego cannot legitimately refuse to give his daughter in marriage to a true MBS (*sago*). Similarly, ego is under an obligation to provide a wife for any individual to whom the *sago* term is applied, i.e., all members of a lineage which has given a woman in the previous generation. Reciprocally, *nesago* (FZS) designates a potential wife-giver.

The application of these cross-cousin terms is adjusted to reflect the present state of reciprocity. In the generation following a sister exchange, the (male) members of both lineages are *nesago* to each other. Each is a potential wife-giver to the other but neither is under the obligation of unfulfilled reciprocity which the *sago* terminology conveys. The alternate classifications following exchange and nonreciprocal unions are illustrated in figures 25 and 26.

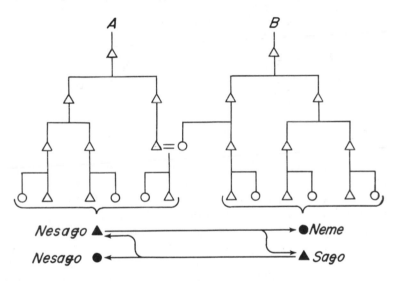

▲ Any male ego of the bracketed generation
● Any female ego of the bracketed generation
⟶ Addresses as (kin term)

FIG. 25.   Cross-Cousin Terminology Following a Nonreciprocal Union

---

11. More specifically, this condition is a product of equations such as FBW = "M," FBWFBS = "MB," and their reciprocals.

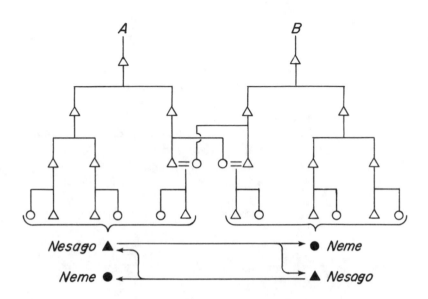

FIG. 26.   Cross-Cousin Terminology Following a Sister Exchange

The daughters of MBS and FZS are both *aua* and are equally marriageable following an exchange of women. However, the Omaha features of the terminology may be extended for an additional generation following a nonreciprocal union. In this context, MBSS is *sago,* MBSD is classified with M, MZ, and MBD as *neme,* and FFZS is *nesago* (fig. 27). The unbalanced state of reciprocity and the obligation to provide wives thus continue to be encoded in kinship classification. This adjusted classification is also conducive to the restoration of balanced reciprocity; the women of the lineage which has provided unreciprocated wives are rendered unavailable to the wife-owing line by the *neme* ("M") terminology, while women of the wife-owing (FFZSon's) patriline are marriageable *aua.* In other words, MBSD unions can be terminologically precluded when reciprocity is unbalanced.

It is evident here that Etoro cousin terms are employed in order to preserve rights to women and to enforce reciprocity in the exchange of women. The primary terminological equation of MBD with M may be regarded as a device which serves to prevent, or at

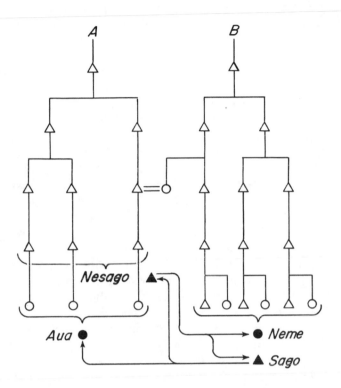

FIG. 27. Kinship Classification in the Second Generation Following a Nonreciprocal Union

least minimize, a unidirectional flow of women by relegating female matrilateral cross-cousins to an incestuous kinship category. As previously noted, marriage with *nesago* (FZD) is not incestuous although such relatives are outside the category of permitted unions. If both female cross-cousins were called *nesago* there would be a strong statistical bias in favor of MBD marriage for several reasons. First, such unions would be preferred as agnatic parallel marriages which create matrilateral consanguinity within the lineage. Second, MBDaughters are more numerous than any other type of kinswoman of marriageable age available to any particular ego. (The reasons for this will be elaborated in subsequent discussion.) Although the Omaha features of the terminology serve to repress a bias in favor of MBD marriage, these features are, of course, important in other respects as well—particularly in the multiplication of matrilateral sibling relationships. It is nevertheless tempting to speculate that the equation of MBD with M originates from an attempt to ensure balanced reciprocity in the exchange of women.

While kinship regulates marriage, it is also apparent from the preceding discussion that terminological designations are themselves conditioned by the reciprocal or nonreciprocal nature of the previous unions through which genealogical connection is established. In other words, the relationship between genealogy and terminology is not determinate but is mediated by intervening factors such as reciprocity. The significance of these intervening factors is amplified in concrete instances by the fact that any particular alter is usually related to ego in several ways. At the very least, there is a selection between relationships traced through alter's mother and father respectively; characteristically there are several additional possibilities traceable via alter's agnates and their spouses. A purely genealogical solution to the terminological classification of any particular individual (other than a true kinsman) is therefore indeterminate and recourse to nongenealogical considerations is necessary in order to establish one designation from among the multiple possibilities. The general strategy which the Etoro employ is to maximize the number of sibling (and F/S) relationships with the members of "brother" lines and to maximize the number of cross-cousin (and MB) relationships with members of exchange groups. This general strategy is apparent in the distribution of a given ego's classificatory kinsmen among lineages presented in tables 33 and 34.[12] The two most important factors which enter into the resolution of the classificatory options which arise from genealogical indeterminancy are:

1. the type of relationship (sibling or exchange) between ego's and alter's respective lineages,
2. the state of reciprocity between exchange groups.

---

12. Tables 33 and 34 have been presented in order to illustrate the effect of lineality on kinship classification. The data on which these tables are based were collected for other purposes and do not exhaustively describe the distribution of classificatory kinsmen among lineages for this particular ego. A number of recently deceased individuals are included in the tabulations and many children are excluded. Data regarding the kin classifications applied to members of Masianifi, Owaibifi, and Nemisato are unavailable and these lineages are consequently omitted from both tables.

TABLE 33

Distribution of Classificatory Kinsmen among Lineages for One Individual Ego of Nagefi Lineage

| Lineage | Brother Lines | | | | Exchange Lines | | | | | | Both | |
	Nado (F)	Giãpu (MH)	Neto (B)	Mano (S)	Nebabo (MB)	Sago (MBS)	Nesago (FZS)	Nemano (ZS)	Nebase (WB/ZH)	Nesuã (DH)	Naua/Aua	Total
Major brother lines												
Turusato	6		12	1							3	22
Alamafi	6										2	8
Salubisato	4		4									8
Kobifi	6		5	2								13
Gemisato	2		2								3	7
Haũasato	5						1				2	8
Subtotal	29		23	3			1				10	66
Partial brother lines												
Sarado	3	1	5	1	3		2	1			3	19
Poboleifi	1	1	3				1				7	13
Somosato	1		1								2	4
Subtotal	5	2	9	1	3		3	1			12	36
Major exchange groups												
Kaburusato							10	4	6		11	31
Ingiribisato			1	2			3	2	3	1	20	32
Haifi	2		1		4		5		2		2	16
Kiwa					1		7					8
Subtotal	2		2	2	5		25	6	11	1	33	87
Minor exchange groups*												
Tifanafi						1					2	3
Hilisato			1		1	2						4
Samadabe					4	2						6
Subtotal			1		5	5					2	13
Minor exchange groups†												
Kasayasato							2				1	3
Waysato	2		2								6	10
Kudulubisato		1					1				1	3
Subtotal	2	1	2				3				8	16
Grand total	38	3	37	6	13	5	32	7	11	1	65	218
Percentage of total	17.4	1.4	17.0	2.8	6.0	2.3	14.7	3.2	5.0	0.5	29.8	

*Recent unions with Nagefi.

†No unions with Nagefi in the last two generations.

TABLE 34

Distribution of Classificatory Kinswomen among Lineages for One Individual Ego of Nagefi Lineage

Lineage	Brother Lines				Exchange Lines					Both		Total
	Nawisi (FZ)	Nadifi (Z)	Mano (D)	Nibia (MBW)	Neme (M)	Nesago (FZD)	Nemano (ZD)	Nesaro (BW)	Nesuä (WM)	Naye	Aua	Total
Major brother lines												
Turusato	2	9	1									12
Alamafi	2	2										4
Salubisato	5	5										10
Kobifi	4	7	2									13
Gemisato	3	1										4
Haũasato	9	1										10
Subtotal	25	25	3									53
Partial brother lines												
Sarado	1	8		1	5	2				2		19*
Poboleifi		2				3				4		9
Somosato	2	1								1		4
Subtotal	3	11		1	5	5				7		32
Major exchange groups												
Kaburusato					6	2	5			1	3	17
Ingiribisato			1			1		1	2	5	3	13
Haifi					5	4		1	1	1	1	13
Kiwa					5	5						10
Subtotal			1		16	12	5	2	3	7	7	53
Minor exchange groups†												
Tifanafi					4							4
Hilisato					2							2
Samadabe					4							4
Subtotal					10							10
Minor exchange groups‡												
Kasayasato					1					1		2
Waysato						1				2	1	4
Kudulubisato							1			3		4
Subtotal					1	1	1			6	1	10
Grand total	28	36	4	1	32	18	5	3	3	20	8	158
Percentage of total	17.7	22.8	2.5	0.6	20.2	11.4	3.2	1.9	1.9	12.7	5.1	

*One additional woman of Sarado is called by the term for MB (*nebabo*).

†Recent unions with Nagefi.

‡No unions with Nagefi in the last two generations.

The allocation of particular women to the kinship categories which delineate prohibited and permitted unions frequently involves a selection among several classificatory designations according to these criteria. Thus, while prohibited and permitted unions are delineated in terms of kinship categories, recruitment to these categories is not purely genealogical. The same may be said of other terminological categories. *Sago* designates an individual to whom ego is obligated to provide a wife and may be either a MBS or a MBSS depending on the state of reciprocity.

The preceding discussion suggests that some of the important functions of classificatory kinship systems may pertain to the variable application of the terminology by individuals in different social situations. The relationship of kinship to social process is difficult to perceive when the analysis of a terminological system is limited to genealogical considerations alone and when the system itself, in its entirety, is taken to be a constant.

MARRIAGE RATES

Classificatory relationships between the members of lineages which exchange women can be traced in as many ways as there are prior marriages between these groups, and marital eligibility (in terms of kin category designations) is often contingent on a selective recognition of appropriate relationships. A potential spouse may be both "FZSD" and "MBD" so that a prospective union can be considered either incestuous or ideal depending on which of these relationships is acknowledged. Among major exchange groups— where this type of situation frequently occurs—the potential "MBD" classification is usually overlooked in order to facilitate the desired concentration of marriages. This is apparent from the data presented in table 35 which shows the multiple relationships between spouses in thirty-eight recent unions. Although 36.8 percent (14/38) of the wives could be classified as "MBD" on purely genealogical grounds, the Etoro acknowledge this relationship in only one instance, i.e., informants describe only one marriage (number 7 in table 35) as an incorrect "MBD" union.[13] This designation is based upon the principles of reciprocity discussed above; in the other thirteen cases the marriage is either part of a current exchange of women or follows a previous exchange (in that the wife is "FZD" or "FZSD" as well as "MBD"). A classificatory

---

13. The woman was also enticed to desert her original husband in this case so that the union was not approved or sanctioned by the wife-giver.

TABLE 35
Kin Relationships between Spouses in a Sample of Current Marriages

Case	FZSD	FFZD	FFZSD	ZSD	DD	MBSD	FMBD	FMBSD	FZD	MBD	B/Z-B/Z Exchange	B/Z-F/D Exchange	Unrelated
						Ego's Wife Related as His:							
1	x*							o†				x	
2	x					x							
3		x				x			x	x	x		
4		x				x			x	x	x		
5						x			x	x			x
6							x						x
7									x				
8									x	x			
9									x	x			
10	x												
11	x												
12	x					x							
13	x												
14	x		o			x							
15	x									x			
16	x									x			
17	x			x									x
18						x							
19				x	x	x							x
20								x					
21	x								x	x	x		
22	x								x	x	x		
23	o												
24	o									x			
25												x	x
26									x	x			
27							x		x	x			
28							x				x		
29							o	x		x			x
30							x						x
31		o				x		x					
32–38													7
Total number of relationships	14	3	1	2	1	5	7	5	9	14	5	8	8

Note: This sample includes the marriages of all zero generation men and women of eight lineages (Nagefi, Turusato, Salubisato, Sarado, Kaburusato, Ingiribisato, Haifi, and Katiefi). Unions of these zero generation egos with spouses in the plus one generation are included, as are unions with spouses of lineages other than those listed above. Zero generation men's and women's marriages that are not intratribal or do not represent women's first marriages are excluded. In all, the sample includes 62.3 percent (38/61) of all zero generation intratribal women's first marriages. The sample is representative with respect to the larger lineages (and probably for the society as a whole). The unions which are excluded are primarily those between the smallest descent groups. These declining patrilines generally do not maintain genealogies which are sufficiently complete at the upper levels to reveal the multiple kin relationships between spouses.

*x = classificatory relationship.

†o = true relationship.

194

matrilateral cross-cousin relationship is thus covertly acceptable in the context of current or ongoing exchange, but not when it represents a unidirectional flow of women in consecutive generations.

Twenty-one percent (8/38) of the spouses in the sample are not genealogically related through intermarriage between their respective lineages in the past two generations,[14] while 79 percent (30/38) can trace at least one recent genealogical connection and typically two. More than half (17/30) of the related spouses are both patrilaterally and matrilaterally related[15] and the remainder are about equally divided (six to seven) in this respect. The sixty-one relationships which comprise the total are also very equally distributed (thirty to thirty-one) with regard to the laterality of the wife's genealogical connection to her husband. However, there are only three cases in which ego's wife is related solely through women received in the past (as "MBD," "MBSD," and "FMBSD") and the union is also not part of a current exchange. Few marriages are thus inconsistent with the ideal of balanced reciprocity over the long term. The equivalence of patrilateral and matrilateral connections between spouses is itself a result of previous reciprocity in exchange; the characteristic multiplicity of kin relationships is a product of the concentration of marriages between exchange groups.

Concentrating marriages is clearly considered more important than strict adherence to the rules which prohibit cross-cousin unions. Indeed these incorrect marriages succinctly illustrate the dual emphasis on reciprocity and concentration. In nine of the fourteen cases in which the wife is a classificatory cross-cousin, she is both "MBD" and "FZD"; in three additional cases she is simultaneously "MBD" and "FZSD." The co-occurrent relationships follow from prior sister exchanges and cross-generational B/Z-F/D exchanges (fig. 28), respectively. If the prohibition of "MBD" unions were strictly observed, intermarriage following both types of exchange would be delayed an additional generation. Disregarding this prohibition thus facilitates the intergenerational concentration of marriage.

---

14. One of these eight men traces a FFFZSSSD relationship to his wife and several others maintain that previous intermarriages with their wife's line have occurred in the +3 or +4 generation although the linking relatives are no longer recalled. Classificatory relationships traced through a "FZ" of a brother lineage are adduced in other cases.

15. A relationship which is established through women received by the husband's lineage in the past is referred to as matrilateral in this context, i.e., a matrilateral connection here includes those traced through "FM" as well as "M."

Etoro Social Structure

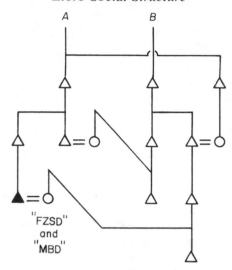

FIG. 28. Spouse Related as "FZSD" and "MBD" as a Consequence of Cross-Generational Exchange

Classificatory "MBD" unions are, concurrently, agnatic parallel unions which establish bonds of matrilateral siblingship (MBDS/MFZS) within the lineage.[16] Matrilateral cross-cousin unions are functional in this respect and serve the objective of concentrating marriages as well. The substantial frequency of this particular violation of marriage prohibitions is both understandable and expectable for these reasons. However, "MBD" marriage may also be disadvantageous in that it depletes the number of individual matrilateral sibling relationships between lineages; MBDS is an agnate rather than a member of a "brother" lineage. Similarly, an overly extensive concentration of marriages with only one or two exchange groups—at the expense of contracting marriages elsewhere —narrows the lineage's external base of support. In other words, the dispersion of both sibling and affinal bonds is decreased by matrilateral cross-cousin marriage. Whether this dispersion decreases to a dysfunctional level depends upon the frequency of such unions—and the prohibition has the effect of limiting this frequency. Both the prohibition of "MBD" marriage and the substantial but nevertheless limited violation of it are functional.

---

16. The spouse is usually of FBWBDaughter's or FFBSWBDaughter's lineage rather than a member of ego's true mother's lineage so that the matrilateral sibling relationship ("MBDS"/"MFZS") links FFBSons or more distant agnates (not F and S).

The incidence of "MBD" marriage is also influenced to some extent by demographic factors. The age differential between spouses affects the number of available mates of each genealogical type which are of marriageable age. Girls of ten traditionally married men ten years senior and women give birth to their first child at the age of twenty. A man is thus thirty years older than his first child and a woman twenty years older.[17] Kinswomen in ego's generation who are related through FZ and FFZ consequently tend to be older than those related through M and FM respectively. Since men marry younger women, matrilateral kin in ego's generation are more likely to be of the appropriate age than patrilateral kin. In short, classificatory MBDaughters and FMBSDaughters *of marriageable age* are more numerous than other kinswomen. Furthermore, the number of available mates affects the frequency of any given type of union.

The ages of various types of kin, relative to ego and to the appropriate age of ego's wife, are presented in table 36. The determination of these relative ages proceeds from the following assumptions:

1. Men and women are, respectively, thirty-seven and twenty-seven years older than their median child (who is assumed to be seven years older than the first child of a union).
2. Siblings are considered to be the same age (since they are equally likely to be either older or younger).

It is also assumed that the relative age of a true kinswoman is the mean age for classificatory kin of the same type (i.e., that the latter are equally likely to be either older or younger). Classificatory kin are presumed to be normally distributed around this mean with respect to age. The number of available mates of a particular classificatory kin type will then depend upon how closely the mean relative age of the type corresponds to the appropriate age for ego's spouse (which is ten years younger than ego).

The mean relative age for "MBD" and "FMBSD" is precisely ten years younger than ego while that for "FZSD" is twenty-seven years younger or seventeen years less than the ideal age. Classificatory MBDaughters of marriageable age should therefore be more numerous than "FZSDaughters." More specifically, only father's equal aged lineage sisters' elder sons' elder daughters will be of marriageable age for a median-age ego; only the youngest of a group of

---

17. The changes in these relative ages which are currently taking place do not affect the age distribution of the current adult generation's kinsmen included in table 35.

TABLE 36

Expected Age Differences between Ego and
Selected Potential Spouses

Type of Kinswoman (Delineated by Genealogical Relationship)		Mean Age Relative to Ego	Mean Age Relative to Appropriate Age for Ego's Spouse
	MBD	− 10	identical (0)
Matrilateral	FMBSD	− 10	identical (0)
kin	MBSD	− 47	− 37
	FMBD	+ 27	+ 37
	FZD	+ 10	+ 20
	FZSD	− 27	− 17
Patrilateral	FFZSD	+ 10	+ 20
kin	FFZD	+ 47	+ 57
	ZSD	− 64	− 54
	DD	− 64	− 54

same generation agnates will find the median-aged "FZSDaughters" (who are most numerous) to be of marriageable age. The eldest lineage members of a particular generation will generally find that nearly all their "FZSDaughters" are too young at the time they are seeking a first wife (although more of these kinswomen will be available should they later take a second wife). Comparatively, the age distribution of same generation agnates and that of their "MBDaughters" (and "FMBSDaughters") correspond perfectly when the ten-year age differential between spouses is taken into account.

The general point which I wish to make is that each man generally has many more "MBDaughters" of marriageable age than "FZSDaughters" and that some men have no appropriately aged "FZSDaughters" at all. (These conclusions are borne out by available genealogical data as well as by the model presented here.) The attainable frequency of the preferred union is thus less than 100 percent[18] while the prohibited match is nearly always possible.

───────────────

18. FZSD marriage becomes increasingly possible during a period when the age differential between spouses is expanding—and increasingly difficult in the following generation. If a man is twenty years older than the spouse he seeks, FZSDaughters are more readily available. However, the son of such a union will be thirty-seven years older than his FZSD, rather than twenty-seven. The son's MBD would be twenty years younger, as the mean age difference between ego and MBD is always the same as that between husband and wife. These prospective changes in mean relative age (and marriage possibilities) do not affect the incidence of FZSD relationships in table 35 as the women are nearly all over the age of twenty-one and were married before the age differential had increased. However, one might predict that the frequency of FZSD unions will increase in the next fifteen years and decrease thereafter.

This raises an interesting question, namely, is the frequency of each genealogical type of kin relationship between spouses a simple mathematical function of the number of available mates of that type? In general terms, this is indeed the case as table 37 indicates. The incidence of a particular type of kin relationship between spouses decreases as the mean relative age of the kin type increases (and an increase in the latter is commensurate with a decreasing number of available mates). However, a perfectly consistent covariation occurs only when several different kin types are grouped together on the basis of identical or nearly identical relative age and then divided by the number of types in each age grouping. The effects of ideological preferences and prohibitions are evident when individual kin relationships are singled out. There are an equal number of MBD and FZSD relationships between spouses (fourteen for each) even though there are more MBDaughters of marriageable age. The respective frequencies of MBD and FZSD unions may therefore be explained as the vectorial product of divergent demographic and ideological forces. Preference and prohibition alone would produce a preponderance of FZSD over MBD relationships while the number of available mates would, in itself, favor the opposite distribution. The equivalent frequencies represent a balance of these two forces.[19]

The relatively strong influence which number of available mates exerts on the frequencies of different types of unions is explicable in terms of the importance of exchange relationships between lineages. When one of a bachelor's major exchange groups contains a girl of the appropriate age, the young man's father is likely to be successful in arranging a future marriage. The exchange relationship between the two lineages often takes precedence over individual kin relationships which would otherwise pro-

---

19. The effect of numerical availability is modified by other factors as well. The incidence of "MBD" and "FMBSD" relationships should be equivalent, on the grounds of number of available mates alone, but there are fourteen of the former and only five of the latter. This difference is due to the fact that "MBD" marriages are also agnatic parallel unions while FMBSD marriages are not. Similarly, there are nine "FZD" relationships and only one "FFZSD" relationship although the mean relative age for both kinswomen is the same. The paucity of "FFZSD" relationships follows from the substantial frequency of preferred FZSD unions. When ego's F married his FZSD, then ego's FFZSD is his mother (or "mother's sister"). Under these circumstances, a "FFZSD" match entails a unidirectional flow of women.

TABLE 37

Numerical Distribution of Selected Genealogical Kin Relationships
between Spouses According to Expected Age Differences

	Kin Types			
	MBD FMBSD	FZSD FZD FFZSD	MBSD FMBD	ZSD DD FFZD
Mean age (in years) relative to the appropriate age for ego's spouse	identical (0)	± 17–20	± 37	± 54–57
Number of relationships of each type among recently married spouses*	19	24	12	6
Number of relationships divided by the number of kin types in each relative age grouping	19/2=9.5	24/3=8.0	12/2=6.0	6/3=2.0

*Data from table 35.

hibit the match. The incidence of each type of genealogical relationship between spouses will then be responsive to the numerical
availability of appropriately aged mates of that type, since availability itself is conducive to the occurrence of a union. In other
words, demographic factors come into play because lineage relationships are more important than individual kin relationships; the
significance of these demographic factors is a product of the larger
structure.

A classification of recent marriages (from table 35) according
to Etoro preferences in selecting among multiple kin relationships
between spouses is presented in table 38. By this classification 68.4
percent (26/38) of the unions are with genealogically related *aua*,
21.1 percent (8/38) with unrelated *aua*, 7.9 percent (3/38) with *nesago* ("FZD"), and 2.6 percent (1/38) with *neme* ("MBD"). Thirty-
two percent (12/38) of the total marriages are classified as FZSD
(*nesago iẽ mano*) unions. (In all, 36.8 percent [14/38] of the wives
are related as true or classificatory FZSD, but two of the latter are
also true FMBSD and FFZD respectively and the true relationship
takes precedence in the Etoro view.)

The thirty-eight recent marriages include four unions with unrelated women of partial brother lines and these account for half of the
unions with unrelated *aua* (the remainder involving potential exchange groups which are infrequently a source of wives). The conditions under which partial brother lines will contain unrelated

TABLE 38

Kin Relationship between Spouses According to Etoro Preferences
in Reckoning Relationships

	FZSD	FFZD	FFZSD	ZSD	DD	MBSD	FMBD	FMBSD	FZD	MBD	Unrelated	Total
True	2	1*	1	0	0	0	1	1*	0	0		6
Classificatory	10	2	0	1	0	2	3	2	3	1		24
Total	12	3	1	1	0	2	4	3	3	1	8	38
Percentage of total	31.6	7.9	2.6	2.6	0.0	5.3	10.5	7.9	7.9	2.6	21.1	

Note: True relationships preferred over classificatory, "FZSD" over all other classificatory relatives, and remainder in preference order from left to right.
*Also classificatory FZSD.

women have been discussed in chapter 4. Such unions do not violate any marriage rule, although they are usually disadvantageous because they establish matrilateral sibling relationships with members of major exchange groups in the following generation. Less than 20 percent (44/221) of all recorded intratribal unions (excluding widow remarriages) are within the de facto moiety, i.e., between "brother" lines (table 39). The three largest lineages (Sarado, Kaburusato, and Ingiribisato) are involved as either wife-givers or wife-takers in 61.4 percent (27/44) of these unions. Large lineages contain a proportionately greater number of individuals who are unrelated to some members of their brother patrilines because the percentage concentration of sibling relationships between two descent groups (following from parallel marriage) declines as lineage size increases. At the same time, these large lineages are frequently unable to secure a sufficient number of wives from their smaller major exchange groups and consequently seek wives from partial brother lines. Inasmuch as delayed reciprocity is tenuous in such instances, they frequently find it necessary to provide sisters or daughters in direct exchange in order to secure brides from these partial brother lines. These marriages within the moiety engender sibling relationships with some potential spouses of major exchange groups (in the following generation) and further reduce the supply of women available to the larger lineages. The dispersed wife-taking of the previous generation also reduces the degree of matrilateral consanguinity within the lineage so that the entire sequence of events establishes the preconditions for fission. The unions with partial brother lines are generally contracted

TABLE 39

Specification of Marriages by Lineage, Moiety, and Tribe

Man of: \ Woman of:	MOIETY I											MOIETY II												Total Intratribal	Percentage with Opposite Moiety	Extra-tribal Petamini	Extra-tribal Onanaf	Total Intra- and Extratribal	Percentage Extratribal
	Nagefi	Turusato	Alamafi	Salubisato	Kobifi	Gemisato	Hausato	Sarado	Poboleifi	Masianifi	Somosato	Kaburusato	Ingiribisato	Haifi	Tifanafi	Owaibifi	Katiefi	Hilisato	Samadabe	Kasayasato	Waysato	Kudulubisato	Nemisato						
MOIETY I																													
Nagefi			1										2	3	1		2	2	1				1	11	90.9	1		12	8.3
Turusato												2	2	4			1	1		2	1			17	100	1	1	19	10.5
Alamafi												2	1	1			4			1				9	88.9	1		10	10.0
Salubisato												2	1			1						1		5	60.0	1		6	16.7
Kobifi							1					1	2		1	1		1						11	90.9	1	1	13	15.4
Gemisato												1	3			1						1		9	77.8	1		10	10.0
Hauasato												1	1	1		1	1					1		7	100	1		8	12.5
Sarado					4							1	1	1	2		5	2				1		21	76.2	3		24	12.5
Poboleifi			1										1	2						2	1			9	55.6	1		10	10.0
Masianifi									1	1		1												3	100	1	1	5	40.0
Somosato								1				1									2	1		1	100			1	00.0
MOIETY II																													
Kaburusato	5	4	1	1			3			2	2	1	1											23	82.6	5		28	17.9
Ingiribisato	2	1	3	3	2	1	2	4	2	3														24	79.2	1		25	4.0
Haifi	4		1	1		2	2	4	1			2						1						17	76.5	4		21	19.0
Tifanafi	1				1		1																	2	100			2	00.0
Owaibifi																	1				1		1	2	00.0	1		3	33.3
Katiefi	1		1	2	2	1	4	1						1										13	100	4		17	23.5
Hilisato				2	2	1						1	1											7	42.9			7	00.0
Samadabe	1								1			1												2	50.0	1	2	5	60.0
Kasayasato	1			2		1	1			1		1												7	71.4	2		9	22.2
Waysato	1				1	1	1	1	4						1		1						1	15	60.0			15	00.0
Kudulubisato					1	1	1	1																4	100			4	00.0
Nemisato	1					1																		2	100		4	6	66.7
Extra-tribal																													
Petamini		1			1		3					4				1	1						3						
Onanaf		2			2															1	2		4						
																								221	80.1	27	12	260	15.0

Note: Although the number of recorded unions (260) is close to three times the number of extant unions (93), the data are probably no more than 75 percent complete. Marriages in the second ascending generation tend to be forgotten when the alliance has been reduplicated in the current generation. Genealogical revision also reduces the number of agnatic parallel marriages in the senior generation because the son's sons of lineage sisters married to different men are given as the descendants of a single individual. Both of these factors diminish the recorded

by only one segment of the lineage (which is unrelated to the wife-giver) and this segment subsequently splits off to form a new lineage. The emergent patriline becomes an exchange group of its former partial brother lines—and consequently a member of the opposite moiety—merely by continuing the pattern of intermarriage which initiated fission.[20] This reestablishes a balanced supply of women between exchange groups and between moieties. The recorded marriages within the moiety—primarily contracted by the three largest lineages—therefore represent essential processes of readjustment. These readjustments are easily effected because both lineage segments and moieties are defined in relation to exchange and the matrilateral siblingship relationships which follow from parallel marriage.

MARRIAGE RULES AND THE STRUCTURE OF INTERGROUP RELATIONS

Although Etoro moieties are predominantly exogamous they are not recognized as distinct social groups which regulate marriage. Most women of ego's moiety are ineligible as wives because they are his "Z," "FZ," or "D," but any woman of the moiety who is *aua* may be married. Marriageability is thus determined by kinship rather than moiety membership (and this also facilitates the processes of readjustment). Recognition of the moieties as exogamous, sociocentric groups which delineate marital eligibility is neither necessary nor necessarily functional. Indeed a formal conceptualization of these de facto units is inherently incompatible with the Omaha features of the kinship terminology which are instrumental in generating this division of the society into two largely exogamous groups of "brother" lines.

Conceptualization of the moieties as exogamous units involved in the regulation of marriage would entail the recognition of MBD marriage and such unions constitute classificatory mother-son incest since MBD is terminologically equated with mother. The acknowledgment of MBD marriage would be necessarily entailed because the moieties are based on kinship rather than descent. A group of "brother" lines constitutes a moiety by virtue of the fact that nearly all of the individual members of these lineages are sib-

---

20. The kinship terms applied by a Nagefi man to members of Sarado (table 34) anticipate impending fission and the emerging lineage's associated change from a sibling to an exchange relationship. One segment of Sarado (including three FBSons) married four women of Gemisato, a partial brother line, in the last generation.

lings to each other. By the same token, nearly all women of ego's generation and his mother's moiety are mother's brother's daughters, i.e., mother's matrilateral sibling's child. If they were not so related to ego's mother they would not be members of her moiety since the moieties themselves are defined by matrilateral sibling relationships. It would not be necessary to conceive of women of the opposite moiety as mother's classificatory kin (and hence ego's kin) if recruitment to moiety membership were based on descent, but this conception is logically entailed by the kin-based delineation of the moieties.

The Etoro resolve this potential difficulty by nonrecognition or denial of the existence of an opposite moiety. Each de facto moiety is cognizant of its own status, as a group of brother lines, but effectively ignores the comparable organization of the other half of the society. It may be recognized, in appropriate contexts, that some of ego's exchange groups are brothers to each other but a systematic appraisal of the entire range of sibling relationships between all non-brother lineages is never required. The logic of "by the same token" therefore does not apply and the fact that ego's spouse is usually his mother's matrilateral sibling's daughter is conveniently disregarded.

The relationship between the Omaha aspects of the kinship terminology and the de facto moieties is instrumental as well as contradictory. The de facto moieties are based on relations of matrilateral siblingship which are a product of the classificatory rule that every woman of mother's lineage, in her generation or adjacent generations, is equivalent to mother as a linking relative. The moieties themselves are thus a product of the classificatory rule (MBD = M) which, in the context of marriage, stands in a contradictory relation to a formal moiety organization. The Omaha features of the terminology could not be dropped in order to accommodate the MBD marriage which moiety recognition would entail inasmuch as the moieties would cease to exist in the absence of these terminological features. The moieties, as they are presently constituted, can exist without contradiction only insofar as they remain de facto units which have no recognized relevance to the regulation of marriage.[21]

---

21. The same dual relation of instrumentality and contradiction obtains with respect to the utility of MBD unions, as agnatic parallel marriages, and the Omaha features of the terminology. A MBD union can only create a matrilateral sibling relationship within the lineage when MBD is classified with mother (so that MBDS/MFZS are "brothers"). The utility of such unions is thus based on the same classificatory principle which renders them incestuous.

A model of exchange between two descent groups incorporating the Etoro preference for FZSD marriage is presented in figure 29. All marriages in the model are B/Z - F/D exchanges and every spouse is simultaneously FZSD, MBD, and FMBSD. (The potential ZD relationship is not recognized when the Z and D are involved in a direct or contemporary exchange.) If the sibling bonds in the diagram are taken to represent classificatory matrilateral sibling relationships, the model conforms to observed intermarriage between the exogamous de facto moieties. It also conforms to Etoro ideology in one important respect, namely, that ego's spouse may always be traced as a classificatory FZSD through father's matrilateral siblings. As mentioned previously, this relationship is frequently established after the marriage has taken place so that WF becomes FZS. This is consistent with ego's recognition of his own moiety as a group of brother lineages but does not entail recognition of the opposite moiety.

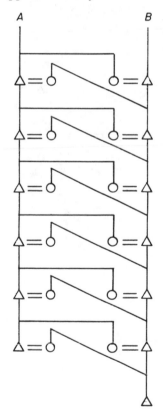

FIG. 29. A Model of FZSD Marriage with Two Descent Groups

If the sibling bonds in the diagram are taken to represent the relationship between lineage brothers and sisters, the model illustrates one of the modalities of intermarriage between exchange groups. Twenty-one percent (8/38) of the recent unions in table 35 are B/Z - F/D exchanges and 13 percent (5/38) of the wives are related as both FZSD and MBD, and 60.5 percent (23/38) as either FZSD, MBD, or both. These are the two most statistically prevalent relationships between spouses.

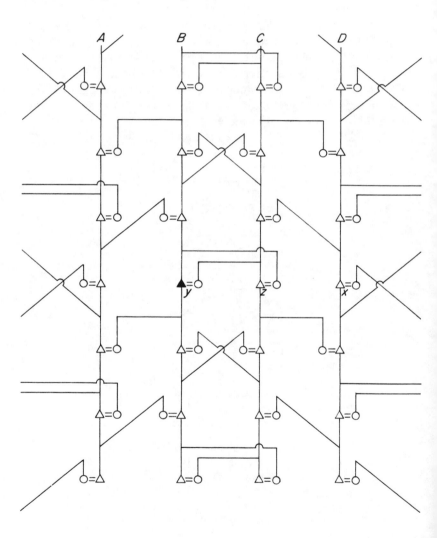

FIG. 30.   A Model of FZSD Marriage with Four Descent Groups

A model of exchange between four descent groups incorporating the preferred FZSD union is presented in figure 30. In this model every spouse is FZSD and also MBSD (and DD) or FMBD in every third generation—but never MBD. One third of the unions are sister exchanges and another third are daughter (F/D - F/D) exchanges. Each lineage intermarries with two other descent groups but contracts two-thirds of its marriages with one and only one-third with the other. Finally, each lineage is linked by matrilateral sibling bonds to the fourth patriline which is an exchange group of its exchange groups. Ego's MBDS and FMBDS are members of the fourth line in two out of three generations and of ego's line in the remaining generation. However, the male of this fourth line is either FMBDS or MBDH to ego in every generation. Descent groups A and C, and B and D are thus "brother" lineages, or at the societal level, may be taken to represent the de facto moieties based on matrilateral siblingship.

This model more nearly corresponds to each lineage's conception of its relationships to other lineages, the latter including both exchange groups (major and minor) and sibling groups. The model also illustrates several of the modalities of intermarriage between exchange groups not included in the previous formulation, e.g., sister and daughter exchange, FMBD, MBSD, and DD unions—all of which occur with limited frequency as the diagram indicates. (Marriage with MBD is excluded, as the Etoro prefer to believe, although this exclusion is at variance with empirical reality.)

The four-line model illustrates an important point concerning the manner in which each lineage's network of sibling and exchange relationships intersects with comparable networks of other lineages. Brideprice payments and witchcraft compensations are accumulated through donations by all bilateral kin and affines, including members of both sibling and exchange groups, and these payments are redistributed by the recipient to the same types of kin. Wealth items involved in these transactions may therefore be redistributed to the same lineages from which similar items were originally elicited. In the limiting case, a particular individual may be both donor and recipient in the two phases of a single transaction. Although the limiting case is an infrequent occurrence, it provides the simplest illustration of the structure of these transactions, which is the structure of generalized exchange. The man x (fig. 30) contributes a wealth item for brideprice to y (x's MBDS = B) who transfers the brideprice to z (y's WB), and z redistributes a portion of the payment to x (z's MB). The individual x is therefore brideprice donor and recipient to y and z, respectively (just as in generalized exchange he would be bride-giver and receiver) and the structure of the transaction is $x \rightarrow y \rightarrow z \rightarrow x$. ($x$ will not receive the same item he gave, although it may be an item of the same type.)

Sequences of this type are enjoined by the principles of matrilateral siblingship and the continuity of exchange relationships. Any two lineages (B and D) which consistently exchange women with the same third lineage (C) will be brothers to each other (as a consequence of parallel marriage) and bilateral kinsmen and affines of their mutual exchange group. Whenever one of the two brother lineages draws upon its matrilateral siblings in accumulating a payment to be made to its exchange group, and the latter redistributes the payment to affines, cross-cousins, and so forth, then the flow of goods will correspond to a cycle of generalized exchange. This is inherent in the definition of matrilateral siblingship by which a pair of lineages become brothers through their mutual exchange relation to a third lineage.

In actual cases the cycles are more complex than the limiting case described above and generally involve lineages rather than individuals, but the basic structure is nevertheless apparent. An example of a more complex sequence of brideprice accumulation and redistribution involving a marriage between lineages B and C (see fig. 30) would be:

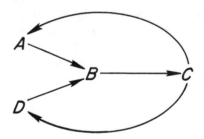

Here B receives contributions to brideprice from sibling line D and exchange group A, B transfers the brideprice to C, and C redistributes the payment to its sibling line A and exchange group D. Since each lineage generally has three major exchange groups and at least three major brother lines, a sequence based on a six-line system more nearly accounts for the total flow of valuables (with the exception of those accumulated from and redistributed to agnates). When *A*, *C*, and *E* are brother lineages and *B*, *D*, and *F* their exchange groups, the sequence is:

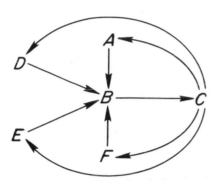

Both the two- and four-line models presented above have been constructed so as to conform to the preference for FZSD marriage and are adduced primarily to illustrate the concomitants of this form of marriage. It is important to note, however, that the complementary distribution of sibling and exchange relationships—which is largely a product of the kinship terminology and the principles of matrilateral siblingship—is independent of any specific preferred union. This complementarity determines the way in which each lineage's network of sibling and exchange relationships intersects with that of other lineages (such that one lineage's exchange group is another lineage's sibling line) and engenders a general structure of interlineage relationships within the tribe as a whole. Any preferred union which is consistent with the bilateral exchange of women and provides for the continuity of exchange relationships (as opposed to widely dispersed marriages) is compatible with this more general structure. Marriage with FZSD is not a determinant of the general structure but rather one of several modalities of exchange that are appropriate to it.

A model of the general structure of interlineage relationships is presented in figure 31. The model is constructed on a tribal scale and twenty patrilines are represented, this being roughly equivalent to the number in the tribe as a whole.[22] (The minimum number of lines is four, the maximum is indeterminate.)

This lattice structure is based on the principles of exchange and matrilateral siblingship and on the complementary distribution of these two basic forms of relationship. As mentioned previously, any form of marriage which ensures the continuous bilateral exchange of women is appropriate to the structure. Bilateral exchange is necessary so that brother relationships will be established through both parties to an exchange relationship (i.e., if B is a brother line of D via co-exchange with A, then A will be a brother line of C via co-exchange with B). This feature is essential to an overall complementary distribution of the two types of relationships. The marriage rules which are instrumental to this structure are:

1. The prohibition of MBD unions, particularly those which represent a unidirectional flow of women in consecutive generations. This ensures bilateral exchange (as does the more general emphasis on balanced and direct reciprocity).

2. The prohibition of all classificatory first-cousin unions. This provides that marriages are sufficiently dispersed so that each lineage has several exchange groups. (The general objective can be achieved even though this rule is frequently violated.)

3. The prohibition of unions with classificatory sisters. This very important rule, underwritten by the strongest negative sanctions, is necessary for the sociocentric properties of the structure to emerge. In the absence of such a rule each lineage's network of sibling and exchange relationships would not mesh with the networks of other lineages.

---

22. All adjacent groups, on a horizontal or vertical axis, are major exchange groups and any pair of lineages which exchange women with the same third descent group are brother lines. The four corner lineages each have two major exchange groups, those on the sides have three, and the interior lineages have four. These correspond to small, average, and larger lineages, respectively. The odd and even numbers represent the de facto moieties composed of groups of brother lineages. A large patriline, number eight for example, has four major exchange groups (3, 7, 9, and 13), four major brother lines (2, 4, 12, and 14) which are related as matrilateral siblings through two mutual exchange groups, and three minor brother lines (6, 10, and 18) related through a single mutual exchange group. A large lineage's brother lineages—related through major exchange groups alone—are therefore nearly coextensive with the de facto moiety.

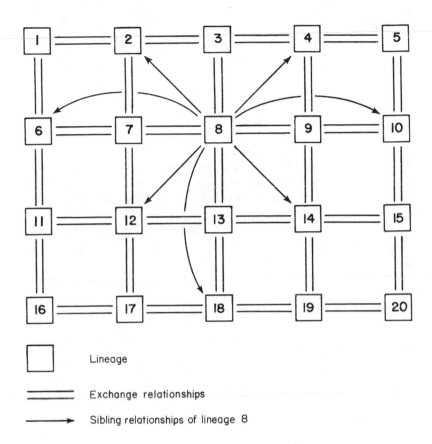

FIG. 31. A Model of the General Structure of Interlineage Relationships

4. The preference for marriage with genealogically related *aua* which engenders a concentration of marriages between exchange groups. This produces congruence in the matrilateral sibling relationships of lineage members so that brother relationships link lineages as units rather than individuals.

It may be noted in passing that this lattice structure makes intratribal conflict of any scale virtually impossible as almost all the potential allies of any given lineage will also be potential allies of an opposed lineage. (Lineages which are adjacent in the diagram are generally also fairly close together on the ground so that two patrilines with relatively discrete sets of allies are at opposite ends of the tribal territory.) Intratribal conflict therefore mobilizes many more mediators than participants. Bow and arrow fights occasionally occur between longhouse communities (over pig theft, women, witchcraft, etc.) but generally do not escalate and rarely last for more than a day or five days at most.[23] There are no enduring relations of hostility within the tribe. However, the entire tribe may be mobilized to fight the Kaluli, who are traditional enemies of the Etoro, since the two tribes almost never intermarry. The number of men drawn into an external conflict increases in relation to the casualties sustained. Several brothers will recruit their close agnates, affines, cross-cousins, and close matrilateral siblings for a raid. If any of these are killed or wounded, their affines, cross-cousins, etc., will join in. Three or four casualties sustained by members of lineages which occupy nonadjacent points in the overall structure are sufficient for total mobilization. Given the residential dispersion of lineages among longhouse communities, sufficient casualties may result from a single Kaluli raid. On one well-remembered occasion an Etoro force of over one hundred men carried out a retributive raid against the Kaluli in which they killed all the residents of a large longhouse community—probably about forty to fifty people—and returned to Etoro territory with the dismembered bodies while losing only one man in the encounter.

MARITAL PAYMENTS AND AFFINAL EXCHANGE

Having discussed marriage rules and rates and their relationship to the general structure of sibling and exchange relationships between lineages, we now turn to consideration of the marriage contract, the betrothal and brideprice payments by which it is sealed, the affinal relationships which follow from it, and subsequent exchanges between affines and cross-cousins.

Marriage negotiations involve little more than securing the girl's father's agreement to the union itself. There is a general

---

23. An individual is obligated to join his longhouse of residence in such a fight. Men related as agnates, affines, cross-cousins, or matrilateral siblings may find themselves on opposite sides. When this occurs, their participation will be unenthusiastic. Although a man may shoot at anyone other than close consanguineal kinsmen and affines, most wounds are sustained at the hands of relatively distant or unrelated individuals.

consensus within the tribe (at any particular point in time) concerning the appropriate size and composition of the brideprice payment and this issue is easily settled. The agreement to wed is formally concluded by a betrothal payment of one pig or one pearl shell. This initiates two separate sequences of transactions between the parties to the union: a series of reciprocal food exchanges and a nonreciprocal transfer of material goods (including brideprice) from the groom to his future wife's father.

During the betrothal period the young man presents several large packages of cooked sago grubs (prepared in sago) to his prospective wife's father and the latter counters with a perfectly equivalent return gift several months later. On another occasion, seventeen smoked marsupials are exchanged in the same manner. Equivalence is characteristic of affinal food exchanges which occur throughout the duration of the union. The premarital food exchanges are consistent with this and anticipate the affinal relationship (discussed more fully in a subsequent section of this chapter).

At irregular intervals the prospective groom also presents material gifts to his future wife's parents, none of which are reciprocated. No particular items are specified but all trade goods are considered appropriate. Most of the current gifts are of introduced items such as steel axes, bush knives, cloth, mirrors, matches, beads, salt and shillings. The trade beads, cloth, and steel tools have replaced traditional strung seed necklaces, bark cloth, and stone counterparts. Salt imported from Wabag was also given in the past but has similarly been replaced by trade-store salt. Long rolls of smoke-dried tobacco are one of the few traditional items that are still given. A barkcloth cape (or fabric counterpart) is presented to the bride's mother while the remaining gifts go to the bride's father. These gifts demonstrate the young man's generosity and industry (in pursuing trade) and serve as recommendations of his character, indicating that he will faithfully honor his obligations as an affinal relative.

The prospective husband generally brings some small gift whenever he visits his future wife's community, an infrequent occurrence. A man cannot speak directly to or touch his wife's parents so the presentation must be made through a third person, usually an age-mate who resides at the girl's longhouse. The young man also does not converse with his bride-to-be. He sits on one side of the communal section of the longhouse smoking and talking with his age-mates and WB while she sits on the other side whispering and giggling with her girl friends. After fifteen or twenty minutes of mutual embarrassment, the young man departs for his own community.

The girl's childish behavior communicates the idea that she is not yet prepared to wed. A more mature response to the prospective husband's visits, later in the betrothal, signals her readiness. A girl grows up with the expectation of marrying a particular man and does not think to question the arrangement itself. However, she may delay the event and will not normally be pressed into marriage before she is ready. The marriage of her age-mates and the inducement of adult status militate against protracted delays. Moreover, the transition to the status of wife is gradual in every respect so that a girl has little reason to postpone the union. Marriage does not entail the wife's separation from her family and close kin; a recently married girl will generally live with her parents and brothers whether she moves to her husband's community or is joined by him. The demands on her labor are no different after marriage than they were before. Girls help their mothers in gardening and sago production from an early age and assume a full work load as soon as they are physically capable of it.

A husband acquires exclusive rights of paternity and sexual access and rights to the domestic services of a woman through the payment of brideprice. However, a woman's brother retains a limited claim to her labor. He may, by custom, request that his sister assist in weeding his garden; she is obliged to do so and is entitled by her labor to a small share of the harvest. (An unmarried young man has more extensive claims on his married sister and may depend upon her for food and articles of manufacture such as net bags.)

A woman's relationship to her family and natal lineage is in many respects unchanged by marriage. A wife retains undiminished rights in the land of her natal line and may garden there as she wishes. (Indirectly, a man thus obtains unrestricted access to garden land in his wife's lineage territory through marriage.) A married woman also continues to look to her brother and close agnates as protectors of her welfare. Obligations toward a woman, outside the domestic sphere, are shared equally by her husband and brother. This division of obligations is particularly evident with regard to witchcraft. When a woman is named as a witch her husband and brother are each responsible for accumulating half of the required compensation. A woman's brother (and close agnates) therefore continue to be responsible for her after marriage and this responsibility is not limited to situations where the husband is derelict in fulfilling his obligations. The strength of the sibling bond is not diminished by marriage. A brother's obligations are not wholly transferred to the husband but are instead shared equally by both men.

Brideprice

There is a general consensus within the tribe concerning the appropriate size and composition of brideprice at any particular point in time. The standard for current betrothals is thirty-four items including five major valuables (typically one pig and four mother-of-pearl shell ornaments) and twenty-nine minor valuables (usually twenty-eight cowrie necklaces and one steel axe). The negotiated brideprice in five current betrothals is equivalent to the expressed standard in three cases and differs from this by only one major valuable more and less in the other two (i.e., six major and twenty-eight minor items or four major and thirty minor items). This represents a variation of only 5.4 percent in total value, calculated in cowrie string equivalents.[24]

Brideprice payments have undergone considerable inflation in recent years. The current standard, valued at 46.5 cowrie string equivalents, is approximately 90 percent more than the accepted brideprice payment about fifteen years before this study. At that time (ca. 1953) an appropriate brideprice consisted of seventeen items, including one pig, two pearl shells, and fourteen cowrie shell necklaces (equal to 24.5 cowrie strings). The composition of brideprice payments has also changed dramatically. Before 1953, mother-of-pearl shells were not included in brideprice or compensation and appear to have been entirely absent from the Etoro area. Marriage payments then consisted of pigs, cowrie strings, and stone axes. Stone axes have not been given for about ten to twelve years but were not replaced by steel axes until four or five years before this study. At an even earlier date, perhaps in the 1940s, dog teeth necklaces were the major wealth item in brideprice. These very substantial changes are probably due to disruption of trade networks following contact in other areas. (The Etoro simply say that dog teeth became unavailable and pearl shells eventually replaced them.) However, the amount contributed by the groom (approximately 50 percent) appears to have remained relatively constant in spite of these changes in the composition and amount of the payments. This suggests that the marriage payment is defined in relation to the general availability of wealth items—of whatever

---

24. Total value is here determined by reducing brideprice payments to cowrie string equivalents. One mother-of-pearl shell can be obtained for three to four cowrie shell necklaces (depending on the quality of each) in extratribal exchange and these major items are consequently valued at 3.5 cowrie strings.

sort—and is pegged at approximately twice as much as any single individual can acquire through inheritance and diligent trade.

The brideprice which is actually transferred at marriage is generally larger than the negotiated amount and corresponds to the standard for current betrothals. This means, in effect, that the groom tacitly agrees to give whatever is considered to be the appropriate amount at the time the union takes place. In the most recent union the prospective WF requested four cowrie strings in addition to the thirty-four items already promised and the groom quickly acquiesced after a pro forma protest.

Brideprice valuations also vary in accordance with the marital experience of the woman. Most widows are retained by the deceased husband's lineage through the levirate or are given to "brother" lines without payment of brideprice. When a widow is remarried for brideprice, the accepted amount is half that for a woman's first marriage. Adherence to this customary valuation is reflected in the fact that, until recently, the marriage payment included exactly half of a pig. There is greater variation in the amount of brideprice requested for a divorced woman since a divorcée is, by definition, a witch (see chapter 8). A woman who has been named as a witch on several occasions is sometimes given for the asking as it is believed that only a witch would knowingly marry a witch. Sister exchange does not have any effect on brideprice; the customary payments are made by both men just as they would be for any other union. (The two marriages are celebrated on different occasions, about four to six months apart.)

The brideprice contributions of various kinsmen and affines are presented in table 40.[25] The groom himself provides 48 percent of the marriage payment (in total value) and 73 percent of the major items. These are acquired through inheritance, witchcraft compensation paid at father's death, and by extratribal trade. Pigs, casso-

---

25. The sample includes the brideprice payments of men of five different lineages and the cases are equally divided between small and large patrilines. The unions span a period from 1950 to 1968, although most are post-1960. The number of items varies from eleven for the earliest case to thirty-eight for the most recent. Five men's second marriages are included and two of these involve divorcées. Fewer items are required in the latter cases and there are also fewer contributors in all men's second marriages as older men have more wealth items at their disposal. The contributions of ego and his true brother would be proportionately less if these cases were excluded; the average number of contributors would be about 11.5 rather than 9.5 (ego included).

waries, cassowary bone knives, hornbill beak ornaments, feathers, bows, arrows, sago, and tree oil are all traded to the Huli on expeditions that travel as far as Tari. Small cassowaries are the most valuable locally available item and can currently be exchanged for two pearl shells. Bamboo tubes of tree oil, obtained from the Onabasulu to the southeast, can also be traded for pearl shell ornaments. Both of these items are included in the brideprice of Highlands tribes.

The groom's true brother contributes more than any other

TABLE 40

Contributors to Brideprice

A Summary of Fourteen Cases

Relationship of Contributor to Groom	Number of Contributors	Percentage of Total: Number of Contributors	Number of Major Items	Percentage of Total: Major Items	Number of Minor Items	Percentage of Total: Minor Items	Combined Value of Major and Minor Items	Percentage of Total: Combined Value
Ego	14	10.6	33	73.3	92	33.6	207.5	48.1
True brother	13	9.8	3	6.7	29	10.6	39.5	9.2
Close agnates								
FB, BS	6	4.5	1	2.2	6	2.2	9.5	2.2
FBS	6	4.5	2	4.4	7	2.6	14.0	3.2
Subtotal	12	9.0	3	6.6	13	4.8	23.5	5.4
Distant agnates								
FFBS, FFBSS, etc.	15	11.4	1	2.2	20	7.3	23.5	5.4
Matrilateral siblings								
MZS, MBDS, etc.*	35	26.7	3	6.7	57	20.8	67.5	15.8
Patrilateral kin								
FZS, ZS	21	16.0	—	—	28	10.2	28.0	6.5
Matrilateral kin								
MB, MBS	14	10.6	1	2.2	22	8.0	25.5	5.9
Affines								
WB	1	0.8	1	2.2	—	—	3.5	0.8
ZH	7	5.3	—	—	13	4.8	13.0	3.0
Subtotal	8	6.1	1	2.2	13	4.8	16.5	3.8
Grand total	132	100	45	100	274	100	431.5	100

*Matrilateral "fathers" and "sons" are also included here, i.e., FMZS, MZSS.

single individual (father being deceased in all cases). Close agnates (other than brother) and distant agnates each give equal amounts (5.4 percent of total value) although there are generally many more of the latter than the former. However, most of the distant agnates who contribute to brideprice are also matrilateral siblings of the groom. Those who are not matrilaterally related provided only 2.4 percent of the total value of brideprice in these fourteen cases. This clearly documents the point that such kin are effectively outside ego's network of personal allies and supporters. Matrilateral siblings of other lineages also contribute 50 percent more (of the total value) than all agnates, excluding true brother, and comprise the largest single group of contributors (27 percent). Mother's brothers, sister's sons, and cross-cousins (true and classificatory) also provide a larger percentage of the total value of brideprice (12.4 percent) than do agnates (other than true brother). There are no significant differences between these matrilateral and patrilateral kin in the value of brideprice contributions. The contributions of affines are small due to the fact that only men taking a second wife have a WB at the time of marriage. If the groom has a ZH he is usually recently married and will have expended his valuables for his own brideprice. About 60 percent of the total value of brideprice not provided by ego himself is contributed by close consanguineal kin and immediate affines (e.g., true sister's husband). The Etoro emphasis on relations of siblingship, close consanguinity, and bilateral kinship is thus clearly evident in brideprice contributions.

The same range of kinsmen and affines who contribute to brideprice are recipients in the redistribution of marriage payments as the two transactions are linked. However, the order of these events is usually reversed due to the age differential at marriage. A man's sister will generally marry some years before he takes a wife. Those who receive valuables in the redistribution of ego's sister's brideprice are formally obligated to contribute to ego's marriage payment (whether ego or his father presides at the distribution). In those cases for which data are available, there is an 80 percent correspondence between recipients and contributors in these two linked transactions.[26] Nearly all the differences are due

---

26. Data on twelve brideprice and compensation transactions in which members of the same network were involved, covering a period of about twenty years, clearly demonstrate that sons succeed to their father's obligations and credits. Men frequently contribute to their ZSon's brideprice in their young son's name, so that obligations between cross-cousins are established.

to instances in which MB (FB, FZH or MZH) receives and MBS (FBS, FZS, or MZS) later contributes. These two transactions are quantitatively dissimilar in that ego himself retains only about 15 percent of the total value of his sister's brideprice although he provides nearly half of his own. The difference is largely accounted for by inflation. Ego receives as much in donations as he redistributes at the time of his sister's marriage but requires a larger marriage payment when he later weds. The increment is provided by his larger personal contribution. There are no significant differences between brideprice accumulation and redistribution in the proportional representation of various types of kin. The single exception is that affines are generally not represented since ego's ZH will not receive part of ego's sister's brideprice (and ego is typically unmarried and has no WB).

The cycles of generalized exchange which describe the flow of brideprice valuables between lineages (discussed earlier) are a product of the complementary distribution of sibling and exchange relationships and the fact that 60 percent of the participants in marriage payment transactions are members of these brother and exchange lines (and are about equally divided between the two).

The marriage payment is presented to the bride's father during the ceremony at which the union is celebrated. There is no specific marriage ceremony which is discrete from the Etoro ceremonial repertoire in general, although one of several standard performances may be occasioned by a marriage. Transactions pertaining to the union take place at intervals between the songs and dances which begin at about two in the afternoon and last until dawn the next day. All the kinsmen of both the bride and groom attend including members of each of their lineage's major brother and exchange groups and residents of both communities, one hundred fifty to two hundred people in all.[27] The ceremony is usually held at the longhouse where the groom resides (irrespective of whether or not he is an agnatic resident).

Marriage payments are nonreciprocal and there is no countergift of pigs or valuables associated with the transfer of brideprice. However, a reciprocal exchange of vegetable foods, consistent with the affinal relationship, takes place during the ceremony. The

---

27. When a ceremony was held at the longhouse where we resided, my wife and I were urged to play the roles appropriate to our status as residents of the host community which entailed taking part in the women's opening dances and the men's fighting force display. This is indicative of the fact that participation is not narrowly restricted.

gift and counter-gift are two perfectly equivalent three-foot high mounds of sweet potatoes and taro. The valuables which comprise the brideprice are displayed on top of the groom's vegetable heap. These are presented to the bride's father (or brother) who usually redistributes them at that time (although he may also do this later, at his own longhouse community). The groom's vegetables are then distributed among the bride's kin and the bride's vegetables among the groom's kin. The parties to the union and their kinsmen also partake of a communal meal of greens steamed in sago but do not share meat as this would be highly inappropriate.

At the conclusion of the ceremony (at dawn), the bride holds up a small piece of cooked marsupial. The groom dashes by her at full speed, snatches the piece of meat from her hand and disappears into the bush not to be seen again for several hours. This represents a symbolic consummation of the union[28] and, given the symbolism, it is not surprising that the communal wedding meal consists of vegetable foods. The Etoro associate eating meat with sexual intercourse (see the *Faitilo* myth presented in chapter 4) and sharing exchange pork with exogamy, "brother" relationships, and co-exchange. A pig which passes between individuals related by marriage cannot be given, by the recipient, to any third party to whom he is related by marriage (except, of course, his wife). A gift of pork from an affine or cross-cousin should only be eaten by "brothers" of the recipient who marry ("eat") women of the same exchange lines (and who share women through the levirate and widow-gift). Those who exchange women also exchange pork and do not partake of the same animal or the same group of women. In other words, only members of the same de facto moiety (and their wives) can share in the consumption of a pig involved in affinal gift exchange (or the marriage payment). (The rule is not affected by residence and does not apply to pork that is not given to affines.)

A man should make a payment of one pig or pearl shell to his wife's father or brother after the birth of his first child. The Etoro denote this transaction as "child payment–final payment" and regard it as the final installment of brideprice. The birth of a child makes the marriage contract irrevocable and jural divorce is not possible after this event. (A man who later decides his spouse is incompatible is advised to resolve the difficulty by taking a second

---

28. The physical consummation of the union traditionally did not take place until some years after the marriage ceremony. Currently, this may occur after about six months, now that girls marry when they are already physically mature.

wife.) The pearl shell given at the birth of a child is also a "final payment" in that there are no subsequent presentations of valuables to the child's mother's lineage (i.e., no illness, injury, or death compensation paid to matrilateral kin).

At this time a man will customarily begin to address his WF by the term for FZS (*nesago*). This change from affinal to consanguineal terminology marks an easing of formality and constraint. The affinal term for WF (and WM) is *nesuā* (reciprocal) and individuals to whom this is applied are treated with the utmost formality and respect. The relationship with WM (*udia nesuā* or female *nesuā*) is *tobi*; ego may not touch or speak directly to his mother-in-law. Her name cannot be mentioned in any circumstances, nor can the word for her name be used in other contexts. This relationship continues to be restrictive throughout the marriage (and the *nesuā* terminology is not changed). The same restrictions concerning physical contact and conversation apply to WF during the betrothal period, although they are adhered to somewhat less rigidly. A gradual reduction of formality follows in the early years of marriage. The change to cross-cousin terms initiates a relationship of equality.

The cross-cousin (*nesago*) relationship is quite the opposite of that with *nesuā*. The Etoro say that a cross-cousin is "just like a brother." This single statement is virtually a précis of Etoro social structure as it could be made only in a society that views the relationship between brothers in terms of consanguinity rather than descent. Cross-cousin terminology carries the implication of consanguinity which is the hallmark of solidarity in Etoro society. The *nesago* term is employed reciprocally between WF and DH (as it is between cross-cousins following a sister exchange) and connotes a relationship of equivalence and mutual support.

The betrothal payment, brideprice, and child payment (and the gifts given to a prospective wife's father) are the only customary transactions between the parties to a union that do not involve direct reciprocity in kind. These three payments are designated by the same term (*su*) which describes compensation payments of all types, including that paid to the surviving kin of a victim of witchcraft (or of a witch execution), compensation for personal injury, adultery, and accidentally killing someone's pig (in a deadfall trap). All nonreciprocal payments are regarded as compensatory in nature. Marriage payments indemnify the woman's family and kin for the loss of her domestic services and reproductive potential and validate the transfer of rights over the woman in the domestic sphere.

In the Etoro view, the marriage payments and the transfer of a woman in marriage do not represent complementary elements of a single transaction in which women move against goods but are rather two separate transactions, each of a quite different order. The exchange of women is governed by balanced reciprocity which can only be achieved by giving women in return for those received. Brideprice is irrelevant in this sphere. (The relations between affines are also placed on a footing of equality by this ideology; DH or ZH owes ego nothing other than women in future generations.) Marriage payments, on the other hand, are essentially compensatory and reciprocity is thus inappropriate to the nature of the transaction. The absence of any counter-gift, such as the "return pigs" given in Enga and other Highlands marriage exchanges (Meggitt, 1965:111), is consistent with this.

Affinal and Cross-Cousin Exchange

Affinal (and cross-cousin) exchanges are transactions of still another order which are distinct from both the exchange of women and marriage payments—neither of which create any outstanding obligations in the realm of material goods. However, affinal exchange is governed by the same principle which governs the exchange of women, namely, that reciprocity must be achieved by giving an item which is equivalent in every respect to that received. Grubs are thus exchanged for grubs, marsupials for marsupials, sweet potatoes for sweet potatoes, and after the union, pork for pork. These exchanges always involve food and parallel the exchange of women in this respect as well, given the symbolic association of eating and sexual intercourse previously discussed.

Affinal exchange and the exchanges which occur between cross-cousins are ideologically merged by the custom of applying the FZS term (*nesago*) to WF after marriage. The exchanges of pork which take place between these two types of relatives are not distinguished since the relatives themselves are equated. Both occur simultaneously and halves of the same pig may be presented to WB and FZS (or MBS) respectively. These exchanges involve classificatory as well as true cross-cousins so that gifts of pork may pass between the members of any two lineages linked by recent intermarriage. All co-resident agnates (and matrilateral siblings) share in the meat received by any one of them. Although the obligation to give is phrased in terms of individual kin and affinal relationships, the transactions serve to maintain amicable relations between lineages which customarily exchange women.

Ideally these presentations should be temporally coordinated so that pork is widely available in all the longhouse communities involved. Several members of one community will announce that they intend to discharge their obligations and some individuals of other communities will usually decide to kill pigs at the same time. A number of pigs will thus be slaughtered simultaneously at two or three different locations. However, neither individuals nor communities kill all their adult pigs on these occasions and there is no general slaughter of pigs within the tribe as a whole. Exchanges occur between the same longhouses at intervals of about twelve to eighteen months but different groups of communities stage these events at different times (generally during the *kahēo* season, however).

Etoro pigs are semidomesticated and spend most of their lives foraging in the bush unattended. They are generally approachable but sometimes cannot be located or captured at the specific time that they are required for affinal exchanges and this limits the scale of the pig killings which take place on these occasions. In one case nine men of four lineages, who resided at two different communities, announced that they would kill a total of thirteen pigs to give to their affines and cross-cousins. However, only six pigs were actually killed on this occasion, while six others eluded their owners. One pig was bashed on the head and presumed to be dead but later revived when it was placed on the coals in order to singe off its hair. It escaped into the bush and attempts to recapture it were unsuccessful. One of the pigs that was successfully slaughtered was not located until ten days after the others were killed.

The exchange of pork between affines and cross-cousins may be either immediate or delayed. On this particular occasion, four of the transactions involved immediate reciprocity, i.e., two men each gave their respective WB and "FZS" a side of pork and received an equivalent gift from him the next day. The return for the six other sides of pork and one complete pig was expected the following year. The relations between recipients and donors are shown below.

Recipient Related to Donor as:	Number of Transactions:
WB	3
ZH	1
WF	2
"FZS"	2
"MBS"	2
MB	1
Total	11

These exchanges ultimately involved the members of six lineages who resided at four different longhouse communities. The transactions are summarized according to lineage and local group in tables 41 and 42 and the genealogical relationships between the participants are diagramed in figure 32. Although various aspects of these transactions can be described in terms of the relationships between donors and recipients according to the criteria of individual kinship, descent group affiliation, and local group membership, the basic structure of affinal and cross-cousin exchanges can be clearly elucidated only by reference to the de facto moiety organization of the society as it is expressed in the dual organization of local groups. This dual organization is implicated by the rules governing pork consumption, particularly the specification that only "siblings" (i.e., members of the same moiety), and their wives, can partake of the same pig. It is considered desirable that pork be available to all the members of a community which kills pigs for distribution—the longhouse being a unit within which food is freely shared on a day to day basis. The celebration is less than ideal when half the local group is excluded. However, the general consumption of exchange pork within a community can only occur if there is a bilateral (and immediate) exchange between the resident members of each "moiety" (fig. 33), or a unidirectional flow of gifts between the dual segments of two local groups (fig. 34), or some permutation of these two pure types. The transactions within and between the two pig-killing longhouses in the particular case at hand incorporate elements of both these structural types (fig. 35) with an emphasis on bilateral exchange. (This emphasis is evident in two other unobserved series of exchanges, although all instances involve some unidirectional sequences.) Many of the presentations occurred within communities because the donors and recipients were co-resident affines. Three pigs were killed at each longhouse and each was in possession of two and one-half pigs following the exchanges.[29]

Sides of pork were also given to members of two communities

29. Figure 35 omits the two sides of pork given to members of communities which did not kill pigs and one prestation (from individual 10 to 4) based on an affinal relationship following from a marriage within the moiety. The latter is omitted only in order to avoid the confusion of listing Kaburusato lineage members as members of both moieties. It presents no particular problem for the Etoro. Both of the man's (4's) wives are of "brother" lines and his role in these exchanges is dictated by his affinal relationships.

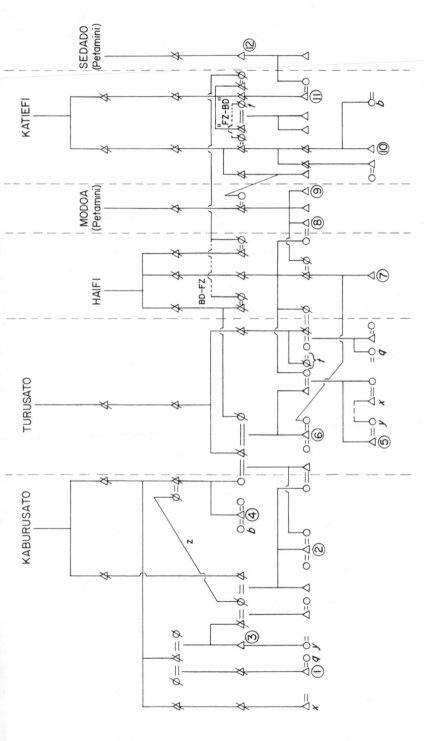

FIG. 32. Genealogical Relationships among Participants in an Exchange of Pork. *Note:* b, q, t, x, and y appear in diagram twice, once as lineal descendants and once as spouses.

Longhouse Community

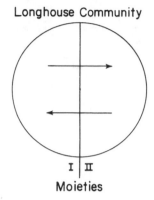

I | II
Moieties

FIG. 33.   Model of Bilateral Exchange of Pork

Longhouse Communities

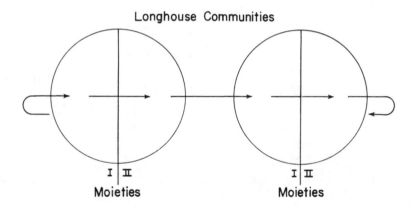

I | II   I | II
Moieties   Moieties

FIG. 34.   Model of Generalized Exchange of Pork

which did not kill pigs. However, in at least one of these cases,[30] all residents of the longhouse received a portion of pork from one source or another. The secondary redistribution of subdivided sides of pork among "siblings" reaffirms "brother" relationships in the same way that affinal gifts reaffirm exchange relationships. Thus, several men of Nagefi and Salubisato, residing at Kaburusato longhouse, were given cuts of pork by their "brothers" of Turu-

---

30. Data is unavailable concerning the redistribution of the side of pig given to a Sedado man as this community is of the Petamini tribe. It is also quite possible that pigs were slaughtered at Sedado and that a simultaneous series of exchanges occurred between communities of that tribe.

TABLE 41

Affinal and Cross-Cousin Exchanges at the Lineage Level

	Lineage Affiliation					
	Kaburusato	Turusato	Haifi	Modoa (Petamini Tribe)	Katiefi	Sedado (Petamini Tribe)
Individuals	2→→6→7→→9 1↓ 5 3↓ 4←				11→12 8←10	

Note: Numerals refer to individuals in the genealogical diagram, figure 32.
Each ⟶ indicates a gift of a side of pork.

sato. The side of pork presented by a Turusato man to his cross-cousin of Kaburusato was also shared by agnates and by several young men of Haifi residing at Kaburusato longhouse. These men of Haifi were thus included in the general distribution just as they would have been if they had resided with their agnate who participated in the affinal exchanges, the only difference being that they received Turusato pork from a matrilateral sibling rather than an agnate.

TABLE 42

Affinal and Cross-Cousin Exchanges at the Residential Level

	*Community of Residence**			
	Kaburusato	Turusato	Katiefi	Sedado
Individuals	1←	2→6←→7→9 3←5→11	11→12 10→8	12

Note: Numerals refer to individuals in the genealogical diagram, figure 32.
*Designated by lineage territory on which longhouse is located.

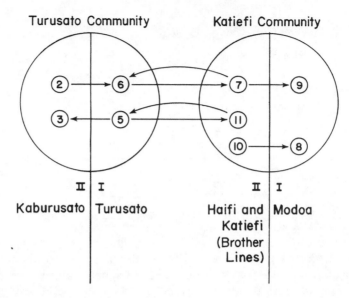

FIG. 35. Affinal and Cross-Cousin Exchange in Relation to the Dual Organization of Local Groups. *Note*: Arabic numerals refer to individuals in the genealogical diagram, figure 32.

CHAPTER 8

The Dissolution of Marriage and the Relational Effects of Widow Remarriage

The durability of the marriage bond takes on added significance in a social order in which interlineage relationships and position with respect to the moiety division are defined by the marriages each patriline contracts. The dissolution of a union, by death or divorce, severs a marriage tie which not only binds exchange groups but also constitutes the point of linkage through which external sibling relationships are traced. Etoro customs concerning divorce and widow remarriage both ensure marriage stability and provide a means for reestablishing those marriage ties which are particularly important in terms of both sibling and exchange relationships between lineages.

WIDOW REMARRIAGE

There is a very high incidence of both widowhood and remarriage among the Etoro. Marriages are of comparatively brief duration relative to the life expectancy of the surviving spouse—usually the wife. More than 70 percent of Etoro wives become widows during the course of their lifetime and almost all widows age forty-five and younger remarry. In short, widow remarriage is of statistical as well as structural significance. (A statistical description of widowhood and remarriage is presented in the Appendix.)

The Etoro employ three forms of widow remarriage: the levirate, the transfer of the widow to a "brother" line without payment of brideprice, and remarriage for brideprice. This multiplicity of

229

customary forms is concordant with the structural significance of affinal relationships and kin ties traced through women. Each type of widow remarriage has distinctive effects on several spheres of relationship; each serves different ends. The decision to employ a particular form of remarriage is also a decision to maintain, consolidate, extend, terminate, or redefine a specific relationship (or set of relationships). Insofar as the lineage has residual rights in a widow, this decision should serve lineage—rather than individual—objectives.

Widow remarriage impinges on five spheres of relationship (illustrated in figure 36):

1. Relations of matrilateral siblingship within the lineage.
2. The affinal relationship between the widow's natal and the deceased husband's patriline.
3. The affinal relationship between the widow's natal and second husband's patrilines.
4. The relationship (of siblingship or exchange) between the first and second husbands' patrilines.
5. The relationship of matrilateral siblingship between the deceased husband's and the widow's lineage sisters' sons' descent groups.

The effect of widow remarriage on each of these spheres of relationship depends on the form selected and on several additional factors, especially (a) whether the original union was part of a parallel marriage and therefore an important point of linkage in both internal and external relationships of matrilateral siblingship; (b) the presence or absence of children of the original union.

In the following pages, the effects of the three forms of widow remarriage on the five spheres of relationship will be discussed, taking into account the two factors noted above. Thirty-six cases will be analyzed in terms of the relation between form of remarriage and the characteristics of the original union (with respect to parallel marriage and offspring). This analysis will also provide a basis for evaluating both the extent to which lineage objectives are satisfied and the degree to which the lineage effectively exercises control over the disposition of widows. Most importantly, however, this chapter provides substantial documentation of the interpretation of Etoro social structure which has been presented thus far.

The levirate accounts for 47.2 percent (17/36) of all widow remarriage and the widow transfer for 30.6 percent (11/36). In 22.2 percent (8/36) of the cases the woman was remarried externally for

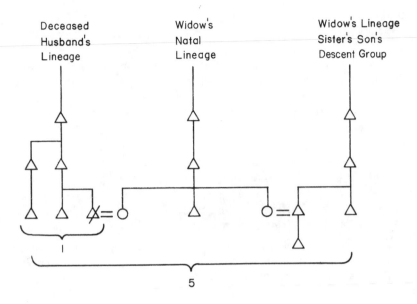

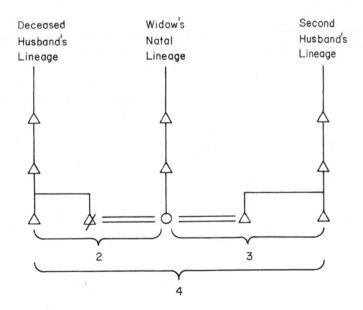

FIG. 36.   Five Spheres of Relationship Affected by Widow Remarriage

brideprice. The destination of a widow should be determined by the lineage membership with the deceased's true brother having a leading role in the decision. Although widows are frequently married by the deceased's true brother himself, the Etoro voice strong disapproval of such unions. The BW (*nesaro*) relationship is *tobi*, and a man cannot speak directly to or touch his true brother's wife during his brother's lifetime.

These prohibitions promote the solidarity of brothers by preventing social intercourse with BW which might lead to suspicions of adultery. If the BW relationship were not explicitly restricted by these taboos, sexual relations would be virtually enjoined by a logical extension of the behavioral rules governing other kin relationships. A man's ZH is culturally defined as an ideal homosexual partner. The logical implications of this for the BW relationship are unmistakable.

$$\frac{\text{cross-sex}}{\text{sibling's spouse}} : \frac{\text{homosexual}}{\text{relations}} :: \frac{\rule{2cm}{0.4pt}}{\rule{0pt}{1em}} : \frac{\text{heterosexual}}{\text{relations}}$$

sexual relations with a person of *same* sex	sexual relations with a person of *opposite* (cross) sex

The "blank" can only be filled by same-sex sibling's spouse—BW for a male ego. The relationship with BW is thus culturally restricted because it is logically enjoined. The prohibition is clearly a denial of the internal logic of this set of behavioral rules. On the other hand, the marriage of a widow to her deceased husband's true brother is concordant with this internal logic even though it is culturally disapproved. The extremely high frequency of this disapproved form of the levirate is partly related to this. This point will be taken up again in the conclusion in the context of a general discussion of structural contradiction.

Ideally, a widow should be given to an agnate other than true brother or to a nonlineage "brother" who is not a close consanguine (such as MZS). The function of this ideology is clear as the widow transfer extends external sibling ties while the remarriage of a widow to the deceased's FFBSS or FBS creates close consanguineal relations of matrilateral half-siblingship between FFFBSSSons or FFBSSons in the following generation. This approved form of the levirate also contributes to the development of congruence in the external sibling and exchange relationships of lineage members whose interests are not otherwise closely identified due to their relatively distant agnatic connection. Remarriage of a widow by the deceased's true brother is less effective in narrowing the consanguineal distance within the lineage as half-siblingship links individuals who are already FBSons. Congruence is established, but between individuals who normally act in concert in any event.

The ideal form of the levirate in which the widow passes to a FBS or FFBSS does not occur frequently in practice. In seventeen cases of the levirate the widow went to a true brother eleven times, to a FBS four times, and to a more distant agnate[1] only twice. The frequency of levirate remarriage with B, FBS, and FFBSS respectively is thus inversely proportional to the genealogical distance between the deceased husband and the second husband (fig. 37), or directly proportional to the degree of consanguinity.

Although all agnates share in the descent group's residual rights in the widow of a deceased lineage member, close agnates

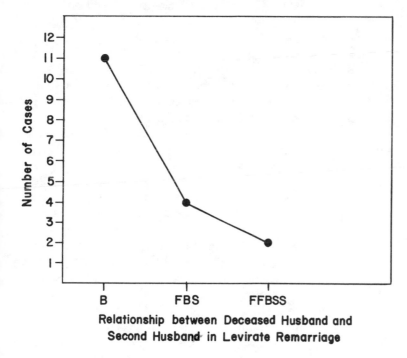

FIG. 37.   Frequency of Levirate Remarriage in Relation to Genealogical Distance between Deceased and Second Husbands

---

1. The two more distant agnates were FFBSS and FFBS. For convenience in exposition both cases will be referred to as FFBSS remarriage.

are more successful in actually obtaining those widows who are retained by the lineage through the levirate. (Two decisions are involved here, internal as opposed to external remarriage and the identity of the second husband.) In practice, then, the levirate operates more in accordance with *preexisting* consanguinity than with the ideal rules—which have the effect of creating closer consanguinity within the lineage when followed. The structural significance of close consanguineal ties between agnates is indicated both by the ideal rule, which has the effect of creating such ties, and by the actual cases, in which widows are awarded on the basis of extant genealogical distance.

The relatively low incidence of the approved FBS/FFBSS remarriage suggests that the development of congruence in the external relationships of distant agnates is but poorly achieved by the levirate as practiced. However, this conclusion is not borne out by a more detailed analysis which will be presented after additional factors are introduced.

Thus far, the levirate has been discussed primarily with regard to relationships internal to the deceased husband's lineage. However, the levirate also has an external aspect in that it reestablishes a defunct affinal relationship between the deceased husband's patriline and the woman's natal group. This affinal bond is not reestablished when a widow is given to a "brother" line or remarried for brideprice. The lineage's decision regarding the form of widow remarriage to be employed in the case of each particular woman is thus also a decision to resurrect some affinal bonds and not others.

The levirate is employed, selectively, to reconstitute marriage ties with major exchange groups. Widows of natal patrilines which are major wife-suppliers are nearly always retained by the deceased husband's lineage. Women obtained outside of these important exchange relationships are more likely to be transferred to "brother" lines or remarried for brideprice. The relationship between types of widow remarriage and the number of women of the widow's natal line married by men of the deceased husband's lineage is shown in table 43 and presented graphically in figure 38.

There are seventeen widows of agnatic parallel unions. Of these, 70.6 percent (12/17) were subject to the levirate, 23.5 percent (4/17) were transferred to "brother" lines, and 5.9 percent (1/17) were remarried for brideprice. (The frequency of these three forms of widow remarriage in all cases is 47.2 percent, 30.6 percent, and 22.2 percent respectively.) The levirate was practiced in 100 percent (8/8) of the cases in which the deceased husband's lineage had received three or four women from the widow's natal descent

TABLE 43

Frequency of Three Types of Widow Remarriage in Relation to
Extent of Agnatic Parallel Marriage

Number of In-Married Women of Widow's Line*	Number of Cases of Widow Remarriage		
	Levirate	Widow Transfer	Widow Remarriage for Brideprice
One	5	7	7
Two	4	4	1
Three	4	0	0
Four	4	0	0

*In the past two to three generations.

group. Comparatively, the widow was remarried externally in 73.7 percent (14/19) of the cases in which the widow's original marriage was not part of an agnatic parallel union.

Of the total sample of widows, those which have been retained by the lineage through the custom of the levirate are, in general, the structurally logical choices. Over 70 percent are the widows of agnatic parallel marriage and as such are particularly suited to

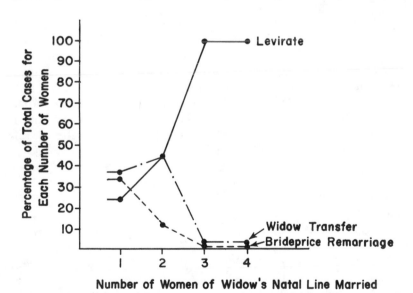

Number of Women of Widow's Natal Line Married
by Men of Deceased Husband's Lineage

FIG. 38. Percentage of Occurrence of Three Types of Widow Remarriage in Relation to Extent of Agnatic Parallel Marriage

fulfilling the functional objectives of the levirate with respect to both external and internal relationships. The levirate serves to re-establish affinal bonds which have been dissolved by death and the most important of such bonds—those with major exchange groups —have been largely reestablished. The levirate also serves to cre-ate close consanguineal relationships of matrilateral half-siblingship between agnates. Applying this form of widow remarriage in the case of those particular women whose original unions were part of agnatic parallel marriages enhances the degree of consanguineal consolidation effected. Two (or more) men who are MZS to each other will be matrilateral siblings to a third man whose father ob-tained one of the mother's sisters in the levirate (fig. 39). Further consolidation can be achieved by repeating this procedure when the second mother's sister is widowed. Finally, the levirate serves to promote the development of congruence and closure in the ex-ternal kin relationships of individual lineage members. Remarrying widows of agnatic parallel unions to agnates of the deceased hus-band produces the maximal congruence attainable through the levi-rate. Figure 39 illustrates how complete congruence may be achieved by applying the levirate to both widows of a single agnatic parallel marriage.

Widows whose original unions were parts of agnatic parallel marriages are not always retained through the levirate because these women can also be effectively deployed in widow transfers to "brother" lines. The Haũasato-Kobifi case discussed in chapter 4 illustrates this. The remarriage of one of a pair of lineage sisters generates multiple matrilateral sibling ties which may be positioned internally or externally according to the relational objectives of the deceased husband's lineage. The potential consolidation of rela-tionships which such a widow represents fails to be realized only if she is remarried for brideprice. Only one of seventeeen widows of agnatic parallel unions was given in this manner.

The decision to maintain a particular affinal relationship by employing the levirate is also affected by the presence or absence of offspring of the original union. Kin ties traced by (and through) the woman's children ensure the continuity of the relationship be-tween the two lineages irrespective of the affinal bond. The levirate is thus much more important when the widow is childless, as the affinal bond is then the only relationship between the two descent groups (stemming from that particular union).

On the other hand, the widow transfer can be effective in creating matrilateral half-sibling ties only when the woman has had children by her first husband. If there are no children, the transac-

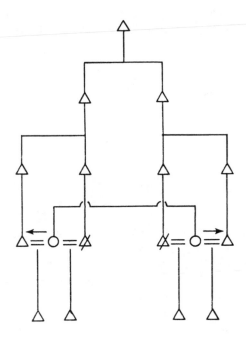

FIG. 39.   Consanguineal Consolidation and Congruence Achieved by the Leviratic Remarriage of Widows of Two Agnatic Parallel Unions

tion reaffirms siblingship in the generation in which it occurs but has little lasting effect. The transfer of a widow who has had children does not affect the widow-giver's kin relationship with the woman's natal line as these children continue to be members of their father's lineage. Such transfers merely fail to reestablish an affinal bond with the woman's natal group when this bond has already been supplanted by ties of kinship.

The type of widow remarriage in relation to the number of children a widow has borne by her deceased husband during the term of their union is shown in table 44 and presented graphically in figure 40.

There are thirteen cases in which childless women were widowed. In 61.5 percent (8/13) of these cases the affinal relationship between the deceased husband's and widow's natal patriline was reconstituted by the levirate, in 23.1 percent (3/13) the widow was remarried for brideprice, and in 15.4 percent (2/13) the widow was transferred to a "brother" line. Special circumstances were in-

TABLE 44

Frequency of Three Types of Widow Remarriage in Relation to
Number of Children by Deceased Husband

Number of Children by Deceased Husband	Number of Cases of Widow Remarriage			Total Cases
	Levirate	Widow Transfer	Brideprice Remarriage	
Zero	8	2	3	13
One	5	2	4	11
Two	2	2	0	4
Three	2	3	0	5
Four	0	1	1	2
Five	0	0	0	0
Six	0	1	0	1

volved in both of these transfers of childless widows. One of the
women was the widow of a man killed in warfare and was given to
an allied "brother" line in accordance with custom; the second
woman was part of a widow exchange between brother lines. In
81.8 percent (9/11) of all widow transfers the widow had one or
more children.

Figure 41 shows the distribution of cases of brideprice remarriage, the widow transfer, and the approved (FBS/FFBSS) and

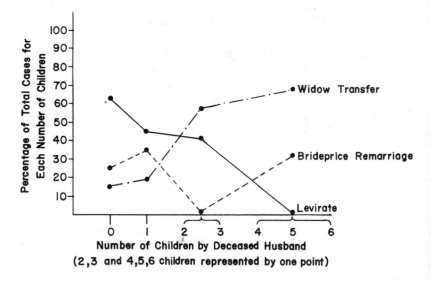

FIG. 40. Percentage of Occurrence of Three Types of Widow Remarriage
in Relation to Number of Children by Deceased Husband

disapproved (true brother) forms of the levirate in relation to two variables, namely (1) number of children by deceased husband, and (2) number of women of widow's natal line married by men of the deceased husband's lineage.

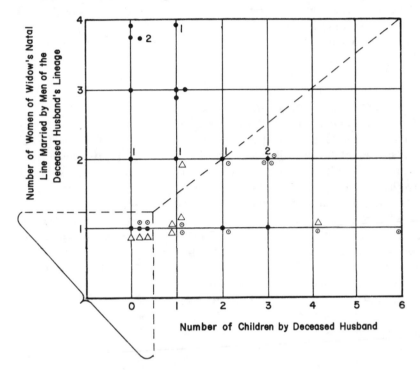

Types of Widow Remarriage

●	Levirate (to true B)
● I	Levirate (to FBS)
● 2	Levirate (to FFBSS)
⊚	Widow transfer
△	Brideprice remarriage

FIG. 41. Distribution of Three Types of Widow Remarriage in Relation to Number of Children and Extent of Agnatic Parallel Marriage

The data presented in figure 41 indicate that widows are generally deployed in accordance with lineage objectives (particularly with respect to external relationships) and that the corporate descent group's residual rights in the widows of deceased members are effectively exercised. There are five childless widows of agnatic parallel unions and all five were subject to the levirate. Marriage ties with major wife-suppliers are thus invariably reconstituted. This promotes the continuity of major exchange relationships both by maintaining the affinal bonds themselves and by providing a second opportunity for the woman to bear children and thus engender kin ties which will persist for some generations. The parallel marriages reestablished by the levirate also represent important points of linkage through which relationships to major "brother" lines are traced.

There are twelve widows of agnatic parallel unions who had borne children by their deceased husbands. Seven of these women were retained through the levirate, four were transferred to "brother" lines, and one was remarried for brideprice. The application of the levirate in these instances contributed to the internal consanguineal consolidation of the lineage and in most cases also increased the degree of congruence in the external relationships of individual lineage members. (The latter point is considered more fully in subsequent discussion.) The widow transfers served to renew, extend, and redefine sibling relationships between lineages in the manner described in chapter 4. The one brideprice remarriage did not further lineage objectives. However, this form of widow remarriage occurred in only 5.9 percent (1/17) of those cases in which the lineage as a group had important interests due to the involvement of agnatic parallel marriage.

There are eight childless widows of nonparallel unions. Three of the women were retained through the levirate, three were remarried externally for brideprice, and two were given to brother lines. Women in this category are not ideal candidates for the widow transfer although the transaction reaffirms siblingship in the generation in which it occurs. Other considerations (see pp. 237–38) were involved in both instances.

Applying the levirate in the case of childless widows of nonparallel unions reestablishes an affinal bond between two lineages, but the relationship that is maintained is generally not an important one.[2] The levirate remarriage of such widows does not contribute to congruence or consolidation of the lineage. It is significant in this respect that all three women went to a true brother of the deceased. (Although the relational effect of these cases is minimal, the lineage retains the labor resources and reproductive potential of the women.)

---

2. In two of the three cases the affinal bond was the only connection between the two lineages, as the widow's original marriage was the only union between them. In the third case one woman had also been given to the widow's natal descent group.

Childless widows of nonparallel unions may be remarried for brideprice without infringing upon the major sibling and exchange relationships of the lineage. The brideprice remarriage of such widows may also be employed to dissolve the affinal component of an ambiguous part-sibling, part-affinal relationship between the deceased husband's and widow's natal descent groups, or to redefine inconvenient sibling relationships with members of the lineage receiving the woman. In short, brideprice remarriage serves lineage objectives when applied to this category of widows. (Several instances will be discussed later in this chapter.)

There are eleven widows of nonparallel unions who had borne children by their deceased husbands. Such widows are well suited to the objectives of the widow transfer and five were remarried in this way. Two women were retained through the levirate. This reestablished unimportant affinal bonds that had already been supplanted by kin ties traced through the widow's children. Applying the levirate to women in this category contributes to the consanguineal consolidation of the lineage, but only marginally to the development of congruence in the external relationships of lineage members—since any congruence effected does not apply to major external relationships. As in the three preceding cases (involving childless widows of nonparallel unions retained through the levirate), both widows were remarried by a true brother of the deceased.

The four remaining widows in this category were remarried for brideprice. All four had daughters but no sons by their first husband and were therefore not ideal candidates for the widow transfer. These remarriages generally followed the pattern noted for brideprice remarriage of childless widows of nonparallel unions (to be elaborated more fully in a subsequent section of this chapter).

It is clear from the preceding summary of cases that the structurally appropriate form of widow remarriage is nearly always employed when important external sibling and exchange relationships of the lineage are involved, i.e., in the remarriage of widows of agnatic parallel unions. This may be taken as evidence that the corporate descent group's residual rights in the widows of deceased members are effectively exercised, particularly in those cases where lineage control over the disposition of the widow is most important.[3]

---

3. Evidence from cases of widow remarriage which occurred while I was in the field also supports this conclusion. There were two cases which I was able to observe and discuss with informants in some detail. One of these is discussed later in this chapter.

In addition, widow transfers and brideprice remarriage generally occur only when they serve the relational interests of the lineage. The widows selected for each of these forms of remarriage are usually appropriate, although not always ideal, candidates. Finally, there appears to be a tendency toward remarriage of a widow by the true brother of the deceased when there are no pressing requirements for alternate deployment of the woman. This raises the question of the effect of the levirate, as practiced, on the internal condition of the lineage (as opposed to its external relationships).

The relative effectiveness of the levirate in promoting the development of congruence and closure in the external relationships of individual lineage members may now be considered. It has already been noted that:

1. The particular widows selected for the levirate are predominantly (70.6 percent) widows of agnatic parallel marriage and as such are ideal candidates for increasing congruence.
2. In most cases, widows retained through the levirate pass to the true brother of the deceased; this adds to congruence between FBSons (in the next generation) but not between distant agnates.

The net effect of these two patterns is the creation of isolated, solidary lineage segments of close consanguineal kin with nearly congruent external relationships. This represents a divisive tendency which is clearly present, and one which also constitutes a process leading to fission. However, a consideration of the distribution of approved (FBS, FFBSS) and disapproved (true brother) forms of the levirate with respect to the characteristics of the particular widows involved (regarding parallel marriage and offspring) indicates considerable amelioration of this tendency. These distributional data are shown in figure 41 and presented in table 45.

Nearly half (5/11) of the disapproved true brother remarriages involved widows of nonparallel unions. These widows are not points of linkage through which important external relationships of matrilateral siblingship are traced; the internal extension of half-sibling relationships to distant agnates (of the following generation) by FBS/FFBSS remarriage would therefore not make a significant contribution to the development of congruence and closure within the lineage. No half-sibling relationships could be established in the three (of these five) cases in which the widow had no children by her deceased husband. In short, widows of nonparallel marriages have little potentiality for augmenting congruence and those who are also

TABLE 45

Approved and Disapproved Forms of the Levirate in Relation to
Characteristics of the Widow's Original Union

*Number of Women of Widow's Natal Line Married by Men
of Deceased Husband's Line*

Type of Levirate	1 (Nonparallel Unions)		2 (Parallel Unions)		3 (Parallel Unions)		4 (Parallel Unions)	
	childless	with children	childless	with children	childless	with children	childless	with children
Number of cases								
Disapproved form								
True brother levirate	3	2	0	0	1	3	2	0
Approved form								
FBS, FFBSS levirate	0	0	1	3	0	0	1	1
Total cases	3	2	1	3	1	3	3	1

Note: The distribution of cases of true brother and FBS/FFBSS levirate is presented in relation to number of women of widow's natal line married by men of the deceased husband's lineage subdivided into childless women and women with children by the deceased husband.

243

childless have no such potentiality. The FBS/FFBSS levirate would not serve any useful purpose under these circumstances.

The remarriage of a widow who is one of a pair of women from the same natal patriline impinges on important relational interests of the lineage as a whole. The two women represent points of linkage through which major external relationships are traced, while internal‑ congruence in tracing these relationships is less than complete. There are four cases of this type and in all four the widow went to a FBS or FFBSS. In three of these cases the widow had children by the deceased husband so that congruence in the external relationships of distant agnates (FFBSSons and FFFBSSSons) of the following generation was established.

There are eight cases involving widows of multiple agnatic parallel marriage (three or four women received from the same natal line) and in four of these cases the widow had borne children by her deceased husband. Only one of the four widows went to a FBS or FFBSS. The further development of already emergent solidary segments is evident in the other three instances involving true brother remarriage, as the brother who received the widow was already married to her lineage sister or true sister. Two of these widows were themselves sisters married to the same man and subsequently passed to his brother, already married to their lineage sister. These women were also part of a sister exchange involving the two brothers' true sister. This instructive case of segment isolation is diagramed in figure 42.

There is a total of seven cases of the levirate involving widows of agnatic parallel unions who had children by their deceased husbands. In four instances the widow was given to a FBS or FFBSS and both congruence in the kin networks of distant agnates and the consanguineal consolidation of the lineage as a whole were promoted. In three cases divisive tendencies prevailed and isolated, solidary lineage segments increased their internal cohesiveness and autonomy by brother remarriage.[4] In all seven cases important external sibling and exchange relationships were maintained while only four of these were also conducive to the development of internal congruence. Thus, the corporate descent group's control over the disposition of widows is more effective in furthering external relational objectives than in promoting internal cohesion.

Although the FBS/FFBSS form of the levirate does not occur in every case where a widow's remarriage may potentially contri-

---

4. There are five additional cases of widows in this category. Four were transferred to "brother" lines and one was remarried for brideprice.

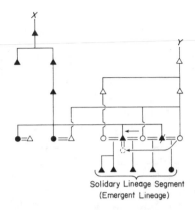

FIG. 42. Segment Isolation as a Consequence of the True Brother Form of the Levirate. *Note:* Members of lineage *X* are shaded.

bute to congruence in the kin networks of distant agnates, it occurs most frequently when this potentiality is present. While FBS/FFBSS remarriage accounts for only 35.3 percent (6/17) of all cases of the levirate, it occurred in 57.1 percent (4/7) of the cases in which lineage congruence was at issue (i.e., in cases of the levirate involving widows of agnatic parallel unions which produced offspring). Conversely, the true brother levirate was practiced in 64.7 percent (11/17) of all cases and in 80 percent (8/10) of the instances in which the remarriage of the woman would have little or no effect on congruence due to the absence of agnatic parallel marriage or of offspring of the deceased husband, or both (see table 46).

TABLE 46

Type of Levirate in Relation to Potentiality for the
Development of Congruence

Form of Levirate	Potentiality for the Development of Congruence in the Kin Networks of Distant Agnates		All Cases
	Present Number of Cases	*Absent* Number of Cases	
Widow remarried by FBS/FFBSS of the deceased	4	2	6
Widow remarried by true brother of the deceased	3	8	11
Total	7	10	17

In conclusion, the incidence of the two forms of the levirate may be seen as the vector of two opposed social forces: (1) the lineage members' attempt to assert the descent group's residual rights in the widows of deceased members and bring about a re-marriage which furthers lineage consolidation, and (2) the true brother's strong claim to the widow based on his close consanguineal relationship to the deceased. In more general terms, this is a contest of allegiance which pits the corporate agnatic descent group against the sibling group. The interplay of these two sets of allegiances is the dynamic of Etoro social life.

Brideprice Remarriage

The remarriage of a widow for brideprice is not a highly regarded form and the fact that it constitutes somewhat of a residual category with respect to the variables considered above is consistent with this. Those widows remarried for brideprice are often inappropriate candidates for widow transfers because they are childless, but need not be retained through the levirate due to the absence of parallel marriage. Thus, brideprice remarriage usually does not impinge on the lineage's objectives of maintaining affinal bonds with major wife-suppliers and consolidating "brother" relationships. This point can be amplified by a consideration of two additional characteristics that are typical of the widows remarried in this way.

1. The widow's original marriage is the only union between the deceased husband's line and the widow's natal line in six of eight cases (the first husband's patriline not only received only the widow, but also gave no women to her natal line in return).
2. The widow has no male children in seven of eight cases.

Both of these characteristics are present in five of eight cases.

The type of widow remarriage in relation to the number of male children a widow had borne by her deceased husband is shown in table 47 and presented graphically in figure 43. The relationship between types of widow remarriage and the number of unions between the widow's natal line and the deceased husband's lineage is shown in table 48 and graphed in figure 44. The distribution of the three types of widow remarriage in relation to both variables is shown in figure 45.

Widow transfers are most effective when the woman has male children by her first and second husbands as "brother" lines will then continue to be linked through the sons and sons' sons of true

TABLE 47

Frequency of Types of Widow Remarriage in Relation to Number of
Male Children by Deceased Husband

Number of Male Children by Deceased Husband	Number of Cases of Widow Remarriage			Total Cases
	Levirate	Widow Transfer	Brideprice Remarriage	
Zero	9	3	7	19
One	7	3	0	10
Two	1	3	0	4
Three	0	2	1	3

matrilateral half-siblings. Classificatory matrilateral siblingship can
be extended through these close consanguineal relationships in
generations following the transfer. A widow who has only daughters
is a less desirable candidate for the widow transfer because the
descendants of these daughters will not be of the deceased husband's lineage. Eight of eleven widows transferred to brother lines
have male children by their first husbands. Two widows were childless and only one had a daughter but no sons. Thus, 73 percent of the
widows given to brother lines have male children while only 47
percent (17/36) of all widows possess this characteristic.

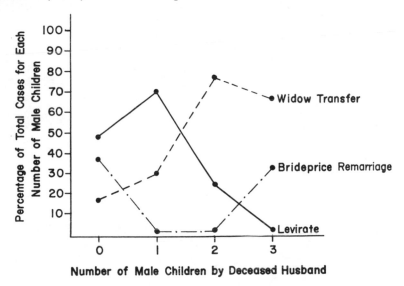

FIG. 43.   Percentage of Occurrence of Three Types of Widow Remarriage
in Relation to Number of Male Children by Deceased Husband

TABLE 48

Frequency of Types of Widow Remarriage in Relation to Extent of
Intermarriage between Widow's and Deceased Husband's Lineages

| Number of Unions* | Number of Cases of Widow Remarriage | | | Total Cases |
	Levirate	Widow Transfer	Brideprice Remarriage	
One	4	6	6	16
Two	2	2	0	4
Three	2	2	0	4
Four	5	1	2	8
Five	2	0	0	2
Six	2	0	0	2

*In the last two to three generations.

Widows remarried for brideprice lack male offspring in seven
of eight (87.5 percent) cases. This form of widow remarriage does
not conflict with the widow transfer as the women involved are
inappropriate candidates for such transfers.

The remarriage of a widow for brideprice does not create matrilateral sibling relationships between the first and second husbands' patrilines such as those that follow from the widow transfer.
A widow transferred to a "brother" line without payment of brideprice is given after the manner of the levirate and this defines the

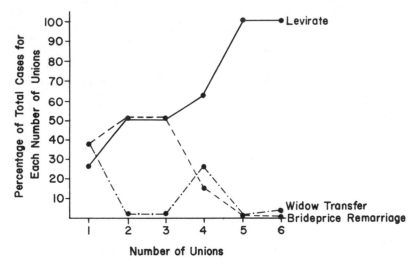

FIG. 44. Percentage of Occurrence of Types of Widow Remarriage in
Relation to Extent of Intermarriage between Widow's and Deceased Husband's Lineages

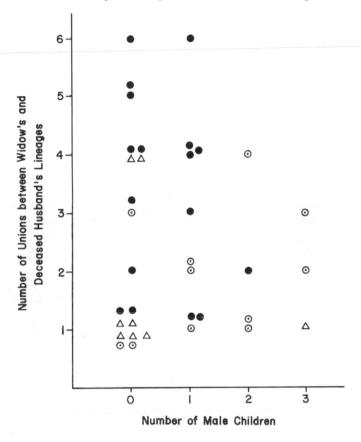

Number of Male Children

Types of Widow Remarriage

● Levirate

△ Brideprice remarriage

⊙ Widow transfer

FIG. 45. Distribution of Types of Widow Remarriage in Relation to Number of Male Children and Unions between Widow's and Deceased Husband's Lineages

relationship between the two lineages as one of brotherhood. The extension of classificatory sibling terms to the same generation agnates of matrilateral half-brothers is appropriate to the idiom of the transaction. However, the payment of brideprice for a widow is quite inappropriate to the Etoro conception of "brother" relationships and the brideprice transaction consequently defines the relation between the deceased and second husbands' lineages as one of exchange. Classificatory sibling terms are not extended. Although the true matrilateral half-siblings of the first and second husband will employ sibling terminology, the same generation agnates of these true kinsmen will not. Thus, any sibling ties arising from brideprice remarriage link individuals rather than lineages. Nevertheless, the inconsistency of these individual ties is one of the reasons that the Etoro disapprove of this form of widow remarriage.

The brideprice remarriage of a childless widow does not create any inconsistent individual sibling ties. When the widow has only female children by her first husband, the sibling relationships of these girls can conveniently be forgotten as soon as they marry. The selection of widows without male offspring (in seven of eight cases) thus largely eliminates the undesirable by-products of brideprice remarriage. It remains an unapproved form but not a deleterious one.

Those widows who are remarried for brideprice are not natally of important exchange groups. The widow's original marriage is typically the only union between the deceased husband's and widow's natal patrilines (six of eight cases). Although these widows could be retained through the levirate, there is no pressing requirement to do so. There is little advantage in reconstituting a defunct affinal bond which provides the basis for a relationship that is itself marginal and insignificant. In some cases, however, brideprice remarriage represents not only a failure to reestablish a relationship between the patrilines linked by the original union but also an attempt to redefine that relationship.

The brideprice remarriage of a childless widow whose original marriage is the only union between the deceased husband's and widow's natal patrilines has the effect of dissolving the relationship between these two descent groups. (The same effect can be achieved if the widow of a single union has only daughters by her first husband as the kin ties traced by a daughter can easily be ignored by her agnates.) The key element in the dissolution of the relationship between the two lineages linked by the original union is not the death of the husband but the remarriage of the widow for brideprice. The brideprice transaction severs the woman's affinal relation to her deceased husband's agnates as the latter act as wife-givers. The widow's husband's "brothers" (*nesaro*) are now the men of her second husband's lineage. Since the widow's HB ties to her first husband's lineage are severed, there can be no ZHB/BWB (*nebase*) relationship between her natal and first husband's patrilines. Such ties would persist if the widow remained unmarried—or if she were given to a "brother" line.

The widow transfer does not dissolve the relationship between the widow's natal and deceased husband's patrilines because the woman's first husband's agnates are her second husband's "brothers." The widow has husband's "brothers" of her second spouse in both lineages—since these lineages are themselves related as siblings. The widow's natal lineage thus maintains ZHB/ BWB (*nebase*) relationships to both her first and second husbands' patrilines. In transferring the widow to a "brother" line after the manner of the levirate, the deceased husband's agnates act as husband's brothers to the widow rather than as wife-givers. The maintenance of ZHB/BWB relationships is thus appropriate to the idiom of the transaction. (As noted previously, the widow's natal and deceased husband's lineages are also linked by kin ties traced through the sons of the woman by her first husband.)

Inasmuch as brideprice remarriage often has the effect of dissolving the relationship between the widow's natal and deceased husband's patrilines it is generally employed when this relationship is undesirable. In one case the widow's first husband was an agnate. After this incestuous union was dissolved by death the woman's natal lineage (also being her deceased husband's lineage) remarried her externally for brideprice. In a second instance the widow's deceased husband's lineage is nearly extinct. The only male member of the line is a childless middle-aged man and the relational effect of the remarriage is a moot point.

Three cases of brideprice remarriage involve the redefinition of relationships between the widow's natal and deceased husband's patrilines.[5] In two of these the original marriage was between partial brother lines and voiding these unions precluded the development (in the next generation) of inconvenient MZS ties between the deceased husband's lineage and its major wife-suppliers (see chapter 4, pp. 101–6). These widow remarriages also negated the affinal component of an ambiguous part-sibling, part-affinal relationship between the widow's natal and deceased husband's patrilines. In both instances the deceased husband was initially given in genealogies as a man who died before marriage and his daughter

---

5. In the three remaining cases there were other ties of kinship and/or affinity between the widow's natal and deceased husband's patrilines. However, two of these cases fulfilled other objectives as explained in subsequent discussion.

was listed as one of his brother's children. (There may be other cases of this type that I did not uncover.)

The remaining case involves recent fission of the woman's natal line. A multiple revision of relationships was achieved by this widow remarriage and a detailed exposition is in order.

Four true brothers of Kaburusato built a separate longhouse at Mamunapia, within Kaburusato's lineage territory, and took the name Mamunasato. Taking this name established both their status as a lineage and their claims, as a corporate descent group, to this land. This offshoot line subsequently moved en masse to the Petamini tribal territory to join affinal relatives, the wives of all four brothers being Petamini women.[6]

The widow in question (*b*) is the daughter of one of these four brothers of Mamunasato. She had been married to an Alamafi man before the fission of Kaburusato. This marriage is the only union between Alamafi and Mamunasato although there are two other unions between Alamafi and the main branch of Kaburusato. The exchange relationship between the latter patrilines is not affected by the remarriage of this widow for brideprice.

The brideprice remarriage of *b*, who is childless, terminated the affinal relationship between Alamafi and Mamunasato by mutual agreement. The woman herself was very much opposed to the proposed second marriage as her husband-to-be had been named as a witch on two previous occasions. She told her deceased husband's brother that she had much affection for him and wanted to be his wife but he refused her suggestion. She then ran away to her FBrothers in the Petamini territory and pleaded that she might stay with them. They promptly returned her to the custody of her deceased husband's brother. Shortly thereafter she became the wife of the witch, an Ingiribisato man.

Ingiribisato and Kaburusato are exogamous "brother" lines and the union thus initiates an exchange of women between Mamunasato and a lineage that was a major "brother" line prior to fission. Mamunasato will have claims to the son's daughters of their widowed sister and her second husband in subsequent generations. This is the first step in Mamunasato's switch to the opposite side of the moiety division. The transition will also be facilitated by the fact that Mamunasato's Petamini wives will engender no MZS ties to Etoro lineages.

---

6. It is expected that the Mamunasato lineage will eventually return. Its members have lived with the Petamini for twelve years.

Alamafi also redefined its relationship to some members of Ingiribisato by this widow remarriage. This may be most easily explained in relation to a diagram (fig. 46). The father (*a*) of the deceased husband (*e*) married a woman (*s*) of Sarado, a brother line of Alamafi. The two true sisters of *s* (*m* and *r*) married men of Ingiribisato. Alamafi thus has matrilateral sibling relationships to Ingiribisato. Indeed, the widow *b*'s second husband is a MZHBS (="MZS") and MZHB to the deceased husband (*e*).[7] Although the deceased husband and second husband were formerly "brothers," the brideprice transaction redefines this relationship. The second

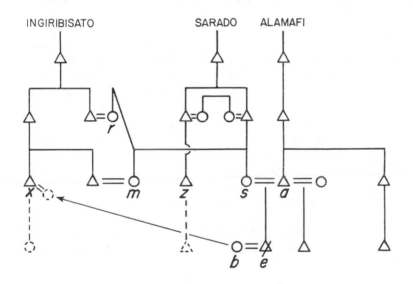

FIG. 46.   Genealogical Relationships between Individuals Involved in an Alamafi Widow's Remarriage for Brideprice

---

7. It is of interest that *z*, a "MB" of both the deceased husband (*e*) and second husband (*x*), played a major role in arranging this widow remarriage. The daughter of *x* will be a "FZSD" to *z*'s son and the preferred marriage is with FZSD. (The fact that MZSons have the same MB is an important link between them.)

husband (*x*) is now addressed by Alamafi men as *naua,* the kin category appropriate to unrelated individuals.

Alamafi and Ingiribisato are on opposite sides of the moiety division. Alamafi is an Etoroi lineage and Ingiribisato is one of the four major wife-suppliers to this group. However, these two patrilines have not intermarried as a consequence of the matrilateral sibling relationships between them following from Alamafi's (or *a*'s) past marriage to Sarado, its partial "brother" line. The remarriage of an Alamafi widow to an Ingiribisato "brother" for brideprice does not itself initiate an exchange but it negates the sibling relationship which has blocked intermarriage. If *a*'s marriage to *s* is forgotten, as seems likely, the sibling relationship will be completely erased.

The effects of this widow remarriage on several spheres of relationship may be summarized as follows:

1. The affinal (and exchange) relationship between the widow's natal and deceased husband's patrilines.
    a) The exchange relationship between Kaburusato (the widow's natal line prior to fission) and Alamafi (deceased husband's line) was unaffected.
    b) The affinal relationship between Mamunasato (the widow's natal line after fission) and Alamafi was terminated.
2. The relationship between the widow's natal and second husband's patrilines.
    a) The remarriage laid the groundwork for a future exchange relationship between Mamunasato and Ingiribisato which were formerly brother lines.
3. The relationship between the first and second husband's patrilines.
    a) The remarriage contributed to the negation of a partial sibling relationship between Alamafi and Ingiribisato, facilitating future intermarriage.

Widow remarriage for brideprice may thus be employed by the deceased husband's lineage to redefine relationships between (1) the widow's natal and deceased husband's lines, and/or (2) the deceased husband's and second husband's patrilines. The effect of the first type of redefinition is to negate the affinal component of an ambiguous part-sibling, part-affinal relationship and to prevent the emergence of inconvenient MZS ties traced through the widow's lineage "sisters." The second type redefines existing MZS ties (from previous generation unions) which block desired marriages to lineages of the opposite moiety. In the case previously discussed (and in two additional cases) former "MZSons" ("brothers") now address each other by the kin terms appropriate to the exchange of women. In all, six of eight cases of brideprice remarriage entail some redefinition of relationships; one case is immaterial due to imminent extinction of the deceased husband's lineage, and one involves the widow of an agnatic parallel union who had borne three sons by her deceased husband and who should have been retained through the levirate or transferred to a "brother" line.

Brideprice remarriage also creates a quasi-affinal relationship between the widow's natal and second husband's patrilines. (Men of the two lineages are related as WB/ZH but not as wife-giver/wife-receiver.) The second husband's lineage tacitly accepts this relationship in contracting the marriage, but the widow's natal line usually has no control over the location of this affinal tie since it has no voice in the disposition of its widowed sisters. Nevertheless, most of these affinal bonds are appropriate to existing relationships—six out of eight are between lineages of opposite moieties.

The effects of the several forms of widow remarriage on the five spheres of relationship are summarized in table 49.

DIVORCE

The dissolution of a union by divorce is a serious matter when marriage is both a transaction between descent groups and a point of linkage through which sibling and exchange relationships are traced. Etoro customs minimize both the incidence of divorce and the adverse relational effects.

The Etoro recognize two situations of marital separation which may be termed jural and de facto divorce. Jural divorce involves a bilateral agreement between the husband and the woman's agnates to terminate the union. Either brideprice is returned in full or the divorced woman is replaced by a lineage sister. However, jural divorce is considered to be inconceivable after a woman has borne a child.[8] Divorce may be initiated by the husband prior to this event, but only if his wife has been named as a witch (responsible for a death).

---

8. The birth of the first child cements the marriage contract. The husband should make a payment of one pearl shell to the wife's father or brother at this time. This transaction is denoted as "child payment–final payment" and is regarded as the final installment of the brideprice.

TABLE 49

Relational Effects of Widow Remarriage

Form of Widow Remarriage	Internal to Deceased Husband's Lineage	Between Widow's Natal and Deceased Husband's Patrilines	Between Widow's Natal and Second Husband's Patrilines	Between First and Second Husbands' Patrilines	Between Deceased Husband's and Widow's Lineage Sisters' Sons' Patrilines
True brother levirate	Promotes the development of isolated, solidary lineage segments of close consanguineal kin with nearly congruent external relationships (particularly in cases involving widows of agnatic parallel unions).	Affinal bonds are reconstituted; the continuity of major exchange relationships is promoted. If the widow is childless, the levirate also provides an additional opportunity for her to bear children and to establish enduring kin ties between the two lines.			Increases the number of individual ties of matrilateral siblingship between the two lineages.
FBS/FFBSS levirate	Creates close consanguineal relations of matrilateral siblingship between FFBSSons and FFFBSSSons in the following generation. Also contributes to the development of congruence in the external relationships of lineage members (particularly when widow's original union was part of an agnatic parallel marriage).	Same as above			Increases the number of individual ties of matrilateral siblingship between the two lineages, and extends these ties to new segments of the deceased husband's lineage.
Widow transfer	Contributes to congruence in the external relationships of lineage members.	ZHB/BWB relationships are maintained. Consanguineal kin ties between the two lineages are traced through the woman if she has had offspring by the deceased husband.	A ZH/ZHW relationship is created; consanguineal kin ties are traced through the woman.	Matrilateral sibling relationships are established, renewed, or extended (most effective when the widow has children by her first and second husbands).	"MZS" relationships are maintained, particularly if the widow has had children by her deceased husband.
Brideprice remarriage		ZHB/BWB relationships are terminated; kin ties between the two lines are not traced through the woman. Inconvenient, ambiguous affinal relationship may be obviated in this way.	A quasi-affinal relationship (ZH/WB but not wife-giver/wife-receiver) is created. Consanguineal kin ties are traced through the woman.	Wife-giver/wife-receiver relationship established. Partial sibling relationships may be negated. *Nawa* terminology is employed.	Classificatory MZS ties are not traced by the deceased husband's agnates. Classificatory matrilateral siblingship is thus terminated. (True MZS ties are traced by the widow's male children by her first husband, if any.)

A woman cannot initiate a jural divorce. De facto divorce refers to the situation in which a woman takes up residence with another man and bears a child by him. The birth of this child terminates the woman's jural union and confers a degree of legitimacy on her de facto union. Until this birth occurs, a woman continues to be regarded as the rightful wife of the man she has deserted.

The frequency of divorce in Etoro society is quite low (tables 50, 51, and 52) as a consequence of the narrowly restricted grounds for divorce and the strong sanctions against it. The Etoro do not recognize any situation in which a woman may legitimately divorce her husband; a man may secure a divorce only if his wife is childless and has also been named as a witch. A union is therefore susceptible to divorce only in the early years of marriage, and only under extraordinary circumstances. It is particularly important to note that these circumstances are supernatural rather than personal, and as such are beyond the control of either husband or wife. A man cannot name his wife as a witch (except on his deathbed). Thus, while the husband alone can initiate a jural divorce, he cannot personally establish the only culturally recognized grounds for dissolution of the union.

A divorced woman is by definition a witch and it is firmly believed that only a witch will marry a witch. A divorcée's prospects for a more favorable second union are consequently rather dim. This is to say that a woman might precipitate a jural divorce only at the cost of being named as a witch and subsequently married to one. The social disabilities of this position are enormous. Being named as a witch is not to be taken lightly inasmuch as the disadvantages include a reduced life expectancy. An individual who has once been accused of witchcraft tends to be named again and a person who is held responsible for three or four deaths is invariably executed.[9]

Although the culturally recognized grounds for divorce are

---

9. The social sanctions which restrict the frequency of divorce may also restrict the ethnographer's ability to record all instances. However, there are several reasons for believing that the reported figures (tables 50 and 51) are reasonably accurate. The number of women named as a witch (before bearing a child) is necessarily limited and not all of these childless witches are subsequently divorced. Of seventeen acknowledged female witches only four were reported to have been divorced (three of these being twice divorced). These seventeen witches represent about 10 percent (17/171) of the women in the sample (see Appendix, p. 299). A low rate is also indicated by the fact that there were no jural or de facto divorces during the fifteen months I was in the field.

TABLE 50

Cumulative Marital Experience among the Etoro

Category of Union		Frequency		
	Intratribal Unions	Etoro Man– Extratribal Woman Unions	Extratribal Man–Etoro Woman Unions	All Unions
Sample I: Women's first marriages				
Marriages terminated by:				
Death of one spouse	48	14	7	69
Jural divorce	3	0	1	4
De facto divorce	2	0	0	2
Extant marriages	65	20	8	93
Total marriages	118	34	16	168
Sample II: Women's second and subsequent marriages				
Marriages terminated by:				
Death of one spouse	7	3	1	11
Jural divorce	3	0	0	3
De facto divorce	0	0	0	0
Extant marriages	13	1	5	19
Total marriages	23	4	6	33
Total Sample: Women's first and subsequent marriages				
Marriages terminated by:				
Death of one spouse	55	17	8	80
Jural divorce	6	0	1	7
De facto divorce	2	0	0	2
Extant marriages	78	21	13	112
Total marriages	141	38	22	201

defined in terms of supernatural rather than personal characteristics, these supernatural characteristics (witchhood) are socially ascribed. The Etoro complex of beliefs and cultural rules concerning divorce makes the social body the arbiter of marital dissolution rather than the parties immediately concerned. The institution of divorce thus serves social rather than purely individual ends. Recently contracted marriages which create friction between affinally related descent groups tend to be dissolved. Such marriages are generally characterized by frequent incidents of domestic strife. When this occurs, the wife is likely to be named as a witch. A

TABLE 51

Divorce Rates among the Etoro

Category of Union	To All Marriages (Expressed in Percent)				To Terminated Marriages (Expressed in Percent)				To All Marriages Less Deaths* (Expressed in Percent)			
	(a)	(b)	(c)	(d)	(a)	(b)	(c)	(d)	(a)	(b)	(c)	(d)
Sample I: Women's first marriages												
Ratio of:												
Jural divorces	2.5	0	6.3	2.4	6.3	0	14.3	5.8	4.3	0	11.1	4.0
De facto divorces	1.7	0	0	1.2	4.2	0	0	2.9	2.9	0	0	2.0
All divorces	4.2	0	6.3	3.6	10.5	0	14.3	8.7	7.2	0	11.1	6.0
Sample II: Women's second and subsequent marriages												
Ratio of:												
Jural divorces	13.0	0	0	9.1	42.9	0	0	27.3	18.8	0	0	13.6
De facto divorces	0	0	0	0	0	0	0	0	0	0	0	0
All divorces	13.0	0	0	9.1	42.9	0	0	27.3	18.8	0	0	13.6
Total Sample: Women's first and subsequent marriages												
Ratio of:												
Jural divorces	4.3	0	4.5	3.5	10.9	0	12.5	8.8	7.0	0	7.1	5.8
De facto divorces	1.4	0	0	1.0	3.6	0	0	2.5	2.3	0	0	1.7
All divorces	5.7	0	4.5	4.5	14.5	0	12.5	11.3	9.3	0	7.1	7.5

Note: (a) = Intratribal unions; (b) = Unions consisting of Etoro man and extratribal woman; (c) = Unions consisting of extratribal man and Etoro woman; and (d) = All unions.

*Extant marriages and divorces.

TABLE 52

Number of Divorces Experienced by
Each Ever-Married, Living Woman

	Number of Times Divorced					*Total*
	Never	*Once*		*Twice*		
		Jural	De Facto	Jural	De Facto	
Number of women	165	1	2	3	0	171

woman who flagrantly violates the cultural norms which define a wife's role at the same time displays the attributes which are considered to be an outward sign of a witch's evil inner nature. This latter point is illustrated by the following story:

A man and his wife went to cut down a sago tree. They went to work sago because there were many people at the house. The woman was beating the sago when her child defecated on the ground. The woman said to her husband, as he watched her beating sago, "You pick it up and throw it away." Her husband, angry, returned to the house and complained to his brothers, "My wife told me to clean up her child's feces." His brothers replied, incredulously, "Your child defecated and she told *you* to clean it up?"

The man and his brothers cut firewood; they harvested tree-fern fronds; they heated stones. When the stones were heating, the man said, "I am going to tell my wife you shot a cassowary." The man went to the place where his wife was beating sago and told her, "They killed a cassowary. Your husband's brothers (*tisaro*) shot a cassowary." His wife exclaimed, "My husband's brothers! Hot shit!" and she prepared to return to the house. As they climbed to the house the woman cut some vine for string and put it in her net bag; she gathered cooking leaves and put them in her net bag; she harvested tree-fern fronds and put them in her net bag. Up at the house she exclaimed, "Husband's brothers! Hot shit![10] A cassowary! I brought some sago."

Suddenly the man and his brothers pushed the woman over into the stone-heating fire. She was burned all over. They burned her in the fire and killed her. They wrapped her in the sago she had worked, in the cooking leaves she herself had gathered, along with her own ferns

---

10. Etoro stories frequently employ this type of play on words. The translation here is nearly literal, the Etoro phrase being "recently deposited feces." Of particular importance here is the fact that the woman employs this crude expression in directly addressing her husband's brothers, who are *tobi,* and to whom she should not speak at all (except through intermediaries).

and tied it all up with her own string. After she was cooked in this way, they ate her.

The Etoro practice cannibalism but consume only the bodies of witches and enemies killed in intertribal warfare. It is therefore implicit in the preceding story that the vulgar, insensitive wife is indeed a witch. The woman's deviations from the culturally defined role of wife are the behavioral concomitants of this supernatural condition.[11] (The story also suggests how an ill-favored union may be terminated after a woman has borne a child.)

The Etoro rules concerning divorce provide a mechanism whereby incompatible, socially disruptive unions may be terminated in the early years of marriage while at the same time preventing easy access to divorce. Serious incompatibility and disruptiveness are not in themselves grounds for divorce but can be translated into a witchcraft accusation against the wife—the necessary precondition for dissolution of a (childless) union. The husband himself cannot lodge such an accusation and consequently cannot pass judgment on his own marriage. This rests largely with his close kinsmen.

Although a woman must be named as a witch to be divorceable, witchcraft accusations directed against recently married, childless women do not always lead to termination of the union. Whether or not a man chooses to divorce a wife under these circumstances depends not only on the relationship between husband and wife, but also on the relationship between the husband and the victim (also the accuser). One woman was named as the witch responsible for the death of her husband's FBW. The marriage continued. A few years later this woman was named as the witch responsible for her husband's true father's death and the union was then terminated. This second witchcraft accusation clearly reflects tensions between the woman and her husband's closest kin. In these circumstances a man's kinsmen may exert considerable pressure on him to secure a divorce, irrespective of his personal wishes. The case at hand is particularly instructive in this respect as the marriage was a love match (a rare event in Etoro society).

---

11. Another story deals with dereliction of responsibilities by a husband. A man refuses to share with his wife a marsupial he has caught. In retaliation, the woman kills him by witchcraft. However, the wife is then killed by her husband's brothers. Thus while an irresponsible husband may be bewitched, an irresponsible wife *is* a witch. The former is subject to supernatural punishment, the latter to death.

The second husband carried on an adulterous affair with the woman and married her after she was subsequently divorced by her first husband (as a witch).[12]

Although this divorce ended one affinal relationship, it had the effect of maintaining the exchange relationship. The woman's behavior and her witchcraft had become a source of friction between the two lines and the divorce was less disruptive than the continuation of the marriage would have been. In addition to the friction that had already been generated, it was quite likely that the woman would again be accused of witchcraft in connection with a death, and more than likely that she would be executed as a result. This case aptly illustrates the point that divorce serves social rather than individual ends.

In a jural divorce the husband is entitled to a full return of the brideprice. In some cases there is also a sororal replacement of the divorced woman. This sororal replacement may take one of two forms: a lineage sister of the divorcée may be given to the husband himself, or to one of his close agnates (B or FBS). In either case, the affinal relationship between the two lineages in reconstituted. (In both cases the original brideprice is returned to the husband so that a customary brideprice presentation may be included in the marriage ceremony at the time of the second union.)

Jural divorce is followed by sororal replacement when the original union is part of a major exchange relationship. The affinal bond was reestablished in all three cases in which there were three or more unions between the lineages of the divorced couple but not in the four cases in which there were only one or two unions between the two lineages.[13]

---

12. The tendency for a jurally divorced woman to be divorced a second time (table 52) is correlative of the tendency for a once-named witch to be named again.

13. The Etoro maintain that the sororate is also practiced when a young woman recently given in marriage dies without having borne a child. However, these circumstances apparently arise very infrequently, probably because the mortality rate for young women between the ages of ten and twenty is lower than that of any other segment of the population. In any event, informants were able to provide information on only a single case. In this instance, the sororate claims of the widower were rejected on the grounds that (1) all girls of the lineage of the deceased wife were already betrothed, and (2) the balance of exchange favored the husband's patriline by four to one. The position of the widower evoked the sympathy of his kinsmen and several individuals volunteered to contribute to brideprice for another marriage. A second union was arranged by the widower's FBSWZH (= "Brother").

A jurally divorced woman is made available for remarriage by her agnates. Inasmuch as it is believed that only a witch would be foolish enough to marry a witch, any man who offered for the divorcée would be automatically suspect. As a result, only a man who has already been named as a witch is likely to seek the hand of a divorced woman. The brideprice is generally reduced to about half that of the original union. In one of the cases in which the woman was twice divorced she was given away for the asking. All divorcées have remarried.

The remarriage of divorced women who have been named as witches is facilitated by the Etoro belief in the birth oracle which may disprove responsibility for a particular death. If the first child born to a witch (or his wife in the case of a man) is of the opposite sex from the person she (or he) is alleged to have killed by witchcraft, then the allegation is held to have been false and the compensation must be returned. A child of the same sex as the deceased confirms the witch's guilt. There is consequently a 50 percent chance that a divorced woman will later be absolved of the alleged witchcraft which led to her divorce.

De facto divorce refers to the situation in which a woman leaves her husband for another man and bears a child by him. This occurs very infrequently as there are very few men who are willing to undergo the risks and disabilities which this course of action entails. The rightful husband and her agnates will seek to reclaim the woman by force. In the event of a fight, the woman's consort cannot expect assistance from anyone save his closest kin. No Etoro community will serve as a refuge for the parties to an illicit match. In a society of less than four hundred people there is not a single longhouse that does not contain kinsmen of the aggrieved parties—the husband and the woman's agnates. The attachment can be maintained only if the couple resides outside of the tribal territory until the woman has borne a child. In one case the man and woman did not return until she had borne three children and then only following the death of her rightful husband. In the second case the woman ran off with a man of the Petamini tribe and never returned.

A situation which is in some ways quite similar to de facto divorce occurs when a young man elopes with a girl betrothed to another individual. Several instances of this provide additional information on the legitimization of a de facto union. No one will seek to reclaim the woman after she has borne a child. However, complete social recognition follows only if brideprice is paid and here the "husband" encounters a serious difficulty—almost no one will contribute to brideprice under these circumstances. In the single case in which brideprice was paid the husband accumulated the entire amount himself by many long trading expeditions. (He also single-handedly stood off the woman's betrothed and four of his supporters in an arrow duel at the time of the elopement, receiving several wounds in this encounter.) This man is highly respected. But most men are unable to accumulate an entire brideprice payment by themselves and are consequently subject to occasional snide allusions to their "thievery."

De facto divorce rarely occurs when a woman has had children by her jural husband. A single instance to the contrary involved exceptional circumstances. The woman was natally of the Mamunasato branch of Kaburusato. She was married to a man of Haũasato before the Mamunasato segment split off and formed a separate lineage. After Mamunasato migrated to the Petamini tribal territory she ran off with a man of that tribe and joined her agnates, taking her two small children with her. This action was possible only because it was supported (and perhaps contrived) by her natal line. Normally, a woman's agnates would see to it that she returned to her rightful husband. However, Mamunasato had no desire to maintain this particular affinal relationship after fission.

CHAPTER 9

Structure and Empirical Events

The objectives of this study are to provide a detailed ethnographic account of the main features of Etoro social organization and to explore the nature of structure and the relationship between structure and empirical events.[1] The questions I have examined in the preceding chapters are, to a large extent, those which are contained in and prompted by the data themselves—an inductive bias which I have found to be inherent in the ethnographic enterprise. However, these data are also particularly relevant to several major theoretical issues to which I now turn.

The central question concerns the relationship between structure (or models thereof) and empirical events; the characterization "loose structure" which has been applied to New Guinea societies embodies a regional variant of it. Resolution of this central issue depends, in my view, on the development of a theory of structural contradiction. However, this presupposes a reconsideration of the structural principles which have been employed in model construction—principles formulated so as to display the "functional consistency amongst the constituent parts of the social system" which Radcliffe-Brown (1952:43) enunciated as a sociological law. Specifically, it will be necessary to reconsider the relationship between siblingship and descent, principles which are contradictory rather than functionally consistent in many societal contexts. I will attempt to demonstrate that the essence of social structure is the

---

1. The term "event" (or "events") is herein employed to refer to empirical instances of social behavior, in a sense corresponding closely to the primary dictionary definition of the word (i.e., the fact of taking place, occurrence). My utilization of the phrase "structure and event" is to be understood in these terms and should not be confused with the specialized usage whereby "event" connotes incidents (of a historical nature) which are extrinsic and external to the structure but nevertheless impinge upon it.

organization of such contradictions and that contradictions are, moreover, empirically manifested in events.

SIBLINGSHIP AS A PRINCIPLE OF RELATIONSHIP

Etoro social structure is of particular interest in that it displays the operation of siblingship as a major principle of relationship in the politico-jural domain commensurate with, and functionally alternative to, the principle of descent. Although the sibling group has for some time been recognized as a structural *unit* in every society (Radcliffe-Brown, 1950:83), siblingship has generally not been regarded as an important principle of *relationship,* particularly at the group level. For Radcliffe-Brown, the structural significance of the "unity of the sibling group" turned on the fact that sibling equivalence provided a medium through which classificatory kin relationships were extended and thus formed the basis for wider structures of kinship. Fortes has expanded on Radcliffe-Brown's principle by pointing out that siblings are identified in the structure of the lineage, as well as within the familial domain, and that siblingship is consequently a lineage status in addition to being a familial one (Fortes, 1969:77). This is manifested in the substitutability of same-sex siblings in jural and ceremonial contexts. Siblingship here enters into the jural domain, but as a status (vis-à-vis third parties) rather than as a connective relationship. The direct relationship between siblings is conceived as one of moral equality consequent upon their common filiative status, and this is "reflected at the level of lineage structure in the segmentary organization of the lineage" (1969:77). Although one might well argue that such important features of segmentary organization as complementary opposition are based on siblingship rather than descent,[2] Fortes clearly does not here (or elsewhere) accord siblingship this organizing role. Rather it is only "reflected" in a structure which is based on, and organized by, the principle of descent. Indeed, British social anthropologists have consistently viewed siblingship in terms of unit rather than in terms of relationship. Fortes speaks of "corporate

---

2. Fortes himself makes the key point that equivalence can be expressed in terms of opposition, although he regards this as a paradox and fails to perceive the deeper significance of it. He states that "We can see that if sharing by equal division is a jurally enforceable rule, then fission, partition of patrimonial property, and, in the extreme case, dissension and dispersion might well be the paradoxical climax in the assertion of jural equivalence among siblings" (Fortes, 1969:78).

descent groups designed to contain the sibling group as a unitary element of its internal structure" (1969:78).

The connective dimension of siblingship is particularly evident in the mythologically specified "brother" relationships between Etoro patrilines. In these myths, the widow of one lineage's apical ancestor is selected as a wife by a totemic snake who thereby founds a second lineage through the progeny of this union. (The genealogical relationship between such patrilines is schematically illustrated in figure 47.) Although both lineages are composed of patrilineal descendants of the widow, she is not a member of either group by birth. The principle of patrilineal descent thus excludes the only ancestor these two lines have in common. Moreover, there is no form of descent which is consistent with both the internal structure of the lineage and its external relations.

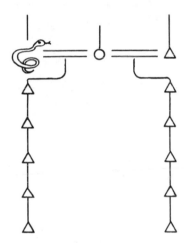

FIG. 47.   Genealogical Dimension of Mythologically Specified Brother Relationships between Lineages

The relationship between such pairs of lineages is of the same order as that between siblings both in cultural idiom and in sociological principle. The relationship is mediated by the apical female and is one of equivalence with respect to several dimensions which she symbolically represents. Most importantly, the woman represents an exchange group in common and this in turn entails equivalence with regard to wives, matrilateral filiation, and classificatory mothers. Equivalence in wives is expressed in the levirate and the widow transfer (of which this mythological female is the object) and these are indicative of siblingship, as is matrilateral co-filiation. The relationship involves co-exchange as well as co-filiation and cannot be reduced to the latter without distortion. This raises certain questions concerning the analytic definition of siblingship which will be considered shortly. Nevertheless, it is clear at present that such pairs of lineages stand in a relation of matrilateral half-siblingship and that they regard each other as "brother lines." Siblingship thus defines relationships in the politico-jural domain. More specifically, recruitment to the Etoro lineage is exclusively patrilineal[3] while alignment is based on siblingship (and exchange) rather than descent. This differentiation between descent as a principle of recruitment and siblingship as a principle of alignment has general applicability.

The recognition of siblingship as a principle of relationship (rather than merely a unitary element of structure) necessitates a redefinition of the term, and one that will effectively extract siblingship from the familial context which has heretofore served as its primary referent. This can be accomplished by drawing on the relational concept of transitivity (Feibleman and Friend, 1945:21). A relationship between two elements (X and Y) is transitive when it is contingent upon, and in this sense defined by, their respective relations to a third element (M). (Transitive relations are thus inherently indirect, being mediated by a third element.) I will be concerned with only one specific type of transitivity, that in which the relationship of each of the two elements (X and Y) to the mediator is identical. To be perfectly explicit, I am concerned with situations in which (1) the relation between X and Y is defined by the relation of X to M and of Y to M, respectively, and (2) X and Y are each related to M in the same way (i.e., $X:M::Y:M$). The elements X and Y are thus equivalent in the environment or context of this particular mediating term (by definition). However, the precise nature of the relationship of each element to M is neither specified nor significant to the resultant equivalence and is capable of total variation. For example, the elements X and Y could both stand in opposition to M, being linked through their identical opposition.

The nuclear sibling relation conforms to these specifications

---

3. Patrilineal descent is necessary but not sufficient for recruitment to lineage membership. This insufficiency does not alter the fact that Etoro lineages are of virtually pure agnatic pedigree (reaffiliation being rare to nonexistent) although it does mean that recruitment is more exclusive than patrilineal descent alone would require. It is also important to recall that patrilineal descent is the idiom of lineage definition as evidenced by the fact that genealogical revision recasts matrilateral consanguinity in patrilineal terms and reformulates kin relationships in terms of ancestry.

with respect to an extensive (but cross-culturally variable) range of mediating elements. Moreover, there are a number of additional relationships involving kin outside the nuclear family and also extending beyond the domain of genealogical kinship per se which similarly meet the specifications. Therein lies an important advantage in defining siblingship in terms of equivalent transitive relations: it allows one to perceive the operation of an abstract relational property in a number of diverse contexts without the reduction of an entire range of phenomena to one of its expressions. However, we may set aside these claims for the moment in order to register a more pragmatic consideration. In point of fact, it is not possible to define siblingship without invoking transitive relational properties. Fortes's summation of the general properties and defining characteristics of siblingship (1969:270) exemplifies this:

> . . . siblingship connotes common parentage, which, in terms of the calculus of filiation means co-filiation. Siblings have common filiative credentials, and this is what we subsume under the rubric of the equivalence of siblings. That this equivalence *inter se* in the familial domain is graduated by order of birth and modified in accordance with the values attached to difference of sex in a given society is well known. . . . Here it is more relevant to recollect, also, that siblings may be differentiated *inter se* by the calculus of filiation, as bilaterally co-filiate (full siblings), or unilaterally so (half siblings), as jurally assimilated (step-siblings), or incorporated (adoptive siblings).

To refer siblingship to "common parentage" is to say that the relation between any two siblings (X and Y) is mediated by their respective (equivalent) relations to a third element, the parental pair (M), i.e., to invoke a transitive relation. Other mediators of the nuclear sibling relation include all kinsmen to whom connection is established through this parental pair, and co-filiation thus similarly involves transitive relationship, or more precisely, an extensive series of such relations.

It is important to note that co-filiation does not exhaust the potential equivalence of siblings as there are additional elements which can mediate a transitive relation between them. Any two siblings of a set of three have a co-affinal relation to the spouse of the third, e.g., ZH for a pair of brothers. Under conditions of fraternal polyandry and sororal polygyny same-sex siblings have identical relations to their common spouse and to all their spouse's kin. Very similar results are achieved simultaneously when two brothers marry a pair of sisters (i.e., in true parallel marriage). The brothers have isomorphic relations to WF, WM, WB, WMB, etc., and the sisters likewise have isomorphic relations to HF, HM, HZ, HMB, etc. Brothers who marry into the same lineage will have classificatory WB (and other) relationships in common. Cross-sex siblings involved in a sister exchange will have spouse's parents in common, and their respective relationships to the latter may be equivalent in some respects although differentiated in others. In the Etoro case, brother and sister have analogous relationships of sexual partnership to the sister's spouse. These examples should suffice to illustrate that the equivalence of siblings is not restricted to filiative equivalence; siblings may have common affinal relatives in addition to their common filiative credentials. In other words, equivalent transitive relations may be mediated by affines as well as consanguineal kin. Moreover, at the unit level of organization "brother" relationships may be culturally specified through co-exchange as well as through common ancestry.

Analysis of siblingship as a relationship rather than a unitary element of structure clearly indicates that equivalent transitivity precisely describes the mode of connection. I would furthermore propose that siblingship may be recognized as the effective principle of organization whenever a relationship conforms to the specifications $X{:}M{::}Y{:}M$ irrespective of the nature of the three elements (X, Y, M). The principle of siblingship is thus applicable to the nuclear family relationship but is not defined by it. It should be noted that a relationship can never be adequately defined by the elements it relates, but only by the manner in which they are articulated. Identification of the elements which may enter into a particular type of relationship is a delineation of domain or sphere of operation. This is preeminently an empirical question, and not a matter of definition.

The idiom of siblingship may be defined, for any culture, by the sum of all relations which are phrased in terms of brotherhood and by the emergent properties and logical implications of this set taken as a whole. The idiom of siblingship is related to the principle in that culturally specified relations of "brotherhood" characteristically evidence equivalent transitive properties. This correspondence suggests that recognition of such properties may provide the basis on which brotherhood is imputed. The mediating terms may be genealogical but are by no means exclusively so, nor is the idiom of siblingship restricted to the sphere of genealogical kinship. Indeed the applicability of this hypothesis to nongenealogical brotherhood is particularly striking, and is exemplified by usages such as "brothers in Christ." It seems clear enough that the condition of brotherhood devolves upon an equivalent transitive relationship mediated by this religious figure. Similarly, the members of a Walbiri patrilineage assert that they are "brothers in spirit" as a consequence of the fact that each possesses elements of the totemic lodge spirit (or dreaming) which have been incorporated into his spiritual makeup through initiation (Meggitt, 1962:207, 213).[4]

The Etoro explain a terminological condition of matrilateral siblingship by reference to the fact that a pair of individuals have "mothers of the same lineage," i.e., by invoking an equivalent transitive relation. Such conditions of brotherhood can also be accounted for in terms of genealogically based terminological equations supplied (although not volunteered) by informants, i.e., M = MZ = MBD, etc., such that all women of mother's lineage are equivalent as linking relatives. I would suggest that both the Etoro formulation and the genealogical rules proceed from the same underlying principle of relationship, and that the condition of brotherhood which both explain or account for is imputed upon recognition of an equivalent transitive relationship.

Although culturally specified relations of brotherhood characteristically evidence equivalent transitive properties, the converse does not hold. The presence of such properties is not sufficient for the ascription of siblingship because an equivalent transitive relationship in the context of one mediating term may be asymmetrical and nonequivalent in other contexts. For example, the Etoro lineage and its associated *Sigisato* spirits are linked through their co-ownership of the lineage territory. Although the spirit group and agnatic group stand in an equivalent relation with respect to this territory, other aspects of their relationship are asymmetrical and the relationship is not phrased in terms of classificatory "brotherhood."[5] Nevertheless, it is important to recognize that the connec-

---

4. Both the applicability of the hypothesis advanced above and the analytical utility of the proposed principle of siblingship are particularly well illustrated in an analysis of the Fijian kinship system performed by a native Fijian, R. R. Nayacakalou. He states that, "When the principle of the unity of siblings [enunciated by Radcliffe-Brown] ceases to provide a workable basis for the classificatory principle it is supplemented by cold hard logic. Thus a man can be a classificatory brother to another man through a third man if they are both related to the third man in the same type of way. Thus if A is a classificatory father to B, and C is also a classificatory father to B, then A and C are classificatory brothers, even if no genealogical tie can be traced between them" (Nayacakalou, 1955:48).

5. The relationship is not phrased in terms of brotherhood in the literal sense, in that *Sigisatos* are not designated or described as "brothers" (or by any kin term). However, these spirits are helpful, protective, and beneficent toward lineage members and their behavior is thus consistent with that of a "brother."

tive bond between lineage and spirits is based on a commonality of
land ownership (rather than ancestry) and that siblingship is the
effective principle of organization. (This example is also intended
to illustrate the contention that an abstract definition of the principle of siblingship in terms of $X:M::Y:M$ allows one to perceive the
operation of it in diverse contexts.)

Recognition of siblingship as a major principle of relationship
will serve to disentangle several divergent concepts which have
been agglomerated under the rubric of descent—specifically, recruitment and alignment. The recruitment dimension is embodied
in Fortes's (1959:207) definition of descent as a relation between a
person and an ancestor which is mediated by a parent (a transitive
but asymmetrical relationship). In this definitional rendering, descent is a principle which confers entitlement to group membership. In addition, Fortes (1959:206) maintains that

> . . . any two or more persons whose pedigrees converge in a single
> common ancestor can be said to be linked by descent.

In this sense of the term, descent entails co-membership and is
fundamentally a principle of alignment or mobilization (equally applicable to both individuals and co-ordinate segments). However, it
would be more precise to specify the linkage between individuals
whose respective pedigrees converge on a single ancestor as one of
co-descent, i.e., as an equivalent transitive relationship mediated
by an ancestor. Thus, siblingship is the effective principle of organization[6] in the alignment aspect of descent (but not in recruitment). Siblingship is, moreover, the idiom of the relationship.

The mythologically stipulated "brother" relationships between
Etoro patrilineages clearly illustrate the structural separability of
recruitment and alignment principles. The pedigrees of the members of two patrilines converge in a single (putative) female ancestor who, by patrilineal recruitment, is not a member of either
group. Thus, one ancestor serves as the fixed point from which

---

6. To the best of my knowledge, brotherhood is universally imputed
among co-members of a descent group and among members of co-ordinate
segments. This is consistent with the hypothesis that recognition of
equivalent transitive relational properties provides the basis for the ascription of brotherhood. In the case of clans it would indeed be difficult to
argue that the classificatory siblingship is extended from the nuclear family
context along specified paths of genealogical connection inasmuch as such
connections are not known.

recruitment to membership is computed while his spouse is the axis of alignment. Comparatively, in segmentary lineage systems (as an ideal type) the ancestor of recruitment to primary segments is the son (or patrilineal descendant) of the ancestor of alignment. The Etoro differ in two respects: first, in the relationship between these two antecedent figures, and second, in that the equivalent (or symmetrical) relationships of co-aligned segments to their mutual point of attachment are relations of apical affinity rather than co-descent. In other words, siblingship is mediated by an exchange group. (In formal terms, $X:M::Y:M$ describes the relationship between aligned units [X and Y] in both cases. They differ with respect to the identity of M and consequently in the nature of the relationships of X and of Y to M.)

The significant point here is that a single relational property forms the basis of the relationship between nuclear siblings on one hand and between co-members of a descent group and between co-aligned segments on the other. Recruitment is based on a quite different relational property (asymmetrical transitivity), although a similar element (i.e., a lineal antecedent) appears in both sets of relational equations. To say that recruitment and alignment are based on the same principle (i.e., descent) is analogous to maintaining that $X-1$ and $X+1$ are both based on the same principle because both include the element X.

The agglomeration of divergent types of relationships under a single rubric invests social systems with a high degree of functional consistency among their constituent parts inasmuch as several organizational domains appear to be ordered by the uniform operation of a single principle, namely, descent. Under these analytic circumstances it is difficult if not impossible to detect a functional inconsistency, that is, an unresolved conflict between two aspects of a social system (Radcliffe-Brown, 1952:43). Radcliffe-Brown's law is thus true by the definition of terms. The distinction which I have proposed is preliminary to an investigation of the interplay between descent (as a principle of recruitment) and siblingship (as a principle of alignment). This investigation will reveal that the appearance of consistency conceals an underlying contradiction. I have already discussed the contradiction between siblingship and descent in Etoro society and will consider other examples rather than reiterate this analysis.

The appearance of functional consistency which results from assimilating divergent relational properties to a single concept exists primarily at the level of model rules. However, since the types of relationship are not in fact the same, an inherent inconsistency is displaced from the level of rules to the relation between model and reality. In other words, the contradiction which is analytically denied in the structural model emerges in the form of a discrepancy between that model and "what's happening on the ground." A substantial portion of this discrepancy can consequently be resolved by analytic application of the principle of siblingship in the appropriate contexts, that is, by revising the model. It will be useful to examine this aspect of the relationship between structure and empirical events before investigating the role of contradiction. Although I will argue that the degree of correspondence between model and reality can be significantly augmented by the application of the concept of siblingship, I do not intend to imply that siblingship should be installed in place of descent as a unitary principle of organization applicable to every aspect of the social system. Nevertheless, I will focus on those areas in which the concept of siblingship is applicable, ignoring for the moment those areas in which it is not. In other words, I will argue a case for siblingship, leaving synthetic consideration of the interplay of structural principles for later discussion.

From the vantage of descent theory the Etoro social system appears anomalous and ridden with inconsistencies, in brief, "loosely structured." This is primarily due to the fact that descent is neither the only nor the major principle of organization in Etoro society. Thus, from another (nondescent) perspective, there is a central unity to the social system. The complementary opposition between the categories of siblingship and exchange provides a single structural master plan which orders relationships at virtually every level of organization. This complementary opposition is inherent in the kinship terminology and is expressed in the (de facto) moieties and the dual organization of local groups. Similarly, lineages are aligned through matrilateral sibling relationships mediated by exchange groups. Siblingship is a pervasive structural principle which governs relationships in the politico-jural domain (as above) and in the sphere of egocentric kinship where congruence in individual kin networks—the hallmark of the nuclear sibling set —delineates mutual support groups.[7]

---

7. Congruence in individual kin networks refers to the condition whereby two (or more) individuals have relatives in common, although both individuals need not be related to these relatives in precisely the same way. The equivalence of siblings entails congruence, but the co-relationships are also identical. The concepts of equivalence and congruence differ in degree (of commonality) rather than kind.

The complementary opposition between siblingship and exchange also orders the relationships between men and spirits. I have discussed the manner in which the lineage and its *Sigisato* spirits are linked through their co-ownership of the lineage territory in a relationship based on the principle of siblingship. The second major group of spirits are the *Kesames* which include spirits of the dead and the progeny of their afterlife. A medium acquires a wife from the latter group of *Kesames* and she bears a child (or children) by him. This spirit wife and child provide the medium's connection to the several other-worldly abodes of the *Kesames*. Thus while men and *Sigisatos* are linked by siblingship, men and *Kesames* are joined in marriage.[8] Moreover, myths relate the activities of two types of totemic snakes, the pythons of siblingship and the pythons of exchange. The former reveal "brother" relationships through their selective marriage to the widows of apical ancestors of other lines while the latter analogously reveal exchange relations by their choice of unmarried young women as wives.[9]

Social process is also explicable with reference to this model. Although fission is not genealogically predictable in terms of cleavages based on descent alone, it is not arbitrary and unstructured as Barnes (1962) has argued with respect to New Guinea Highlands societies. Both the event and the lines of cleavage are structurally predictable in terms of congruence in the external relations of lineage members, such congruence being based on close patrilineal connection,[10] agnatic parallel marriage, and the matrilateral sibling relations which follow from agnatic parallel marriage and the levirate.

The characterizations "loose structure," "structural flexibility," and so forth which have been applied to New Guinea societies connote problematic relations between model and empirical reality, ideology and statistical norms, and between structure and social process. A resolution of these problematic relations may be sought in two quite different ways. On one hand empirical arrange-

---

8. A seance entails a direct exchange whereby the medium's soul occupies the "body" of his spirit wife or child or *Sigisato* in one of the spirit worlds and the *Kesame*'s or *Sigisato*'s spiritual essence occupies the medium's body in the longhouse.

9. The organization of the spirit world will be more fully explored in a separate publication.

10. Congruence co-varies with degrees of consanguinity (computed in terms of generational removal of the nearest common nuclear sibling bond). For example, FBSons have FZ, FZchild, etc., in common.

ments may be presumed to be inscrutable to structural analysis so that analytic attention is directed to conditions of environment, demography, warfare, etc., which are expected to provide an explanation of this perceived disorder in nonstructural terms. On the other hand, one may seek to construct a structural model which will account for the observed processual and empirical data.[11] The recognized inapplicability of African (or descent theory) models to most of the New Guinea ethnographic material has given a strong impetus to the former approach and the results have significantly increased our understanding of ecological and demographic processes and the extent to which they influence the structure and composition of territorial segments. However, one may object to the presumption of inherent disorder which has occasionally been associated with this perspective. For example, Barnes points out that fission in New Guinea Highlands societies is not predictable in terms of descent theory and goes on to conclude that the process is arbitrary, although relatable to warfare. Barnes (1962:9) then proceeds to hypothesize that

> the disorder and irregularity of social life in the Highlands, as compared with, say, Tiv, is due in part to the high value placed on killing.

The apparent line of reasoning here is that processes which are inexplicable in terms of one theoretical model are completely unstructured. Moreover, the model comes to define the essential qualities of the data themselves (and hence the explicandum) by its very inability to account for them—the "disorder and irregularity of social life" are clearly identified as the critical features to be explained. This, in turn, discourages attempts to apply alternative structural models since the problem is not to discover the order in the material, but *to account for the inherent disorder,* and this can only be achieved by utilizing a nonstructural approach.

The conclusion that New Guinea societies display inherent disorder clearly does not follow from the explanatory inadequacies of descent theory. However, this fallacious reasoning evidently informs many arguments intended to justify, legitimize, and promote nonstructural approaches which are presented as solutions to this very "problem." The misconception is so widespread as to be enshrined in texts on social organization. Buchler and Selby (1968:

---

11. Burridge (1959 and 1969) and Wagner (1967) have pioneered the development of such models in New Guinea and their work has fostered many insights which are incorporated into my analysis of the Etoro.

76–77) note the limited applicability of models based on descent theory "as abundant and increasing data from New Guinea is showing us daily," proceed to instance a tenuous relation of structure to empirical data in these societies and go on to conclude:

> if we are to render a sufficient account of the social structure of the New Guinea peoples, and a fortiori of any peoples, we must consider not some hypostatized theory of the social order, considered by itself, but rather the interplay of ecosystems, economics, and psychology along with morals, and minimally ascertain the relationship between ideal behavior, and the element of choice and the frequency of choice.

If, on the contrary, one were to present a structural model which is not tenuously related to the empirical data, then the dilemma would become a nonproblem, the sufficient account of social structure would be in hand, and one might consequently dispense with this concatenation of borrowed analytic frameworks which—however useful in other respects—do not render an account of social structure but rather constitute attempts to explain empirical data in nonstructural terms. There is, in short, an alternative solution. I submit that the structural model of Etoro society which I have presented dissolves the problematic relations between model and reality, ideology and statistical norms, and between structure and social process, which are the criteria of "loose structure." I would furthermore suggest that "tight" structural models might be constructed for other New Guinea societies that have heretofore appeared "loose," and I have sought to develop a concept of siblingship as a principle of social organization with this objective in mind.

An attempt to document this suggested general applicability of the principle of siblingship case by case would prove exceedingly cumbersome in the present context. However, it may be pointed out that siblingship subsumes certain aspects of descent; utilization of the concept therefore has the potential for resolving a discrepancy between ideology and statistical norms whenever such discrepancy arises from identification of an ideology as "patrilineal" on the grounds that co-members of groups and/or aligned segments are said to be "brothers" although, statistically, they are not *genealogically* related as patrilineal descendants of the same ancestor (or hierarchy of ancestors). In other words, co-membership and alignment phrased in terms of ideological "brotherhood" is not necessarily inconsistent with omnivorous recruitment and the resultant presence of significant numbers of genealogical nonagnates in local groups. On the contrary, the principle of siblingship may uniformly order both relations between members of local groups and the alignment of territorial segments. Indeed, it appears to be a general feature of "loosely structured" New Guinea societies that "brother" relationships are preeminently mediated by territory (irrespective of ancestry) and the fact that brotherhood is imputed between agnates and genealogical nonagnates who are (or have come to be) co-owners of the territory of the local group is indicative of this. Such local groups are organizationally founded on siblingship as a principle of co-membership, not on descent or cumulative patrifiliation as principles of recruitment.[12]

In summary, I am suggesting that the principle of siblingship provides both the organizational basis of local groups and the mechanism of their alignment and that one may consequently perceive a unitary design in these social systems which contributes to resolution of the problematics of loose structure. I do not suggest that there is any one uniform, paradigmatic model that is applicable to all New Guinea societies, but propose, alternatively, that it would be possible to construct a series of models based on the principle of siblingship (and constituting medial permutations of it)[13] which would describe and interrelate the central organizing principles of these social systems. It is sufficient for present purposes to point out that the principle and idiom of siblingship are not at variance with the range of statistical norms which have been reported for New Guinea societies, that a model constructed on this basis would therefore be relatable to empirical reality, and that social processes such as the conversion of nonagnates into "brothers" are structurally intelligible in these terms.

The principle of siblingship, as I have defined it, perhaps approaches the specifications for the cams of Lévi-Strauss's meta-

---

12. Further indications of the role of siblingship as the principle of organization of local groups are evident in customs such as that of the Bena, "whereby a bride, after she has resided in her husband's group for a time, will pick a 'brother' from among her husband's local group" (Langness, 1964:178). For a general discussion of the emphasis on "brotherhood" (rather than ancestral pedigree) in the New Guinea Highlands see de Lepervanche (1968) and Strathern (1972).

13. The equivalent transitive relationships which serve as a basis for alignment are in some instances mediated by antigamy and exogamy (i.e., by equivalent relationships to an external source of women) and by co-ownership of territory which develops from an intermingling of individual gardening sites (cf. Rappaport, 1967:20–26; and Ryan, 1959).

phorical automatic jigsaw. I refer to the often quoted reply to May-bury-Lewis in which Lévi-Strauss (1960:52) argues that

> . . . Mr. Maybury-Lewis remains, to some extent, the prisoner of the naturalistic misconceptions which have so long pervaded the British school . . . he is still a structuralist in Radcliffe-Brown's terms, namely, he believes the structure to lie at the level of empirical reality, and to be a part of it. Therefore, when he is presented a structural model which departs from empirical reality, he feels cheated in some devious way. To him, social structure is like a kind of jigsaw puzzle, and everything is achieved when one has discovered how the pieces fit together. But, if the pieces have been arbitrarily cut, there is no structure at all. On the other hand, if, as is sometimes done, the pieces were automatically cut in different shapes by a mechanical saw, the movements of which are regularly modified by a camshaft, the structure of the puzzle exists, not at the empirical level (since there are many ways of recognizing the pieces which fit together); its key lies in the mathematical formula expressing the shape of the cams and their speed of rotation; something very remote from the puzzle as it appears to the player, although it "explains" the puzzle in the one and only intelligible way.

The nexus of siblingship is the relational property equivalent transitivity (embodied in the formula $X:M::Y:M$) which is the key to the structure of the social puzzle and generative of the models which are expressed in "the rules governing the constitution of social groups and their inter-relations,"[14] and in other aspects of the culture. It explains the puzzle at several levels, including the rules which define the shape of the pieces and the way in which they fit together.

Utilizing the principle of siblingship one may proceed from formula to model to rules to groups and their interrelations but not to the totality of actual behavior "on the ground." Explication of the latter nevertheless continues to be the final objective (and it should be clear that I am among those who feel deviously cheated by models which depart from empirical reality inasmuch as I have specifically sought to develop specimens which would resolve a discrepancy between the two). In general terms, the problem concerns the relationship between structure (or models thereof) and empirical events. This is a critical issue and one may detect a disjunction or problematic relation between structure and event in nearly every theoretical framework currently employed. It will be

---

14. This phrase is excerpted from Schneider's (1965:26) description of the objectives of alliance theory.

useful to discuss several of these in order to precisely specify the issues involved (but with no comprehensive critique intended).

CONCEPTS OF STRUCTURE

A concept of social structure which "has nothing to do with empirical reality but with models built up after it" (Lévi-Strauss, 1953:525) does not envision analysis of the relationship between the two. This question does not concern Lévi-Strauss and he has repeatedly made this clear when reproached for not having answered it. Thus, he informs Maybury-Lewis that a concept of structure which is dissociated from the empirical level can "tell us more, and differently from, the data" (Lévi-Strauss, 1960:51).

Structure, conceived as a set of jural or ideal rules, cannot account for or explain that portion of actual behavior which does not conform to cultural specifications. The discrepancy is frequently of substantial proportions and it calls into question the general relationship between rules and behavior and hence structure and event. Evans-Pritchard's (1940 and 1951) account of the Nuer provides a classic example of this disjunction, embodied in the Nuer "paradox" whereby the unchallenged status of the agnatic principle somehow accounts for the event of matrilocality and the frequent tracing of descent through women. (Both the concept of structure and the paradoxical data will be considered more fully in a subsequent section of this chapter.) Improved models may reduce the discrepancy but nevertheless cannot account for behavior which violates the rule system of the structural model.

Analytic concepts based on choice and decision have been specifically developed by Firth, Leach, and others in order to deal with the empirical facts of behavior. However, this approach invariably leads to the conclusion that structure is a residual abstraction which is a product of events and therefore cannot explain or account for their occurrence. In brief, choice and decision explain events without relating them to the structure while Lévi-Strauss and his adherents explicate structure without relating it to events. Hence, the issue is disjoined and each side speaks to the deaf ear of the other. An examination of Firth's analytic concepts and their subsequent development will clarify this point.

Firth has been particularly concerned with the formulation of a theoretical framework for analyzing the patterning of behavioral events. However, the concept of structure which he presents is employed as an explanatory principle within this framework only to a very limited extent (while causal and contributing factors are sought at the organizational level of analysis). In Firth's view, structural forms constitute precedents which affect behavior through their influence on the expectations of social actors. These precedential forms (consisting of major patterns of relationship) limit the range of alternatives and thus provide a framework for individual actions and decisions. After the fact, such events become part of the body of precedent so that an enduring shift in the pattern of actual behavior effectively redefines the structure (Firth, 1951:40, and 1964:35–45). At any given point in time structure imposes limitations on behavioral events, but in the long run it is a direct product of the cumulative weight of past action. The logical thrust of Firth's thesis is that the statistical norms of one era become the jural rules of the next.

Firth's basic position concerning the temporally immediate relation between structure and event may be characterized as structural possibilism. Structure imposes *negative* constraints on social action which limit but do not determine behavioral events. The positive causal factors which impinge on individual action are located outside the structure, within the realm of social organization. In this context Firth examines the process by which actions and social relations are ordered in reference to given ends. Behavior is regarded as a product of the principles of responsibility, accommodation, status involvement, and economy of effort (Firth, 1964:80). The emphasis here is on those factors which bear on the strategy of individual decision making in a given social context. Structure is a purely passive element consisting of a range of alternatives that present a choice—but one which is ultimately decided on other grounds.

Firth maintains that structure may change as a result of individual decisions which "carry action right outside" the structural framework (1964:35). This postulated plasticity drains the concept of structure of causal efficacy with respect to behavior. If individual decisions can change the structure, then one may logically deduce that the continuity of structure is contingent upon continuity in the decisions which produced it. This must necessarily be the case, since, if it were not, the structure would have changed (Linnekin, 1972). It may also be logically inferred that this constancy of decisions is based on a like continuity in the factors which impinge on individual decisions (the factors being organizational by analytic definition). This is clearly implied inasmuch as a change in these factors would alter the pattern of decisions and hence change the structure. It is thus logically unnecessary to postulate that the precedential forms which constitute structure have any bearing on behavior whatsoever. The causal factors which originally engendered a pattern of action by influencing individual decision must reproduce that pattern in every generation in which it remains the same, and they consequently constitute a *sufficient* explanation of it. In this framework, structure thus becomes the residuum of action, related to empirical events as product rather than as an ordering force or principle.

The internal logic of Firth's analytic framework has been progressively developed into an explicit doctrine by a succession of authors who have been influenced by his ideas. Leach (1960:124) maintains that, in some cases, social structure may be usefully conceived as "the statistical outcome of multiple individual choices rather than a direct reflection of jural rules." Elaborating on this view of structure as emergent and posterior to event, Murdock (1960) suggests that jural rules themselves are the outcome of individual choice. More recently, Murdock has developed this position to its logical conclusion. He argues that the concepts of structure and culture are mere "epiphenomena" and cannot be employed as explanatory principles. They are, at best, "the results of the interaction of individual human beings; as reified abstractions they can never be the causes or operant factors in behavior" (1971:22).

The choice and decision framework does not elucidate the relationship between structure and empirical events but rather explains events at the individual level in nonstructural terms. Structure is, at most, passive and plastic, at least, a purely residual category. The progression from the former view to the latter represents the fruition of a reductionism which is embraced at the onset by selecting individual acts as the significant unit of analysis. It is interesting in this respect that individual decisions are guided by social ends in Firth's framework and by individual self-interest in Leach's development of it (see Leach, 1954:8). Murdock seeks causality at the level of stimulus and response in accordance with behavioral psychology. A reductionist hypothesis charts its own developmental career whereby theoretical advance requires further reduction. The endpoint is a cul de sac.

Other conceptions of structure place a heavy emphasis on culturally expressed rules. In this view, the cultural idiom is the essence of structure and empirical events are primarily grist for a society's ideological mills. Sahlins's paper concerning the relation between the ideology and composition of descent groups is one of the more explicit statements of this position (written in response to the aforementioned views of Leach and Murdock). Sahlins (1965: 104) argues that, "in major territorial descent groups, there is no particular relation between descent ideology and group composition." Territorial segments which are identical in their empirical composition and genealogical constitution may be either cognatic or agnatic in structure depending on the ideology of their cultural constituencies. The same nonagnatic genealogical connections which are accredited by the former societies are simply discounted by the latter. Empirical events of recruitment are thus subject to arbitrary cultural interpretations and de facto arrangements do not impinge on structural principles. Structure is not "the precipitate of practice" (Sahlins, 1965:106), as Leach and Murdock have argued.

Sahlins's position presupposes that structure has only a weak to nonexistent impact on the occurrence of behavioral events. The general relation between the two is predominantly one of ex post facto revision in which empirical reality is brought into conformity with the native model. The causal dissociation is clear: irregularities in recruitment are a product of demographic and ecological factors while the ideology (which is co-terminous with the structure) is seen as an adaptive response to the selective forces of the social environment (1965:105, 106). In short, structure and event are to be explained in terms of two discrete sets of expediencies —external and internal respectively. These pull in opposite directions, producing a disjunction between ideology and reality.

This theoretical viewpoint accounts for the *discrepancy* between the structural model (of rules) and empirical events which constitute violations of it, but cannot account for the occurrence and patterning of such events in structural terms. Violations are seen as a product of purely external factors and are neither generated nor constrained by the structure. Moreover, an explanation of these rule violations with respect to demographic and ecological factors is conducive to the view that conforming behavior may also be so explained and is not accounted for by the rule itself. If territorial segments which are identical in empirical composition and genealogical constitution may be either cognatic or agnatic, then structure does not covary with these empirical features and, one may infer, does not adequately account for any significant portion of them. In short, structure impinges on events only after the fact and by way of reinterpretation; the causes of events are to be sought at the demographic and ecological levels.

Both the ideological and choice and decision perspectives are useful in many respects and I have utilized elements of each in the preceding ethnographic account. However, neither adequately specifies the structure of a society or elucidates the relationship between structure and empirical events. This may be readily illustrated with regard to the Etoro moieties. These moieties cannot be explained by the imposition of ideology upon empirical reality inasmuch as they are not explicitly recognized by the Etoro and do not exist at the level of the conscious model. On the other hand, they do not constitute a pattern which is a simple product of individual choice and decision since the moiety division persists as invariant structural form irrespective of such decisions. Choice does not create the moieties but merely distributes lineages and lineage segments among them; by his marriage, an individual decides the moiety membership of his descendants. This dual division is a concrete manifestation of the definition of siblingship in terms of co-exchange, a definition which is implicit in the terminological system but explicit only in the ethnographer's model. In other words, the existential locus of the structure lies at a deeper level, in the relationship between rules, not at the level of empirical or ideological reality—although it is expressed in both of these. It is, moreover, rules and the relationship between rules which illuminate the articulation of structure and event.

In summary, elucidation of the relationship between structure and event is contingent upon the concept of structure employed. The conceptualization of structure as a statistical representation of empirical events—the outcome of multiple individual choices—establishes a relation of identity between the two but at the same time reduces structure to a residual abstraction lacking in causal or explanatory efficacy. A concept of structure based on ideology or jural rules may explain the manner in which empirical events are culturally perceived and socially organized (or reorganized), but cannot explain or account for the occurrence of that which is prohibited or the nonoccurrence of that which is prescribed. Neither of these approaches is satisfactory.

The properties which a concept of structure would necessarily have to possess in order to account for empirical events may be readily established by logical inference from the nature of the data to be explained. There are, quite obviously, two types of events —those which conform to ideological rules and those which are violations of them. These stand in a contradictory relationship. Thus, only a concept of structure which incorporates contradictory principles can account for the *occurrence* of both conformity and violation. In short, resolution of this critical issue turns on the development of a theory of structural contradiction.

STRUCTURAL CONTRADICTION

The ideology and practice of the levirate in Etoro society provide suitable material for an exploratory consideration of both structural contradiction and consistency. When a widow is retained by the lineage through the custom of the levirate, the espoused cultural rule dictates that she should marry a FBS or more distant agnate, but never the deceased husband's true brother (who is *tobi*). In actuality, this rule is violated 65 percent (11/17) of the time. If followed, the effect of the positive rule would be to create close consanguineal ties between distant agnates (in the following generation) and to enhance the degree of congruence in the external relationships of lineage members. However, practice corresponds to preexisting close consanguinity rather than the ideal rule. The structural significance of close consanguineal ties is therefore expressed in both the rule and the violation of it.

At this level the structure displays consistency and it would appear that, contrary to my previous statement, both conformity and violation may be explained by a single principle. It would be more accurate to say that both are differential expressions of the same principle. The consistency involves the effect of adherence (i.e., establishing consanguineal consolidation) and the cause or governing principle of the allocation of retained widows in cases of nonadherence (i.e., preexisting consanguinity). Both the effect of one and the cause of the other may be (and are) expressions of the same principle because they do not stand in a contradictory relationship. However, the effects of conformity and violation are exact opposites. The former produces consolidation of the lineage as a whole, which prevents fission, while the latter engenders solidary segments within the lineage, which presage fission. The apparent similarity of causes is also illusory. If the effects of adherence are considered to be their function and function is subsequently equated with motive it would appear that the causes of conformity and violation are the same. This familiar and pervasive fallacy of functional analysis merely obscures the underlying contradiction between structural principles.

This contradiction involves the rules which specify rights to and over property in general and women in particular. An individual has a legitimate claim to his FFBSSon's widow based on the cultural rule that rights to women as wives and rights of disposal over sisters, daughters, and widows are held in common by all lineage members. This rule asserts that the widow is lineage property. A true brother has rights which are identical to those of a FFBSS according to this rule since he is also a lineage member. However, he is arbitrarily disbarred from exercising them in this particular context.[15] A man also has rights in the personal property

---

15. Although the ethnologist may perceive that there are good functional reasons for this arbitrary denial of rights, it is unlikely that a true brother's perception and motives are isomorphic.

of his true brother by virtue of the sibling bond and the rules and ideology of mutual sharing vested in that relationship. A man's brother(s) and sons share in the inheritance of his personal property (and in the witchcraft compensation paid by the witch responsible for his death). Although rights in unmarried women are lineage property, rights over married women are personal property. A marriage continues as a spiritual union during the mourning period and a true brother assumes these personal rights over his deceased sibling's wife. He acts as custodian of the widow throughout this period. Brothers virtually always form a gardening group and ego and his true brother's widow will normally continue to garden together. He will perform the gardening tasks and undertake the other obligations of the deceased husband in producing and procuring food for her. These obligations are also vested in the sibling bond. Moreover, fulfillment of them engenders proprietary rights on the basis of the rule (which is probably universal) that he who contributes to the sustenance of someone develops a claim over that individual as against those who have not so contributed.

An individual thus has rights over his deceased brother's widow on several grounds, all of which are based on, or derived from, the sibling bond. The fact that a true brother should have a leading voice in the decision concerning remarriage may be interpreted as an acknowledgment of these rights. But ideally—according to expressed cultural rules—a true brother's influence in these matters should be strictly limited to the question of disposal and does not entitle him to marry the widow himself. His role should be much like that of a father in arranging his daughter's marriage. (The prohibition of the true brother levirate is structurally analogous to the father-daughter incest taboo but lacks the moral force and negative sanctions of the latter.)

It is clear from the preceding discussion that the cultural rule which stipulates that a widow should marry a FBS or more distant agnate is based on the principle of descent and that the successful assertion of lineage rights is the governing factor in adherence to it. Violation of the rule is a product of the successful assertion of the rights vested in siblingship as against those of the lineage.[16] Both adherence and violation are thus explicable with reference to a structural contradiction between siblingship and descent. It is important to note that the relationship between structure and event is

---

16. It should be recalled that widows are generally deployed in accordance with lineage objectives even though this rule is frequently violated, since violations occur primarily when lineage interests are minimal.

clearly discernible when the structure is conceptualized in these terms. That the occurrence of this particular (patterned) violation is the product of an internal structural contradiction rather than external forces should also be noted. Demographic factors (such as the relative availability of women of marriageable age and the proportion of unremarried widows among them) may affect the frequency of the prohibited true brother levirate but do not dictate the occurrence of this specific practice.

The strong disapproval (or prohibition) of the true brother levirate also entails a contradiction in the "cultural structure" (Bateson, 1958:25), i.e., in the logical integration of cultural rules and premises. To review material previously presented, a man's ZH is culturally defined as the ideal homosexual partner and the logical implication of this is that BW should be the ideal heterosexual partner. This follows from the formulation, cross-sex sibling's spouse (ZH) is to sexual relations with a person of the same sex as same-sex sibling's spouse (BW) is to sexual relations with a person of the opposite sex. Thus, a logical extension of the preference for ZH as a homosexual partner would enjoin sexual relations with BW, while a logical extension of the prohibition of sexual relations with BW would preclude those with ZH. The prohibition of the true brother levirate thus involves a contradiction in the cultural structure which is managed at the conscious level by arbitrary restrictions on the logical extension of each rule. The prohibition also entails an arbitrary restriction (or abrogation) of an individual's rights, as a lineage member, to his true brother's widow. I would suggest the hypothesis that rules which are arbitrary, illogical, and contradictory from the standpoint of the cultural structure tend to be violated more frequently than those which lack these characteristics, other things (such as negative sanctions) being equal. It follows that "deviance" is culturally patterned rather than random and that it is, to some degree, generated by the structure of the society.[17]

A structural contradiction may be defined, in the strict sense, as a condition whereby two rules are at variance such that adherence to one necessarily entails violation of the other. In more general terms, a contradiction may be identified whenever the results

---

17. The thrust of Sahlins's (1965) argument is that one society's cognate is another society's agnate and that deviance is consequently unstructured—a product of demographic forces. This is clearly not the case. For example, among the Huli (Glasse, 1968) segments are attached to the cognatic group structure through a cognate's WB, a form of deviance specific to the structure and absent in patrilineal systems.

of the operation of one rule or principle are inconsistent with, contrary to, and/or invalidative of the results of the operation of a second rule or principle. Contradictions are socially and structurally managed by arbitrary context restrictions, that is, by stipulation of the situations, contexts, or domains to which a given rule applies, and by the denial of its applicability in other contexts.

The organization of contradictions is the essence of social structure. Structure includes not only expressed cultural rules and conscious models which serve to maintain order and equilibrium but also the logical extensions and derivatives of these rules, which are consciously denied and prohibited. Deviant behavior is a product of rules which are endorsed in other domains of the structural system but which are imperfectly contained within these boundaries.

The rigid analytical distinction between domains which Fortes (1959) insists upon is fundamental to analysis of the conscious model and the rule structure of ideal behavior. However, commission of the cardinal sin of confounding domains is not restricted to anthropologists alone, but occurs as well among the people they study. At the surface level, there is a conscious contextual segregation of rule systems; at a deeper level, the relation between these rule systems is contradictory and dialectical. These contradictions are empirically manifested in the totality of observed behavior, as the preceding analysis of Etoro leviratic widow remarriage demonstrates.[18] The Nuer "paradox" provides an additional example of this general principle and will be considered subsequently.

The concept of structural contradiction which I have presented may be applicable to all rule-governed human behavior.[19] There

---

18. This mode of analysis—in which a pattern of behavioral events is interpreted as the result of an interplay between opposed or countervailing forces—has many parallels in the ethnographic literature. Prominent among these are Fortes's (1970:1–32) analysis of Ashanti household composition in terms of the "polar values" attached to paternity and matrilineal kinship and Leach's (1954:167–72) analysis of the effects of an "inconsistency" between patrilocal residence and succession by ultimogeniture upon (aristocratic) Kachin residential patterns. The present work draws on, and is indebted to, these prior analyses. It differs in regarding such polarities and inconsistencies as specific examples of a general phenomenon of structural contradiction and in the formulation of a concept of structure encompassing such contradictions.

19. The basic concept is clearly applicable to individual psychology and analogous theoretical constructs are, in fact, much in evidence in this field (undoubtedly as a consequence of taking deviant behavior as an expli-

are for example, direct parallels in the structure of language and the events of verbal behavior. One may properly say *rowed* but not *goed, isn't* but not *ain't, uncouth* but not *couth,* and *dogs* but not *sheeps.* General rules for formulating grammatical constructions are arbitrarily disallowed in these contexts. However, the prohibited forms nevertheless occur, as speech events, and they are clearly a product of identifiable grammatical rules which are applicable in other contexts. I would argue that they occur, although prohibited, because they conform to the generative rules.

Ain't is a complex but particularly interesting example. There is no acceptable contraction of *am not* and *amn't* apparently is not generated because *m* and *n* do not occur adjacent to one another in the same syllable in spoken English. In other words, there is a direct contradiction between a grammatical and phonological rule. Any form which is generated to fill this void will be likely to conflict with other rules thus leading to further ambiguities. In this particular case the *n* cannot be dropped (forming *am't*) without losing the quality of negation. *An't* or *Ain't* maintains the quality of negation but is devoid of recognizable personal pronoun content or specificity (i.e., *am,* indicating first person singular, is not detectably present). Since there is no personal pronoun content signified in the resultant form of the verb to be, *ain't* does not specify the person of the pronoun subject that accompanies it. It follows that *ain't* is used with you, he, she, and they, as well as with I. These "deviant" speech events are thus derivatives of the solution to the initial grammatical-phonological contradiction but also engender a secondary contradiction in the grammatical system concerning the specification or nonspecification of person in the present tense form of the verb. By logical extension from *he ain't,* one may generate *he go.* This suggests that there may be a dialectical process of language change whereby structural contradictions are productive of "bastard" forms which themselves imply new rules for grammatical formulation. The latter may then be extended so as to initiate a sequence of changes in the linguistic system. Change in social systems may well be governed by similar processes, and I have developed this linguistic example in order to indicate, by

---

candum). Freud's (1938) *Psychopathology of Everyday Life* and Bateson's (1956) theory of the double bind as a cause of schizophrenia provide familiar examples. Interestingly, the same conceptual framework is also implicit in Etoro witchcraft beliefs and in the role of Satan in the Christian pantheon. In both cases, behavioral disconformity is culturally explained by the interplay between opposed domains.

analogy, that the theory of structural contradiction presented herein is not incapable of elucidating social change. This concept of structure is not analytically constrained by equilibrium assumptions.

THE NUER PARADOX

The Nuer "paradox" entails a disjunction between structural principles and behavioral events which is both described and explained by Evans-Pritchard (1951:28) in the following passage.

> I suggest that it is the clear, consistent and deeply rooted lineage structure of the Nuer which permits persons and families to move about and attach themselves so freely, for longer or shorter periods, to whatever community they choose by whatever cognatic or affinal tie they find it convenient to emphasize; and that it is on account of the firm values of the structure that this flux does not cause confusion or bring about social disintegration. It would seem that it may be partly just because the agnatic principle is unchallenged in Nuer society that the tracing of descent through women is so prominent and matrilocality so prevalent. However much the actual configuration of kinship clusters may vary and change, the lineage structure is invariable and stable.

Evans-Pritchard's model of Nuer social structure—based on descent and lineage relations—is basically ideological and perceptual in design. He is particularly concerned to explain how the Nuer cognitively structure concrete reality rather than why they pursue certain courses of action. In this context, the important aspect of the data described above is that the Nuer are capable of imposing ideological order on a diffuse totality of events through selective recognition of their respective structural significance. Evans-Pritchard thus implicitly refutes Radcliffe-Brown's vision of social structure as "concrete, actually existing social relations" inasmuch as he demonstrates that some of these concrete relations are more significant than others and that structure does not exist at the level of empirical reality but in the selective perception of it. We are indebted to Evans-Pritchard for this theoretical advance. However, perception cannot in any sense explain the occurrence of events nor even facilitate their occurrence inasmuch as this kind of cognitive ordering necessarily occurs after the fact. Thus, the lineage structure which is deeply rooted in the Nuer psyche has nothing to do with the prominent tracing of descent through women and the cognatic composition of local communities. These data can be explained, however, by recognition of the role of siblingship in the social order and by application of the concept of structural contradiction developed herein.

The units which are aligned in Nuer society are not patrilineal descent groups as such but territorial sections, each of which has a recognized aristocratic lineage nucleus whose mythological and genealogical relations define the structural position of the territorial unit in a framework of overlapping alignments which are activated through the process of complementary opposition. The relationships between lineage nuclei (and hence territorial sections) are based on the principle of siblingship. The equivalent transitive relationships between co-aligned segments are generally mediated by ancestry and the ancestor of recruitment (to the lineage) is also a lineal descendant of the ancestor of alignment (as discussed on page 273). Groups are invariably united across a sibling bond, but the type of sibling bond is quite variable. In addition to full brother-brother linkages, the variations include brother-sister, patrilateral half-brothers, half-brothers whose mothers were full sisters, true and adopted sons who are "brothers" by virtue of having shared the same mother's milk, and individuals deemed to be "like brothers" as a consequence of shared mythological experiences (see Evans-Pritchard, 1940:229–32). It is quite clear from Evans-Pritchard's account that relations between lineage nuclei are always mythologically encoded so as to establish sibling bonds, but not necessarily those which are consistent with patrilineal descent. In short, siblingship is invariant in the definition of relationships between segments despite the prominent tracing of descent through women. Recognition of the fact that alignment is based on siblingship rather than patrilineal descent thus resolves half of the Nuer paradox since matrilineal connections do not constitute a discrepancy from this standpoint. The disjunction between structure and empirical events is located in the sphere of recruitment (and the contradiction concerns the interplay between the principles which govern alignment and recruitment respectively).

The actual process or mobilization of structurally positioned (or prealigned) segments through complementary opposition is based on the structural distance between the living members of the lineage nuclei involved (Evans-Pritchard, 1940:196, 200). As Evans-Pritchard (1940:201) defines it, structural distance corresponds to genealogical distance to the nearest common ancestor (and hence the nearest nuclear sibling bond). However, the sequence of ascending genealogical linkages need not be exclusively patrilineal since units may be aligned across cross-sex sibling bonds. In other words, structural distance is not computed in

purely patrilineal terms. Moreover, it is clear from the myths which
establish and encode lineage relations that matrilateral siblingship
enters into the computation of structural distance. For example,
two patrilateral half-brothers (Kun and Thiang) whose mothers
were sisters are differentiated from a third half-brother (Jok) of the
same father whose mother is not as closely related to their mothers
as the latter are to each other (fig. 48).[20] The two half-brothers who
are also matrilateral parallel cousins are the respective founders of
the aristocratic lineage nuclei of two primary territorial segments of
the same Eastern Jikany tribe, while the third half-brother is the
founder of a lineage nucleus of a territorial segment of a different
Eastern Jikany tribe. This is quite clearly an evaluation of structural distance in terms of matrilateral siblingship (or matrilateral
co-filiation) and matrilateral gradations of consanguinity since patrilineal descent is a constant in this instance. On the basis of patrilineal descent alone, the structural distance between the members
of the three lineages founded by these brothers is precisely equivalent and the lineages should consequently articulate co-ordinate
territorial segments which are equivalent subgroups of the same
tribe.

Such evaluations of structural distance are the rule rather than
the exception among the Nuer. Evans-Pritchard is aware that the
pattern of segmentation often follows patrilateral half-brother
cleavages, but he does not apply these data to his analysis of structural distance. He notes (1940:247) that the

> Nuer consider that lineage cleavages arise from a fundamental cleav-
> age in the family between *gaatywan,* children of the father, and
> *gaatman,* children of the mother. Where there are two wives and
> each has a son, the lineage bifurcates from this point.

Segmentation and alignment proceed on the same basis; "sons of
one mother" is frequently invoked by the Nuer as an explanation
of patterns of alignment in feud and warfare (1940:143, 146).

On the basis of the material Evans-Pritchard presents, one
may conclude that structural distance between the living members
of lineage nuclei is defined by the number of ascending generations
to the nearest nuclear sibling bond and also by the degree of matri-

---

20. There are several versions of the myth which depict different
relationships between these three women. However, Evans-Pritchard
(1940:232) states that "all accounts make Nyakwini and Nyabor more
closely related to one another than either to Duany."

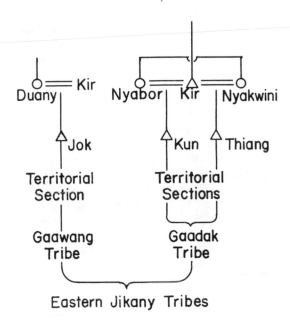

FIG. 48.   Genealogical Relationships Illustrating the Role of Matrilateral Siblingship as a Determinant of Structural Distance among the Nuer. (Based on information in E. E. Evans-Pritchard [1940: 232].)

lateral consanguinity shared by these siblings. (More precisely, structural distance is directly proportional to generational removal of the sibling bond and inversely proportional to the degree of matrilateral consanguinity among members of the sibling set.) Thus, at the same generational range, structural distance is less across a full sibling bond than across one in which brothers have different mothers and, moreover, less when these mothers are sisters than when they are not. These gradations of matrilateral consanguinity follow from matrilateral siblingship; that they enter into the Nuer calculation of structural distance is entirely consistent with the fact that alignment is based on siblingship rather than descent.

This calculation of structural distance creates a contradiction between siblingship as a principle of alignment and descent as a principle of recruitment. Evans-Pritchard (1951:140–41) discusses this contradiction from a somewhat different perspective in his later work on Nuer kinship and marriage.

A Nuer lineage is often named after a woman, its ancestress, because lineages are generally thought of as dividing out from within a polygamous family. They cannot be differentiated by reference to the names of the father of the founders of the different lines of descent, but only by reference to the names of the founders themselves or of their mothers. Thus the typical lineage structure is conceived of as being present in the structure of the polygamous family and in the distribution of huts in the homestead it occupies. . . . *There is involved here a contradiction between the dogma of the unity of brothers, which the Nuer so often enunciate, and both the lineage system and the common experience of family life.* It is a cardinal teaching that all brothers are equal and undivided, for they are sons of the same father and therefore, through their identification with him, equivalent in the lineage. Maternal descent does not count within the lineage and therefore ought not to count within the family, for by the agnatic principle in Nuer social life the family derives from the father. (Emphasis added.)

Evans-Pritchard discusses the manner in which this contradiction is managed in the familial context (1951:142–45) but does not pursue its implications for the lineage system. At the familial level, denial is culturally enjoined and this is implemented by not acknowledging the distinction between patrilateral half-brothers in terminological usage. Such half-brothers are addressed (and referred to) by the term for uterine brothers. However, denial is not entirely effective and the contradiction is manifested in actual behavior—in accordance with the hypothesis developed herein. Thus, the Nuer

recognize that whereas full brothers pool their resources, helping each other even to the point of foregoing their rights, patrilateral half-brothers insist on their rights and try to avoid their obligations, doing for each other only what self-interest demands of them (1951:142).

There is a potentiality that one half-brother may use the brideprice cattle from his uterine sister's marriage to provide a second wife for himself rather than deploying them to secure a bride for his half-brother as the obligations of brotherhood require. A half-brother may also shirk his obligation to marry a wife to the name of a sibling who died without an heir, instead employing his deceased brother's cattle to provide a wife for himself. To prevent this, a man may make prior arrangements for his uterine sister to marry a wife to his name after his demise. This is a telling example of the solidarity vested in matrilateral siblingship and close consanguinity vis-à-vis that vested in agnatic siblingship. The purpose of such ghost marriages is to ensure the continuity of the agnatic line but a son of the same father and co-member of the descent group cannot be counted upon to effect this continuity. It is evident here that gradations of matrilateral consanguinity enter into the calculation of social distance in the familial context just as they enter into the definition of structural distance in the sphere of alignment. The structure displays consistency, but this consistency embodies a contradiction inasmuch as these calculations are specifically denied in the family setting. The totality of behavioral events is explicable in terms of both the contradiction and the cultural denial.

The principle of patrilineal descent ideally determines recruitment to membership in aristocratic lineages and constitutes the idiom of lineage definition. Moreover, the stability and invariance of the lineage structure is indeed essential to the segmentary system as Evans-Pritchard (1951:28) maintains. Recruitment of sister's sons (and their descendants) to lineage membership therefore represents the violation of the fundamental rule of this domain. However, co-alignment and the calculation of structural distance across the same cross-sex sibling bonds utilized in recruitment are perfectly compatible with the principle of siblingship which governs relations in the sphere of alignment. Thus, there is a structural contradiction between siblingship as a principle of alignment and patrilineal descent as a principle of recruitment, and the "deviant" events of matrilateral attachment are explicable in these terms. Cross-sex (as well as same-sex) siblingship and gradations of matrilateral (and patrilateral) consanguinity are structurally and ideologically endorsed in the sphere of alignment and in the calculation of structural distance. Sister's sons are incorporated into patrilineal descent groups by the application of these principles outside their culturally designated domain. The structural contradiction between alignment and recruitment is thus empirically manifested in the presence of accessory branches attached to patrilineal descent groups by cross-sex sibling bonds.

The internal organization of the Nuer local community also reflects the interplay of the principles of siblingship and descent. Evans-Pritchard (1951:23) succinctly describes this organization as follows:

> A Nuer community, whether small or big, is not composed exclusively of members of a single lineage and their wives or, correspondingly, not all members of a lineage live in the same community. On the other hand, in any large village or camp there is represented an agnatic lineage of one or other order and into the growth of this lineage are grafted, through the tracing of descent through females,

branches which are regarded in certain situations and in a certain sense as part of it and in other situations and in a different sense as not part of it. Other lines and persons are grafted into the lineage by adoption, but this can only happen to Dinka and other foreigners, not to men of true Nuer origin. Attached to the lineage, directly or indirectly, are also a considerable number of affines of diverse kinds.

The structural significance of descent is clearly evident in the role of the agnatic core as the central organizational node of the community to which other lines and individuals are attached. On the other hand, all the modes of attachment are structurally predictable in terms of siblingship and, particularly, the jural equivalence of cross-sex sibling bonds in many nonritual contexts. This equivalence is particularly evident in the distribution of bridewealth to maternal kin (Evans-Pritchard, 1951:78). Sisters also have rights in the economic resources of their natal community which they exercise by residing there with their husbands or by returning after they have been widowed, both of these circumstances giving rise to attached sister's son lines (Evans-Pritchard, 1951:26 et passim).

The kinship composition of the local community may thus be viewed as a product of the principles of siblingship and descent. An individual can take up residence in his wife's brother's, mother's brother's, or father's natal community on the basis of cultural rules derived from one or the other of these principles. Any of these modes of residential recruitment is acceptable to the Nuer and there is no deviation from cultural prescriptions which requires explanatory attention. In this organizational domain, siblingship and descent are complementary rather than contradictory. However, the endorsement of the cross-sex sibling bond as a point of connection in residential recruitment quite logically leads to application of the same principle in recruitment to lineage membership, particularly in view of the structural identification of lineage and local community in the segmentary system of territorial alignment. Hence, in recruitment to descent groups, the contradiction is joined and empirically manifested in the prominent tracing of descent through women.[21]

---

21. Recognition of the structural role of siblingship also clarifies other aspects of Nuer society. Evans-Pritchard sought to discover structural consistency in the relation between structural systems, such as the territorial and lineage systems, but was unable to show a similar relationship between these and the age-set system (Evans-Pritchard, 1940:264). This might be achieved by application of the principle of siblingship in that co-membership in an age-set is based on an equivalent transitive relationship mediated by a point in structural time.

In this concluding chapter I have worked toward developing the concepts of siblingship and of structural contradiction in order to elucidate the general relationship between structure and event. These concepts are predominantly derived from my analysis of the Etoro data and the ethnographic account should therefore serve to exemplify their application in a particular case and in the context of a total structural system described in detail. Here I have sought to generalize and extend the range of applicability of these concepts through general theoretical discussion and the utilization of selected examples familiar to the reader. Unfortunately, the generality of a general theory of structure is not easily demonstrated, and I have been able to do little more than chart a theoretical course and illustrate the general outlines of it, leaving a number of loose ends in my wake—a deficiency which I hope to rectify at a later date. I might add that I would have done more were my employer less demanding of a concrete, actually existing manifestation of my efforts. Choice was not mine and decision was dictated by the structure.

There are several additional implications of the concept of structural contradiction which may be briefly mentioned but which cannot be elaborated due to the aforementioned limitations.

The notion of equilibrium which pervades British social anthropology is very closely linked to descent theory. In Radcliffe-Brown's (1952:32–48) formulation, it is unilineal succession which provides for the absence of conflict concerning rights and duties which, in turn, obviates functional inconsistency. The latter exists "whenever two aspects of the social system produce a conflict which can only be resolved by some change in the system itself" (Radcliffe-Brown, 1952:43). Thus it is the consistency engendered by descent which maintains equilibrium. However, if the concept of descent incorporates two contradictory principles, the unambiguous specification of rights and duties is called into question as is functional consistency and consequently the assumed equilibrium. In other words, equilibrium does not adhere in the social facts which Radcliffe-Brown thought to be the epitome of it. Moreover, the concept of structure which I have presented does not entertain these equilibrium assumptions.[22] The relationship between structural domains involves a dialectical interplay at a deeper level and recognition of this creates the possibility of analyzing structural change in structural terms, as a dialectical process, a point which I

---

22. It is important to note that the rejection of the notion of functional consistency does not imply an absence of orderliness.

have briefly touched upon in the discussion of the linguistic usage *ain't.* It is interesting in this respect that Fortes (1969:xii) quotes Saussure's remark that the opposition between synchronic and diachronic viewpoints is absolute and allows no compromise.

A second implication of the concept of structure which I have presented concerns the relationship between the social and symbolic order. If social structure is the organization of contradiction then symbolic structure constitutes the attempted resolution of these contradictions in nondiscursive terms.[23] (I would furthermore suggest that temporary equilibrium is attained by the conscious denial and symbolic resolution of contradiction, a view which invests equilibrium with the tenuousness which history and prehistory document.) The Nuer conception of *Kwoth* (Evans-Pritchard, 1953) is a pertinent example in view of the reinterpretation of Nuer social structure presented herein. *Kwoth* is oneness and at the same time incorporates diverse refractions linked, respectively, to the lineage, local group, family, territorial segment, and so forth. Evans-Pritchard (1953:209) maintains that this reflects the structural relativity of the segmentary social order. However, these diverse representations may also be considered in a generic sense, to be linked to several structural domains. In these terms, the oneness of *Kwoth* embodies a statement of uniformity across domains and an attempted resolution of the contradiction between them. Moreover, the resolution is based on the principle of siblingship, since *Kwoth* mediates an equivalent transitive relationship at any and every level. It is also due to this quality that *Kwoth* may be effectively invoked in situations of social conflict.

---

23. Lévi-Strauss (1967) expresses a similar view regarding the function of myth. However, his development of this position has been hampered by the lack of a theory of social structural contradiction.

Appendix

A STATISTICAL DESCRIPTION OF
WIDOWHOOD AND REMARRIAGE

Tables 53 through 64 in this appendix and tables 50 through 52 in chapter 8 are based on a single sample which includes the unions of all ever-married Etoro men and women in which one or both parties were still alive on May 1, 1968, shortly after the inception of my fieldwork. Completed unions in which both parties were deceased are excluded as information on some points (particularly divorce) may not be reliable. The data are divided into twelve subsamples based on distinctions such as women's first and subsequent marriages and intratribal and extratribal unions. Although these divisions are more important with respect to some factors than others, a single format is used throughout the appendix to facilitate comparison of tables. (Hopefully these subdivisions will also enable other ethnologists to extract a comparable portion of the total sample.) The sample includes:

1. 201 *Unions.* Of these, 112 are extant, 80 were completed by the death of one spouse, and 9 were completed by divorce.
2. 334 *Individuals.* Of these, 171 are women (136 Etoro, 35 non-Etoro) and 163 are men (141 Etoro, 22 non-Etoro). Of the 171 women, 145 were still living as of May 1, 1968, and 26 had died as of that date. Of the 163 men, 111 were still living as of May 1, 1968, and 52 had died as of that date.

Of the 171 Women:

146 were married once and are included once in the total sample of 201 unions.   146 unions

20 were married to 2 men in the sample and each accounts for 2 unions in the total sample of 201 unions. (Of these 20 women, 3 were divorced and remarried once and 17 were widowed and remarried once.)   40 unions

5 were married to 3 men in the sample and each accounts for 3 unions in the total sample of 201

unions. (Of these 5 women, 3 were divorced twice
and remarried twice, and 2 were widowed twice
and remarried twice.)   15 unions
                                          Total 201 unions

Of the 163 Men:

129 were married to 1 woman in the sample and each
   accounts for one union in the total sample of 201
   unions. (Of these 129 men, 3 were divorced and
   died without ever remarrying.)   129 unions

 31 were married to 2 women in the sample and each
   accounts for two unions in the total sample of 201
   unions. (Of these 31 men, 5 were divorced and
   remarried.)   62 unions

  2 were married to 3 women in the sample and each
   accounts for three unions in the total sample of 201
   unions.   6 unions

  1 was married to 4 women in the sample and accounts for four unions in the total sample of 201
   unions. (One of these marriages ended in divorce.)   4 unions
                                          Total 201 unions

Most Etoro women are widowed and remarried during the course of their
lifetime. Etoro men are typically ten to fifteen years older than their wives
(tables 53 and 54) and usually precede them in death. (Tables 53 through 64
are grouped together following page 303.) Nearly 72 percent (51/72) of all
completed unions of Etoro men were terminated by the death of the husband (table 55). There are no significant differences between women's first
and subsequent unions (to Etoro men) in the frequency of termination by
male death. Thus while 32.4 percent (47/145) of all ever-married living
women have been widowed, 12.8 percent (6/47) of the ever-widowed
women have been widowed more than once (table 56). All of these figures
suggest that marriage is frequently of comparatively short duration relative
to the life expectancy of the surviving spouse—generally the wife. This is
also indicated by the high five to seven ratio of completed unions (with one
spouse surviving) to extant unions (table 57).

The frequency of widow remarriage is comparatively high, particularly for women of childbearing age. Forty-one percent of all women
whose first marriage was terminated by the death of their husband have
remarried. Twenty-five percent of all women whose second or third marriages were similarly terminated have also remarried (table 58).

The Etoro say that a widow may remarry "if her genitals are good."
In going over a list of unremarried widows, informants judged all women
under fifty-five years of age, and some women fifty-six to sixty, to be
satisfactory in this respect. This assessment is consistent with the esti-

mated age of all living remarried widows at the time of the second union (table 59). It should be noted that 83 percent of the women were within the childbearing period of twenty-one to forty-five years of age at the time of remarriage and half were twenty-one to thirty.

The 38.9 percent frequency of remarriage for all ever-widowed women understates the actual extent of remarriage among widows of childbearing age. Almost all of these women eventually remarry. Fifty-six percent of the unremarried widows in table 58 are over forty-five and most of the younger women have been widows for less than two years. Table 60 shows the age of all unremarried women who were widows on May 1, 1968; those that died or remarried by July 31, 1969; and the additional women (of various ages) widowed during that fifteen-month period. The number of unremarried widows was the same at the beginning and end of this period as the number of widows who died or remarried equaled the number of newly-widowed women. In other words, the number of widows in the population is (currently) constant over time even though rather extensive remarriage takes place. Indeed, 23.1 percent (3/13) of the surviving widows of childbearing age remarried during these fifteen months, giving a rate of 18.5 percent remarriage per year for widows twenty-one to forty-five. At this rate, nearly all the women in this age category would be expected to remarry. The Etoro share this expectation.

The duration of widowhood for all widows under forty-six is shown in table 61. Sixty percent (6/10) of the women who had not remarried by July, 1969, had been widowed only fifteen or sixteen months and 80 percent (8/10) for less than three years. The duration of widowhood for the two remaining women (20 percent) is uncertain but probably exceeds three years.

Etoro beliefs concerning the proper period of mourning may be undergoing modification. Traditionally, a woman was expected to wait three years before remarriage. Mourning was formally concluded when the bones of the deceased husband were placed in the lineage burial cave and the man's spirit passed into the realm of the remote dead. Prior to this time the deceased husband would communicate with his wife in seances conducted by a medium. The marriage, in a sense, continued.

In 1968–69 some men—young men particularly—maintained that a one-year period of mourning was sufficient in view of the current shortage of marriageable women.[1] Several cases of remarriage after less than three years' mourning occurred while I was in the field. However, burial customs remained unchanged. The bones of the deceased husband had not been placed in the ancestral burial cave in the case of the widow who remarried after fifteen months. No one expressed fear of disapprobation by the ghost, but the widow married her husband's younger brother—a tie too close to admit of any hostility.

However, this particular case was atypical in almost every respect.

---

1. The demographic reasons for this shortage are discussed in chapter 1.

The deceased husband's younger brother is the youngest married man in the society (twenty-one to twenty-five year age group). He was strongly encouraged by his agnates to marry the widow. She looked noticeably pregnant to me—although everyone denied this. The groom was less than enthusiastic about the marriage. His betrothal to a young girl was broken off by her father when it became known that he would marry his deceased brother's wife. In addition, the man paid a brideprice to his sister even though the marriage conformed to the levirate, for which brideprice is not required and almost never paid.[2]

The other case of remarriage before the completion of the traditional three-year mourning period did not involve these extraordinary circumstances. This case thus constitutes the only evidence that a shorter period of mourning is now considered acceptable. This evidence is insufficient as the young men who expressed the view that one year's mourning was sufficient may merely have been engaging in an ad hoc justification of particular instances. In short, nothing definite can be concluded about this possible change in the customary mourning period prior to restudy.

In summary, several points may be noted concerning unremarried widows: (1) 56.3 percent (18/32) are past childbearing age, and (2) 25.0 percent (8/32) have been widowed for sixteen months or less and have thus had little or no opportunity to remarry. All widows of childbearing age are expected to marry, in due course, and the 18.5 percent annual rate of remarriage (for the twenty-one to forty-five year age group) is consistent with this expectation.

Forty-seven percent of the widows who remarried wed bachelors, 29.4 percent went to currently married men, 17.6 percent to widowers, and 5.9 percent to divorcés (table 62). Younger widows twenty-one to thirty years old tend to marry bachelors, widowers, or divorcés while older widows thirty-one to fifty generally go to married men. The large proportion of widows marrying bachelors is a function of the current shortage of marriageable young women. There are presently no young women other than widows available for many men of marriageable age. This is evident from a comparison of the number of unmarried men and women in tables 53 and 54. There are twenty-five never-married men aged twenty-one to thirty-five and only eighteen never-married women aged six to twenty. (The disparity between the number of men and women—irrespective of marital status—is even greater: forty-six men twenty-one to thirty-five as opposed to twenty-seven women six to twenty, or 1.7 men per woman.)

Although only 17.6 percent of the widows married widowers, this accounts for three of the five cases of widower remarriage (table 62). The relatively low percentage of all widows going to widowers is thus primarily due to the fact that there are many more of the former than of the latter.

---

2. I know of only one other case of the levirate in which brideprice was paid. The groom was the FBS of the deceased and the latter's true brother received the brideprice.

TABLE 57

Ratio of Completed Unions with One Spouse Surviving
to Extant Unions
(May 1, 1968)

	Intra-Tribal Unions	*Etoro Man–Extratribal Woman Unions*	*Etoro Woman–Extra-tribal Man Unions*	*All Unions*
Sample I: Women's first marriages				
Extant unions	65	20	8	93
Completed unions with one spouse surviving	48	14	7	69
Total	113	34	15	162
Completed unions as a percentage of the total	42.5	41.2	46.7	42.6
Sample II: Women's second and subsequent marriages				
Extant unions	13	1	5*	19
Completed unions with one spouse surviving	7	3†	1*	11
Total	20	4	6	30
Completed unions as a percentage of the total	35.0	75.0	16.7	36.7
Total Sample: Women's first and subsequent marriages				
Extant unions	78	21	13	112
Completed unions with one spouse surviving	55	17	8	80
Total	133	38	21	192‡
Completed unions as a percentage of the total	41.4	44.7	38.1	41.7

*One woman appears once in extant unions and once in completed unions.

†One woman is counted two times in this group, because her second and third marriages were both ended by the deaths of her husbands. This same woman is also counted once in Sample I, completed unions with one spouse surviving, since her first marriage to an Etoro man also was ended by the death of her husband.

‡Seventeen women are counted twice, two women are counted three times, twenty-six men are counted twice, and three men are counted three times, because they were married to more than one person during the course of their married lives.

Appendix

TABLE 58

Frequency of Remarriage Following the Death of a Spouse for
Completed Unions with One Spouse Surviving
(May 1, 1968)

	Intra-tribal Unions		Etoro Man–Extratribal Woman Unions		Etoro Woman-Extra-tribal Man Unions		Total Completed Unions	
Sample I: Women's first marriages								
Number of widowers	13		5		*		18	
Number remarried	3		1		*		4	
Percentage of total		23.1		20.0				22.2
Number unremarried	10		4		*		14	
Percentage of total		76.9		80.0				77.8
Number of widows	35		9		2		46	
Number remarried	15		2		2		19	
Percentage of total		42.9		22.2		100		41.3
Number unremarried	20		7		0		27	
Percentage of total		57.1		77.8		0.0		58.7
Sample II: Women's second and subsequent marriages								
Number of widowers	2		1		0		3	
Number remarried	0		0		0		0	
Percentage of total		0.0		0.0		0.0		0.0
Number unremarried	2		1		0		3	
Percentage of total		100		100		0.0		100
Number of widows	5		2		1		8	
Number remarried	0		1		1		2	
Percentage of total		0.0		50.0		100		25.0
Number unremarried	5		1		0		6	
Percentage of total		100		50.0		0.0		75.0
Total Sample: Women's first and subsequent marriages								
Number of widowers	15		6		*		21	
Number remarried	3		1		*		4	
Percentage of total		20.0		16.7				19.0
Number unremarried	12		5		*		17	
Percentage of total		80.0		83.3				81.0
Number of widows	40		11		3		54	
Number remarried	15		3		3		21	
Percentage of total		37.5		27.3		100		38.9
Number unremarried	25		8		0		33	
Percentage of total		62.5		72.7		0.0		61.1

*The five unions involving extratribal men and Etoro women are omitted here as it was not possible to reliably distinguish polygynists who lost one of two wives and did not remarry from widowers who lost their only wife and subsequently remarried.

TABLE 59

Estimated Age at Remarriage for Living Widows
Remarried by May 1, 1968

Age Cohort	Number of Women	Percentage of Total Cases
56–60	1	5.6
51–55	1	5.6
46–50	1	5.6
41–45	2	11.1
36–40	1	5.6
31–35	3	16.7
26–30	5	27.8
21–25	4	22.2
Total	18	100.2

Note: Age estimates for widows remarried before contact (in 1964) are based on the ages of offspring by the second husband. Age at remarriage could not be determined in three cases.

TABLE 60

Age-Specific Incidence of Death and Remarriage among Unremarried Widows of May 1, 1968, and Age Distribution of New Widows

Age Cohort	Number of Unremarried Widows on May 1, 1968	Number of Widows that Remarried by July 31, 1969	Number of Unremarried Widows that Died by July 31, 1969	Number of Unremarried Widows Remaining July 31, 1969	Number of Women Widowed between May 1, 1968, and July 31, 1969	Number of New Widows* that Died	Number of Unremarried Widows on July 31, 1969
76–80	1			1			1
71–75							1
66–70				1			2
61–65	4		2	2			6
56–60	6		1	5	1		5
51–55	4			4	1		1
46–50	2		1	1			3
41–45	2		1	1	2		2
36–40	2			2			5
31–35	5	1		4	1		3
26–30	4	2		2	1		3
21–25	1			1	2		3
16–20					1	1	0
Unknown	1			1			1
Total	33	3	5	25	9	1	33

*Includes women widowed nine months or more.

310

TABLE 61

Duration of Widowhood in July, 1969, for Women under Forty-Six
Widowed before May, 1968

Age Cohort	Widow	Duration of Widowhood (in Months)	
		Remarried Widows	Unremarried Widows
41–45	a		less than 36 months
36–40	b		15
31–35	c		16
	d		15
	e		15
	f		less than 24 months
	g	less than 48 months	
26–30	h		16
	i	15	
	j	9	
21–25	k		16
Total	11	3	8

Note: The date that these women's husbands died was determined by informants in relation to the (known) dates of government patrols since contact. Five of the widows were the wives of two men who died after the government patrol that was carried out several months before my arrival.

TABLE 62

Marital Status of Remarried Widow's Second Husband
at the Time of the Union

	Marital Status of Second Husband				Total
	Never-Married	Married	Divorced	Widowed	
Completed unions with widowed women surviving, May 1, 1968	10	6	1	4	21
Completed unions with widowed women deceased, May 1, 1968	6	4*	1	2	13
Total	16	10	2	6	34
Percentage of total	47.1	29.4	5.9	17.6	100

*One man was previously widowed and divorced, as well as being married at the time of his marriage to the widow.

TABLE 63

Age-Specific Incidence of Death and Remarriage among Unremarried Widowers of May 1, 1968, and Age Distribution of New Widowers

Age Cohort	Number of Unremarried Widowers on May 1, 1968	Number of Widowers Remarried by July 31, 1969	Number of Unremarried Widowers that Died by July 31, 1969	Number of Unremarried Widowers Remaining July 31, 1969	Number of Men Widowed between May 1, 1968, and July 31, 1969*	Number of Unremarried Widowers on July 31, 1969
66–70	1			1	1	1
61–65	4			4		4
56–60	7		2	5	1	6
51–55	1			1	2	3
46–50	1			1	1	2
41–45	1			1		1
36–40	0			0		0
31–35	2	1		1		1
26–30					1	1
Total	17	1	2	14	6	19†

*None died or remarried during this time. No man who became a widower after May 1, 1968, died before July 31, 1969.

†The number of widowers on July 31, 1969 (i.e., nineteen) is one less than the number of remaining widowers (fourteen) plus the number of new widowers (six) because one man in the 66–70 cohort who lost a wife previous to May 1, 1968, lost another between May 1, 1968, and July 31, 1969.

TABLE 64

Relationship of Age and Polygyny to Widower Remarriage

Age Cohort	Unremarried Widowers of May 1, 1968, Who Had Not Remarried by July 31, 1969		Ever-Widowed Men Who Had Remarried by July 1, 1969*	
	Sole Wife Died	*One of Two or More Wives Died*	*Sole Wife Died*	*One of Two or More Wives Died*
66–70	0	1		
61–65	2	2		
56–60	4	3		
51–55	1		1	
46–50	1†		1†	
41–45	1		1	
36–40	0			
31–35	1		2	
Total	10	6	5	0

*Includes one man in the 31–35 cohort who was widowed before May 1, 1968, who remarried by July 31, 1969, and four men who were widowed and remarried before May 1, 1968.

†This man is counted twice because he was twice widowed—he was remarried after being widowed the first time, but he was not remarried after being widowed the second time.

Literature Cited

Barnes, J. A.
    1962. African models in the New Guinea Highlands. *Man* 62:5–9.
Bastian, P. G.
    1969. Medical aid for Bosavi cannibals. *Geographical Magazine* 41:
       547–51.
Bateson, G.
    1958. *Naven.* Stanford: Stanford University Press.
Bateson, G., Jackson, D. D., Haley, J., and Weakland, J. H.
    1956. Toward a theory of schizophrenia. *Behavioral Science*
      1:251–64.
Bowers, Nancy.
    1971. Demographic problems in montane New Guinea. In *Culture
      and population: a collection of current studies,* Monograph
      no. 9, edited by S. Polgar. Chapel Hill: Carolina Population
      Center.
Buchler, I. R., and Selby, H. A.
    1968. *Kinship and social organization.* New York: The Macmillan
      Company.
Burridge, K. O. L.
    1959. Siblings in Tangu. *Oceania* 30:128–54.
    1969. *Tangu traditions.* Oxford: Oxford University Press.
Clark, W. D.
    1966. From extensive to intensive shifting cultivation: a succession
      from New Guinea. *Ethnology* 5:347–59.
de Lepervanche, M.
  1967–68. Descent, residence and leadership in the New Guinea High-
      lands. *Oceania* 38:134–58, 163–89.
Ernst, T. M.
    1972. Stealing another man's wife among the Onabasulu of the Great
      Papuan Plateau. Paper presented at the American Anthropo-
      logical Association Annual Meeting, November 30, 1972, at
      Toronto, Ontario.
Evans-Pritchard, E. E.
    1940. *The Nuer.* Oxford: Oxford University Press.
    1951. *Kinship and marriage among the Nuer.* Oxford: Oxford Uni-
      versity Press.

1953. The Nuer conception of spirit in its relation to the social order. *American Anthropologist* 55:201–14.

Feibleman, James, and Friend, Julius W.
1945. The structure and function of organization. *Philosophical Review* 54:19–48.

Firth, Raymond.
1951. *Elements of social organization*. Boston: Beacon Press.
1964. *Essays on social organization and values*. London: Athlone Press.

Fortes, Meyer.
1959. Descent, filiation, and affinity: a rejoinder to Dr. Leach. *Man* 59:193–97, 206–12.
1969. *Kinship and the social order*. Chicago: Aldine Publishing Company.
1970. *Time and social structure and other essays*. London: Athlone Press.

Fortune, R. F.
1963. *Sorcerers of Dobu*. New York: E. P. Dutton and Company.

Freud, Sigmund.
1938. The psychopathology of everyday life. In *The basic writings of Sigmund Freud*, edited and translated by A. A. Brill. New York: The Modern Library.

Glasse, R. M.
1968. *Huli of Papua*. Paris: Mouton and Company.

Hides, Jack.
1973. *Papuan wonderland*. Sydney: Angus and Robertson.

Kaberry, Phyllis M.
1967. The plasticity of New Guinea kinship. In *Social organization: essays presented to Raymond Firth*, edited by M. Freedman. London: Frank Cass.

Kelly, Raymond.
1968a. L'échange géneralisé à Dobu. *L'Homme* 8:54–61.
1968b. Demographic pressure and descent group structure in the New Guinea Highlands. *Oceania* 30:36–63.
1974. Witchcraft and sexual relations: an exploration in the social and semantic implications of the structure of belief. Paper presented at American Anthropological Association Annual Meeting, November, 1974, at Mexico City. (Forthcoming in *Man and woman in the New Guinea Highlands*, edited by P. Brown and G. Buchbinder. Special Publication No. 8, American Anthropological Association.)

Langness, L.
1964. Some problems in the conceptualization of Highlands social structures. *American Anthropologist* 66:162–82.

Leach, E. R.
1954. *Political systems of Highland Burma*. Boston: Beacon Press.

1960. The Sinhalese of the dry zone of Northern Ceylon. In *Social structures in Southeast Asia,* edited by G. P. Murdock. Viking Fund Publications in Anthropology, No. 29. Chicago: Quadrangle Books.

1966. *Rethinking anthropology.* London: Athlone Press.

Lévi-Strauss, Claude.

1953. Social structure. In *Anthropology today,* edited by A. L. Kroeber. Chicago: University of Chicago Press.

1960. On manipulated sociological models. *Bijdragen tot de Taal-, Land-, en Volkenkunde* 116:45–54.

1967. The story of Asdiwal. In *The structural study of myth and totemism,* A.S.A. Monograph no. 5, edited by E. R. Leach. London: Tavistock Publications.

Linnekin, J.

1972. The hard and the soft. Unpublished paper, Department of Anthropology, The University of Michigan.

McElhanon, K. A., and Voorhoeve, C. L.

1970. The Trans-New Guinea phylum: explorations in deep level genetic relationships. *Pacific Linguistics.* Series B: Monograph 16.

Meggitt, M. J.

1962. *Desert people.* Chicago: University of Chicago Press.

1965. *The lineage system of the Mae-Enga of New Guinea.* New York: Barnes and Noble, Inc.

Murdock, G. P.

1949. *Social structure.* New York: The Free Press.

1960. Cognatic forms of social organization. In *Social structures in Southeast Asia,* edited by G. P. Murdock. Viking Fund Publications in Anthropology, No. 29. Chicago: Quadrangle Books.

1971. Anthropology's mythology. *Proceedings of the Royal Anthropological Institute for 1971,* pp. 17–24.

Nayacakalou, R. R.

1955. The Fijian system of kinship and marriage. Pt. 1. *Journal of the Polynesian Society* 64:44–55.

Needham, Rodney.

1974. *Remarks and inventions.* London: Tavistock Publications.

Pouwer, Jan.

1964. A social system in the Star Mountains: toward a reorientation of the study of social systems. *American Anthropologist* 66:133–61.

Radcliffe-Brown, A. R.

1950. Introduction. In *African systems of kinship and marriage,* edited by A. R. Radcliffe-Brown and Daryll Forde. London: Oxford University Press.

1952. *Structure and function in primitive society.* New York: Free Press.

Rappaport, Roy A.
1967. *Pigs for the ancestors*. New Haven: Yale University Press.
Russell, I. A. C.
1953. Pleistocene-Sisa formation. Unpublished report for the British Petroleum Company, Sydney, Australia.
Ryan, D'Arcy.
1959. Clan formation in the Mendi Valley. *Oceania* 29:257–90.
Sahlins, Marshall D.
1965. On the ideology and composition of descent groups. *Man* 65: 104–7.
Schieffelin, E. L.
1972. The gisaro: ceremonialism and reciprocity in a New Guinea tribe. Ph.D. dissertation, University of Chicago.
Schneider, D. M.
1965. Some muddles in the models: or, how the system really works. In *The relevancy of models for social anthropology*, A.S.A. Monograph no. 1. London: Tavistock Publications.
Shaw, R. D.
1973. A tentative classification of the languages of the Mount Bosavi region. In *The linguistic situation in the Gulf District and adjacent areas, Papua New Guinea. Pacific Linguistics*. Series C: no. 26, edited by K. Franklin.
Strathern, A. J.
1972. *One father, one blood: descent and group structure among the Melpa people*. London: Tavistock Publications.
Townsend, Patricia K. W.
1969. Subsistence and social organization in a New Guinea society. Ph.D. dissertation, The University of Michigan.
Voorhoeve, C. L.
1968. The Central and South New Guinea Phylum: a report on the language situation in South New Guinea. *Pacific Linguistics*. Series A: Occasional Papers no. 16, Papers in New Guinea Linguistics 8.
Wagner, Roy.
1967. *The curse of Souw*. Chicago: The University of Chicago Press.
Ward, R. G., and Lea, David A. M., editors.
1970. *An atlas of Papua and New Guinea*. Glascow and Melbourne: Collins-Longman.
Wurm, S. A.
1971. The Papuan linguistic situation. In *Linguistics in Oceania. Current Trends in Linguistics*. Vol. 8, edited by J. D. Bowen, et al. The Hague: Mouton.

List of Figures

List of Tables

Index